Tarot For Dummies®

Cheat Sheet

Tarot Decks

Tarot decks come in many shapes and sizes. A typical tarot deck contains 78 cards and consists of the following elements:

- Major arcana: The first 22 cards in the deck, which have names such as The Fool, Death, and Wheel of Fortune (see Chapter 7).

- Minor arcana: The other 56 cards, which feature four suits, traditionally called wands, cups, swords, and pentacles. The minor arcana contains two types of cards:

  - Number (or pip) cards: The first 40 minor arcana cards, which are numbered from ace through ten (see Chapter 8).
  - Court (or royalty) cards: The last 16 minor arcana cards, which depict kings, queens, knights, and pages (see Chapter 9).

For a small sampling of the variety of tarot decks available, flip through the color insert in the middle of this book.

Magic Mirrors

Tarot cards are like magic mirrors that can help you see yourself and life issues from a different perspective. Achieving this perspective comes down to your willingness to put aside your ego so that your higher soul, spirit, Self might be better seen and heard. Tapping into the power of the tarot requires temporarily giving up

- your preconceived ideas about what you want or feel entitled to.

- how you think things "should be."

- believing that you know what the one and only truth is.

The Simplest Tarot Spread

Less can be best. In Chapter 13, I show you how to lay out and interpret several tarot spreads. The most basic spread is the *touchstone* (meaning "a point of reference") — a simple yet powerful one-card spread. Pulling a touchstone card is a super way of getting acquainted with one tarot card at a time.

To use this spread, select a card at the beginning of the day or before an important event. Turn to that card's interpretation in Chapter 7, 8, or 9 and consider which of the concepts or questions listed there apply to your life situation. Doing so offers you a reference point for the events ahead and a way of reflecting upon what has happened at day's end. Touchstone cards help you see some prospects for the day ahead and, after the day or event is over, reflect upon what you might have missed.

For Dummies: Bestselling Book Series for Beginners

Tarot For Dummies®

Cheat Sheet

Setting Realistic Expectations

As you work with the tarot, keep in mind what the cards can and cannot do. If you set unrealistic expectations, you may miss out on the tarot's possibilities.

What the tarot can do

- Reveal new options.
- Expand how you view your options and possibilities.
- Offer you support, hope, and encouragement.
- Reduce stress and anxiety.
- Empower you to be more conscious of your thoughts, words, and actions.
- Bring mental clarity.
- Bring out or restore your sense of humor.
- Reaffirm what you already know.
- Introduce you to universal truths that help to change your perspective. (For example, "All things happen in divine time.")
- Confirm your intuitive sense of the best course of action to take for the greatest good of all concerned. Often this is something that you might be avoiding because of the discomfort, inconvenience, difficulty, and/or hard work that it entails.
- Remind you that *you* are responsible for your decisions and actions.

What the tarot cannot do

- Predict the exact future.
- Accurately diagnose or treat a medical problem.
- Tell you how to invest money or win the lottery.
- Put a curse or "love spell" on another person.
- Solve legal problems.
- Tell you if you'll meet your "soul mate" on your next vacation.
- Relieve you of your responsibility for your decisions and actions.

Hungry Minds™

For Dummies: Bestselling Book Series for Beginners

Praise For Amber Jayanti and Tarot For Dummies

"Amber's deep knowledge and genuine compassion radiate from the pages of this book, as she gently guides you toward greater understanding. She is a remarkably insightful and empowering tarot consultant. For more than a decade, Amber's teachings have remained one of my most inspiring resources."

— Maria Brignola Lee, MCAT, ADTR, NCC, Dance Movement Therapist

"Amber always manages a sense of humor and continuously shows through her actions that the real key to spirituality is to be able to take the sacred teachings down from the proverbial mountaintop and to apply them to this crazy, wonderful dance of life. She really is a practical mystic!"

— Mary F. Lyell, student of Traditional Chinese Medicine

"Amber's enthusiasm in presenting tarot as a way of self-observation is wonderful. As I acquire knowledge of the principles by applying them to my life each day, I benefit from a clear understanding through using the cards as visions of my life."

— Randall Sulger, founder of Visual Arts Practices

"Esoteric philosophy, such as tarot, is a highly open-ended subject that requires a competent teacher to continue to be an avid student of this study. As her mentor for many years, I know Amber Jayanti as such a student. Amber has had many years to develop and test her unique method of inspiring and teaching students to extend joy in their lives through understanding of this vehicle of ancient wisdom — the tarot."

— Joseph Nolen, former President of Builders of the Adytum (BOTA), teacher, lecturer

"Amber weaves her knowledge of tarot with many other aspects of society to make the presentation relevant to one's life. You have found the right person to explain tarot to the public."

— Das Smyth, CEO, Pacific Rim Media

Tarot
FOR
DUMMIES®

by Amber Jayanti

Hungry Minds™

Best-Selling Books • Digital Downloads • e-Books • Answer Networks • e-Newsletters • Branded Web Sites • e-Learning

New York, NY ◆ Cleveland, OH ◆ Indianapolis, IN

Tarot For Dummies®

Published by:
Hungry Minds, Inc.
909 Third Avenue
New York, NY 10022
www.hungryminds.com
www.dummies.com

Library of Congress Control Number: 2001089325

ISBN: 0-7645-5361-5

Printed in the United States of America

10 9 8 7 6 5 4 3 2 1

1B/RW/QX/QR/IN

Distributed in the United States by Hungry Minds, Inc.

Distributed by CDG Books Canada Inc. for Canada; by Transworld Publishers Limited in the United Kingdom; by IDG Norge Books for Norway; by IDG Sweden Books for Sweden; by IDG Books Australia Publishing Corporation Pty. Ltd. for Australia and New Zealand; by TransQuest Publishers Pte Ltd. for Singapore, Malaysia, Thailand, Indonesia, and Hong Kong; by Gotop Information Inc. for Taiwan; by ICG Muse, Inc. for Japan; by Intersoft for South Africa; by Eyrolles for France; by LR International Thomson Publishing for Germany, Austria and Switzerland; by Distribuidora Cuspide for Argentina; by LR International for Brazil; by Galileo Libros for Chile; by Ediciones ZETA S.C.R. Ltda. for Peru; by WS Computer Publishing Corporation, Inc., for the Philippines; by Contemporanea de Ediciones for Venezuela; by Express Computer Distributors for the Caribbean and West Indies; by Micronesia Media Distributor, Inc. for Micronesia; by Chips Computadoras S.A. de C.V. for Mexico; by Editorial Norma de Panama S.A. for Panama; by American Bookshops for Finland.

For general information on Hungry Minds' products and services please contact our Customer Care department; within the U.S. at 800-762-2974, outside the U.S. at 317-572-3993 or fax 317-572-4002.

For sales inquiries and resellers information, including discounts, premium and bulk quantity sales and foreign language translations please contact our Customer Care department at 800-434-3422, fax 317-572-4002 or write to Hungry Minds, Inc., Attn: Customer Care department, 10475 Crosspoint Boulevard, Indianapolis, IN 46256.

For information on licensing foreign or domestic rights, please contact our Sub-Rights Customer Care department at 212-884-5000.

For information on using Hungry Minds' products and services in the classroom or for ordering examination copies, please contact our Educational Sales department at 800-434-2086 or fax 317-572-4005.

Please contact our Public Relations department at 212-884-5163 for press review copies or 212-884-5000 for author interviews and other publicity information or fax 212-884-5400.

For authorization to photocopy items for corporate, personal, or educational use, please contact Copyright Clearance Center, 222 Rosewood Drive, Danvers, MA 01923, or fax 978-750-4470.

Hungry Minds™ is a trademark of Hungry Minds, Inc.

About the Author

Born and raised: Entered the world in the Big Apple under the sign of Pisces at the end of World War II, making me another infamous "Baby Boomer." Brought up in your typical dysfunctional, yet well-intentioned, family. Had numerous mystical and psychic experiences during childhood. These helped me survive my family situation and permanently altered my view of life.

Pre-tarot: Did well in school, yet lacked a genuine interest and enthusiasm. What I really wanted to learn, but didn't know it, was tarot and other spiritual studies. These subjects were unheard of anywhere in the public education system. Left home at an early age to make my way in the world. Worked as a fashion model until I got tired of being "just a pretty face and body."

The tarot: Love at first sight! I fell head over heels in love with the tarot in 1966. Because a fortune-teller told me "it's unlucky to buy a tarot deck for yourself," I didn't purchase a deck. Luckily, I received my first tarot deck from my best friend for Christmas in 1967 — otherwise I might still be waiting. Read every book I could find on the subject, all of which could be read in a week.

Migration: Where else but to San Francisco's Haight-Ashbury, the heart and soul of the spiritual renaissance? Met people who were interested in the tarot and astrology and yoga. Studied with Jordie Lorring, my first tarot teacher, in 1968. (Jordie, if you just happen to be reading these words, thank you ever so much. Love, Amber)

Study: Became a student of the Builders of the Adytum (BOTA) in the spring of 1968. BOTA is a Western mystery school specializing in the study of the Qabalistic Tarot and Tree of Life. Took astrology classes with a terrific teacher named Chalone Crawford.

Studied Hatha Yoga and meditation at several yoga centers. Initiated into Siddha Yoga by Swami Muktananda in 1974. Traveled and studied Eastern philosophy and spiritual practices in India, Thailand, and the Himalayas. Received an inner certainty about my life's work during my travels.

Founded: The Santa Cruz School for Tarot & Qabalah Study in 1975. The school offers four years of courses — from beginning to advanced Qabalistic Tarot and Tree of Life study.

Books: *Living the Tarot* (Wordsworth Editions, Ltd.); *Principles of the Qabalah* (HarperCollins Thorsons) and its audiotape; *Stepping Through Addictive and Codependent Behavior Using Tarot Symbolism* (self-published); *Silas and the Mad-Sad People,* a children's book on the subject of divorce and separation (New Seed, Stanford University Press).

Music: Produced a CD of *Sacred Qabalistic Chants.* (I love chanting and singing!)

Art: Created an instructive and beautiful 18-by-23-inch full-color poster of the tarot cards placed on the Qabalistic Tree of Life. Even people who are not drawn to studying or meditating on the poster tell me it's a great conversation piece.

Et cetera: Honorary Grandmaster in the American Tarot Association in 1996.

For further information: Visit www.practical-mystic.com or write: Amber Jayanti c/o The Santa Cruz School for Tarot & Qabalah Study, P.O. Box 1692, Soquel, California 95073-1692

Dedication & Acknowledgments

For my dearest, Bernard, my best friend and life partner. To my children, Kurt and Jonah, whom I'm blessed to have in my life. For my 100-year-old Grand Aunt Molly, a truly "Grand" lady.

In loving memory of my teachers Paul Foster Case, Ann Davies, Bagawan Nityananda, and Baba Muktananda, who've inspired me to know my Self.

With deepest appreciation to the Reverend Joseph P. Nolen, who has fired seekers with his "extension of the light" for over five decades.

With special thanks to tarot experts Ronald Decker and Stuart Kaplan.

To those at Hungry Minds, Inc. who helped with the preparation of this manuscript, especially my excellent editors Joan Friedman and Greg Pearson.

With gratitude to Sharon Janis and my agent, Bill Gladstone.

To my students, who've added life and love to the pages of this book and to my life.

Last but not least, to my precious friends who've stood by me through tears and laughter.

Publisher's Acknowledgments

We're proud of this book; please send us your comments through our Online Registration Form located at www.dummies.com.

Some of the people who helped bring this book to market include the following:

Acquisitions, Editorial, and Media Development

Senior Project Editor: Joan L. Friedman

Acquisitions Editor: Michael Cunningham

Copy Editor: Greg Pearson

Technical Editor: Wendy Cohen

Editorial Manager: Christine Meloy Beck

Editorial Assistant: Jennifer Young

Production

Project Coordinator: Nancee Reeves

Layout and Graphics: Amy Adrian, Joyce Haughey, Jackie Nicholas, Barry Offringa, Jill Piscitelli, Julie Trippetti

Proofreaders: John Greenough, Andy Hollandbeck, Marianne Santy, TECHBOOKS Production Services

Indexer: Sharon Hilgenberg

General and Administrative

Hungry Minds, Inc.: John Kilcullen, CEO; Bill Barry, President and COO; John Ball, Executive VP, Operations & Administration; John Harris, CFO

Hungry Minds Consumer Reference Group

Business: Kathleen Nebenhaus, Vice President and Publisher; Kevin Thornton, Acquisitions Manager

Cooking/Gardening: Jennifer Feldman, Associate Vice President and Publisher; Anne Ficklen, Executive Editor; Kristi Hart, Managing Editor

Education/Reference: Diane Graves Steele, Vice President and Publisher

Lifestyles: Kathleen Nebenhaus, Vice President and Publisher; Tracy Boggier, Managing Editor

Pets: Dominique De Vito, Associate Vice President and Publisher; Tracy Boggier, Managing Editor

Travel: Michael Spring, Vice President and Publisher; Brice Gosnell, Publishing Director; Suzanne Jannetta, Editorial Director

Hungry Minds Consumer Editorial Services: Kathleen Nebenhaus, Vice President and Publisher; Kristin A. Cocks, Editorial Director; Cindy Kitchel, Editorial Director

Hungry Minds Consumer Production: Debbie Stailey, Production Director

◆

The publisher would like to give special thanks to Patrick J. McGovern, without whom this book would not have been possible.

◆

Contents at a Glance

Cartoons at a Glance

By Rich Tennant

The 5th Wave By Rich Tennant
EDWARD SCISSORHANDS: TAROT READER

"Gee, Edward - I'd have been happy to cut the deck for you."

page 7

The 5th Wave By Rich Tennant

"This deck was designed by Coco Chanel in the '50's. That's why the queens all carry small quilted handbags."

page 59

The 5th Wave By Rich Tennant
THE SOLITAIRE SPREAD

"...8 of swords on the 9 of cups, 4 of wands on the 5 of pentacles..."

page 169

The 5th Wave By Rich Tennant
TAROT READINGS

"Just try it! If you can reference an astrological chart in a tarot reading, why not a racing form?"

page 253

The 5th Wave By Rich Tennant
ALWAYS KEEP YOUR TAROT DECK IN A SAFE PLACE AWAY FROM CHILDREN

"What does it mean when Pikachu appears between two sphinxes?"

page 301

Cartoon Information:
Fax: 978-546-7747
E-Mail: richtennant@the5thwave.com
World Wide Web: www.the5thwave.com

Table of Contents

Introduction

Welcome to the wide and wonderful world of tarot! Life is a set of picture symbols, and so is the tarot. If you think about it, you've been interpreting picture symbols all your life. For example, when you see a six-sided red sign posted on a street corner while driving, you interpret it as a signal to stop, no matter what language the word is written in. Or, say that one of your bosses smiles at you, and another frowns. It's likely you'd see the "happy face" as friendly and communicating that you're liked, and the "sad face" as unfriendly and communicating that you're disliked. Also, there's an excellent chance you'll see danger and devastation in a house fire, yet feel relief and recovery as the fire truck pulls up.

The tarot is a bona fide form of do-it-yourself spirituality that's been misused, misunderstood, and disgraced for generations. Because of human development, modern technology, and worldwide communications spreading formerly inaccessible teachings, people like you are realizing it's unnecessary to have a middle person between themselves and divinity.

If you're reading these words, you probably believe that all knowledge, wisdom, and truth lie within. You're also probably aware that the true role of spiritual teachings and teachers is to remind you about and put you in touch with the source of knowledge, wisdom, and truth. The tarot is a symbolic system through which hundreds of thousands of people, if not more, accomplish this. It's my honor, privilege, and delight to guide you through the tarot.

My job is to help you make friends with the tarot. I'm offering you suggestions, wisdom teachings, personal and student experiences, and common sense information sprinkled with as many chuckles as possible. In this book, I show you as much of this marvelous system as I think needs presenting for a worthwhile introduction. When you finish this book you'll know whether or not the tarot is a tool you want to know even better. You'll also have some clear ideas about how you can pursue more knowledge.

About This Book

Tarot For Dummies offers the basics of tarot from my point of view. Please be aware that you may encounter very different approaches to the tarot in other books. What you'll find in this book has been taken from my years of studying, teaching, consulting, and "living" the tarot. It is also spiced with comments and experiences from my students and other people who I've met along the way.

For centuries, the tarot has been for the few, not the many. My six primary goals for this book are:

- ✔ To make the tarot accessible and comprehensible to people from all walks of life and backgrounds.

- ✔ To provide you with a clear and simple reference book that can answer your questions about the tarot and demonstrate some of the wonderful things you can do with the tarot.

- ✔ To alter the tarot's long-standing image as a worthless fortune-telling device employed for extracting large sums of money from hapless people.

- ✔ To show that newspaper, TV, and movie accounts of the tarot as a murderer's calling card and tool for practicing black magic are inaccurate.

- ✔ To present the tarot as a nonsexist, nonracist, nonhomophobic, nondogmatic, and multi-denominational system of bona fide spiritual teachings and practices.

- ✔ To demonstrate how the tarot can bring you a deeper and clearer understanding of yourself, others, and the world around you through the universal language of picture symbols.

My Assumptions about You

I'm assuming that you are interested in, if not fascinated with, the tarot. You probably have had your tarot cards read, or have been wanting to have them read for quite a while.

I'm assuming that you're fairly new to reading tarot cards and want to get your feet wet. I'm offering you a warm and friendly wading pool.

I'm assuming that you have a sense of humor. If you can't laugh at your own lack of knowledge or misinformation, close this book immediately.

If you're at an intermediate level, I'm assuming that you're looking to expand your knowledge of the tarot further plus check out how the tarot is linked with astrology and numerology. I'm offering you some new and exciting possibilities while confirming some of what you already know.

If you're an advanced student, I'm assuming that one of the reasons you've picked up this book is because you're interested in one of the tarot's siblings — astrology, numerology, alchemy — or even her parents, the Qabalah. I'll also be so presumptuous as to assume that you may have read and enjoyed some of my more esoteric writing. As an advanced student, I'm assuming you remember that no matter how mundane a teaching seems, the mystic perceives the mystical at its core.

I'm assuming that you're reading this book with an open mind and are wishing to raise your level of awareness. I'm also assuming that you won't agree with everything I say or suggest you do.

My final assumption (this is beginning to sound like a religious rite) is that you know *you* are the final authority on the contents of this book and the tarot. I'm sharing my knowledge and experiences; it's up to you to take what you need and leave the rest.

Whomever you are and whatever your reasons for reading these words, I welcome you with respect and love.

How This Book is Organized

Friendships start by people asking each other questions and sharing information, and this book follows suit. Part I answers the first questions you'd ask about the tarot. It tells you about different tarot decks and suggests where and how you can find your tarot deck. It also explores the tarot's fascinating roots and the many types of tarot practitioners. Part II offers you both an overview and a detailed journey through the tarot deck. Part III introduces you to several enjoyable and interesting ways of using the tarot and shows you how to care for your cards. Part IV provides you with a look at the tarot's relationship with other members of her family. Part V is the standard Part of Tens you find in all *For Dummies* books, with tips guaranteed to give you some giggles that help you keep some important tarot principles alive and well in your life. This book could be the beginning of a beautiful and lasting friendship between you and the tarot.

Part I: It's All in How You See It

This part introduces you to the tarot by answering the most frequently asked questions about this set of picture symbols or archetypes. You'll get a look at the tarot's many types of practitioners, from gypsies to members of the Fortune 500, and go on a shopping spree for your own special tarot deck. I show you tarot decks from antiquity to the 21st century, and I introduce you to the Western mystery school tradition.

Part II: Pick a Card, Any Card: A Guided Tour Through the Tarot Deck

This part gives you an overview of the deck, then takes you on a step-by-step guided tour focusing on each card's basic meaning. I begin with the 22 major arcana cards, continue with the 40 minor arcana number or *pip* cards, and finish with the 16 court or royalty cards.

Part III: The Tarot and You: The ABCs of Tarot Reading (And Then Some)

This part explains methods of finding cards that are relevant to you, your loved ones and friends, history, and special events. It takes you through the hows, whys, and whens of working with the tarot and provides ways of deepening what you've experienced so far with tarot meditation. I show you several interesting and informative tarot spreads along with their interpretations, and I offer some advice if you're considering a career as a tarot professional.

Part IV: The Tarot and Her Family: Seeing Through Other Eyes

This part links the tarot with her kin, the Qabalah and Tree of Life, astrology, numerology, and alchemy. Your understanding of tarot is enhanced as you journey from childhood to old sage by each of the tarot's major arcana cards.

Part V: The Part of Tens

This part should be called "Famous Last Words." The Part of Tens offers tips guaranteed to give you a few chuckles while helping you remember some of this book's key principles. It goes into the "Top Ten Tarot Misconceptions" and "The Ten Cards Most Likely to Cause a Freak-Out." These chapters will aid your perspective and provide you with ideas to keep the tarot's basic principles alive and well in your life.

Icons Used in the Book

In the margins of the pages of this book, you will find little pictures called *icons* to guide you through the ideas I present. Here's a list of what they mean:

This icon points out a tarot principle or point worth remembering. It shows the bottom line.

This icon indicates a potential trap or pitfall that you might encounter while working with the tarot.

This icon points out examples of aspects of the tarot being applied to everyday life.

These suggestions are meant to help you apply tarot principles to your life and practice.

Where to Go From Here

As with other books in the *For Dummies* series, this one is made for skimming, or cover-to-cover reading, or the exploration of specific topics.

- **Skimming:** My goal is to have most parts, chapters, and sections stand on their own, so that you can open this book to almost any place and start reading.

  This might work in some segments, but not in others. For example, unless you are familiar with the meanings of the tarot cards, it would be best to read Part II before going on to Part III. Of course, Part V ("The Part of Tens") can be read any time — first, last, or in the middle of your reading.

- **Cover-to-cover:** If you are interested in all facets of tarot, I suggest starting at the beginning of this book and reading it through to the end. I wrote this book in an order that builds on itself, just in case you are one of those people who likes to start at the beginning and end at the final page.

- **Specific topics:** This book touches on what I believe a beginner would like to know about the tarot, and the topics are listed in both the Table of Contents and the index. If you are interested in finding out about reading the cards right out of the gate, you would skip Part I and go directly to Parts II and III. If you have always wondered how the tarot compares with astrology and other spiritual systems, begin with Part IV.

I recommend that you follow your own inner directives. Read the book in any way that fits your special personality.

Part I
It's All in How You See It

EDWARD SCISSORHANDS: TAROT READER

"Gee, Edward—I'd have been happy to cut the deck for you."

In this part . . .

Part I introduces you to the origins and impact of the tarot. I define the word *tarot* and answer questions that most people have as they begin to work with the cards. To show you that you have lots of company in your interest about tarot, I explain how various groups of people use the cards. Plus, I escort you on a virtual shopping trip by detailing the decks available to you. I show you the tarot's long and mysterious history, introduce you to decks both old and new, and explain the mystery school tradition and its influence on the tarot.

Chapter 1

Making Friends with the Tarot

*L*adies and gentlemen, children of all ages, may I have your attention please! Step right up and make friends with the tarot. In this book, I help you begin to understand what this amazing set of pictures is about and how it can impact your life. I hope to fill you with wonder, eliminate your fears, and illuminate what the tarot is and how it has evolved through the ages.

Before I can accomplish all these goals, I need to start with the basics: What is the tarot, and what is its purpose? This chapter tackles these questions by introducing you to the power of pictures and showing you how you can use the tarot to create positive change in your life.

To experience everything this book has to offer, you must be prepared to take a leap of faith. So slip on your best leaping shoes, grab a hat with wings on it, and come along for a remarkable journey.

Introducing the Tarot

What exactly is the tarot? This whole book is devoted to answering that question, but let's start with the basics. A typical tarot deck is comprised of 78 cards. Twenty-two of these cards make up the *major arcana,* which contain images such as The Fool, The Lovers, The Hanged Man, and The World. (In Chapter 7, I show you each card in the major arcana.) The other 56 cards in a typical tarot deck are the *minor arcana* cards, made up of four suits, generally called wands, cups, swords, and pentacles. The first 40 minor arcana cards are each numbered from ace through ten (see Chapter 8). The last 16 are called *court* or *royalty cards* because they depict kings, queens, knights, and pages (see Chapter 9).

Although I assume that you've probably seen tarot cards before, in case you haven't, flip right now to the color insert in the middle of this book. Doing so will give you a sense of the wide spectrum of tarot decks available, but more importantly, it will show you the first thing you must know about the tarot: The tarot is a set of pictures.

An old Chinese proverb states that "a picture is worth 10,000 words." In tarot-speak, one picture can be seen in an infinite number of ways. Each of us can look at the picture on a tarot card and interpret some of what we see in the same way, based upon our similar human experiences. However, no two people will interpret the meaning of a card in exactly the same way, because our personal experiences color what we see and how we interpret it. A nutritionist won't see the same thing as a shaman, and you won't see the same thing that I see. As I discuss in this chapter, that's part of the reason why the tarot can be so powerful.

Thinking in pictures or symbols is an elementary function of the human mind. Whether you realize it or not, you're constantly interpreting picture symbols. You get these nonverbal messages from your parents, peers, teachers, newspapers, magazines, movies, MTV videos, churches, temples, mosques . . . the list could go on and on.

Most of the time, people don't consciously realize that they are interpreting pictures in certain ways, and that their interpretations impact the way they think, feel, and act. They live "on automatic," and they don't recognize their own power to change their thoughts, feelings, and actions. That's where the power of tarot comes in: Tarot can help you become conscious of how you view the world and yourself. After you become aware of the way that you interpret the pictures of your life, you have the opportunity to change your interpretations for the better.

Harnessing the Power of Symbols

You may not even realize it, but your life is shaped by symbols that are passed to you or inherited from your culture, your race, your peer and social groups, and your family. Newspapers, magazines, TV, and movies have a similar impact. Discovering how these symbols affect your life is essential to understanding how the tarot works. These symbols or *archetypes* — ideas or ways of thinking inherited from all these sources and present in your subconscious — are the models that you pattern your life after.

Becoming aware of archetypes

Archetypes are embedded in your *subconscious* — the part of your mind that is free from conscious awareness. For you skeptics in the audience, let me offer an example of what I mean. The picture symbol of an evergreen tree decorated with lights and other ornaments is an archetype for Christmas. Without consciously thinking about it, you are prompted to think of snow and Christmas presents when you see a picture like this. (And depending on your past experiences, you may feel anything from excitement and hope to depression and anxiety.) Archetypes send shorthand messages to your subconscious and conscious minds, which elicit varying responses.

Personal and impersonal (universal) archetypes

As I see it, there are both personal and impersonal (universal) archetypes or concepts. Personal archetypes are based on your particular experiences whereas impersonal or universal archetypes are based on the experiences of humanity as a whole.

The concept of a horse demonstrates the difference between personal and impersonal archetypes. If you say the word *horse* to one person, it evokes particular associations — images, thoughts, and feelings. One person may associate a horse with fun and freedom, while another (who has been thrown from a horse) associates it with fear and pain. These are personal archetypes. The impersonal, universal archetype — a symbol's mythical and/or culturally based meaning — exists in the collective unconscious (which I explain in the next section). The universal archetypes associated with *horse* include honor, a rise in status, and spiritual or magical, mystical journeys to other worlds. When interpreting tarot cards, both personal and impersonal archetypes should be considered for a balanced perspective. One of the goals of tarot interpretation is bringing these perspectives together.

Although archetypes of both types are powerful, they're not set in stone. Before the invention of the car, the universal archetype of a horse signified honor and status. Luxury cars now signify some of the same things horses once did. Personal archetypes obviously can change as you gain more experiences. If you're fearful of horses, being nuzzled by a foal while feeding her carrots can turn that fearful association around.

Life is a set of pictures. When we change our worn-out associations with these pictures, we change ourselves and, inadvertently, the world around us!

Personal and universal archetypes project ideas that can help you learn about how you should behave and what's important in life. For example, say that a young man keeps seeing the archetype of marriage on the screen of his life because one friend after another gets married. Soon he starts thinking things like, "All my friends are getting married. I'd better start dating more people so I can get married too." Or, conversely, "All my friends are getting married, but my parents got divorced. I'm not going to get married because I know it just leads to pain down the road."

Archetypal patterns take root through duplication. If a symbol keeps bombarding you, it has a good chance of influencing your life. For instance, tattoos have come into fashion. You notice a coffee table book at a large bookstore featuring tattoo art from all over the world. The latest edition of your favorite music and fashion magazine features tattooed performers and models. Without realizing it, you find yourself admiring tattooed bodies at your health club. Your best friend gets a tattoo, and another is talking about designing her own. Because the image keeps coming at you — or *duplicating* itself — you may soon begin daydreaming about the kind of tattoo you'd like and where you'd put it.

Collective unconscious

Your subconscious mind is always receptive and suggestible. These traits make the subconscious mind very similar to what we call the *collective unconscious,* or the "mass mind." The collective unconscious is a collection of memories of all human experiences from the beginning of time. You and everyone else on the planet can tap into the collective unconscious, which is also receptive and suggestible. The subconscious is like a stream, and the collective unconscious is like a river: One flows into the other, and sometimes you don't know which is which. The subconscious and the collective unconscious wield influence over your life that you may not yet be aware of.

Here's an example of how the collective unconscious might affect you. Movies, TV, newspapers, and books often suggest that dark haired, swarthy men wearing sunglasses and shiny suits are mobsters. Unless consciously challenged, this *collection* of thoughts becomes part of your personal subconscious. When your college roommate's father shows up for graduation looking like this archetype, you automatically starting thinking "mobster," whether it's true or not.

Want another example? Here's a true story of how the collective unconscious affected a friend of mine, Rick. When the AIDS virus was first discovered, there was more fear than real knowledge being transmitted by the collective unconscious. Rick, a college professor, picked up the idea that the disease could be caught by using the same glass, plate, spoon, or fork as someone with the virus. When an old friend with AIDS came for dinner, I watched as Rick put on a pair of rubber gloves and threw the man's eating utensils into the trash.

Until you become aware of what's been conditioned into your subconscious mind and the influence of the collective unconscious, you coast through life without consciously realizing why you think, say, and do certain things.

Consider this example: If you were born and raised in Southeast Asia and you saw a man dressed in saffron robes standing in the street extending a bowl for food, the archetype of holiness would automatically rise up from your subconscious. If you were born and raised in the United States, this same image might bring archetypes or associations of poverty and/or worthlessness, incompetence, and helplessness up from your subconscious.

This is just a single example of how archetypes make themselves into reality through your subconscious and the collective unconscious. The process of changing archetypes into reality can cause joy, suffering, and everything in between. If a man keeps thinking of himself as a chiropractor and attends chiropractic college, he will (barring unforeseen circumstances) reach his goal. If a beautiful, large boned woman keeps duplicating the archetype of "only thin is beautiful," she could diet herself into anorexia — and the hospital.

Picturing a new perspective

In the introduction to this chapter, I mention that the tarot is a set of pictures. Now I can get more specific and tell you that the tarot is a group of cards bearing pictures that tap into both personal and universal archetypes.

Reinventing yourself

Archetypes play a role in determining what you think about yourself and other people. They can also impact your success at work, your values, your physical appearance, and even your health. Some of the archetypes that you adopt make you happy, and others make you sad. Archetypes are so powerful that they can even imprison or free you. Do I hear you yelling "How do I get outta here?"

You're in luck. You can reinvent yourself. When used properly, the tarot is a set of archetypal symbols possessing the potential to do amazing things. The renowned mystic P.D. Ouspensky stated that "the tarot contains the means to build anything, even a new world."

The tarot can help you become aware of the archetypes or symbol patterns embedded in your subconscious and the collective unconscious, that keep coming at you with suggestions to be someone other than who you want to be. The tarot can help you separate the archetypes you want from those you don't. The tarot's imagery can help you assign different and better meanings to the picture symbols of your life. The tarot can also help you adopt new and improved habits that support your chosen course of action. For example, when I decided to stop drinking coffee and start drinking more nourishing beverages, I saw myself as the woman in the Strength card and coffee as the lion (see Chapter 7). When I'd feel my desire for coffee roar, I'd call up

Strength's image. It reminded me that I have the final say about acting on my desires. Nine times out of ten Strength got me mixing up a healthy protein shake instead reaching for the java.

About a dozen years ago, I did tarot with Kate. Her tarot reading centered around her feelings of not being smart enough. Kate's parents are brilliant. Although Kate's IQ is at genius level, she felt dumb in comparison to her parents. The cards helped her become aware that her ultra-competitive parents unconsciously sent her picture symbols and ideas that indicated she wasn't nearly as smart as they were. Kate decided that they had sent her these symbols to make her try harder. But instead of trying harder, she felt that she would never succeed in fulfilling her dream of becoming a physicist. Kate kept feeling and thinking that her efforts were hopeless, because she wasn't as smart as dad and mom. The tarot cards' imagery showed Kate how her subconscious adopted the picture symbols for not being smart enough. Becoming aware of these symbols made all the difference for Kate. Last year, I received a letter from her that told me how the cards helped her take the first step in altering her lifelong pattern. Kate now works as a physicist at a world-renowned organization.

Changing an archetype and changing the result

Tarot is a tool that helps you look at the archetypes you're holding and determine if and how you'd benefit from changing them. When you change an archetype — an image, symbol, or concept — you can, in time, change yourself. When you change yourself, you help change the world.

The fall of Communism is a good example of the power of changing an archetype. Person after person in the Soviet Union changed their archetype by picturing themselves and their country as free. And *in time,* the new archetype gathered enough momentum or critical mass to happen. One of the greatest wonders of the tarot is that *over time* it helps to alter erroneous impressions you receive from your subconscious and the collective unconscious. I emphasize the word *time* to help you remember that change takes time. It took time for the Soviets to get fed up, and it took even more time to amass enough energy to make the change and become a free nation.

Because the subconscious makes you do things automatically (without thinking), it is also referred to as the *reactive* or *re-inactive* mind. You can probably recall times when you've said and done things that you wouldn't have if you had thought more about it. Maybe you've looked at your life and asked yourself, "What's wrong with this picture?" What's wrong is the way you see — or do not see — things.

Your training has shown you only a few ways of interpreting life's pictures. You are going to keep interpreting them in the same way until you wake up and ask, "Why am I doing this?"

How you interpret the pictures of your life is based upon your limited understanding of these pictures. When your understanding expands, your ability to look at yourself and your life expands — you start seeing your life from an expanded perspective. This is called "seeing the big in the little" or raising your consciousness.

The tarot offers you an opportunity to look at things from this expanded point of view. This simple shift in perspective has helped thousands of people know who and what they really are, what life is about, and what their place is in the world. The tarot can help you do likewise.

There's a saying in the Ageless Wisdom of the tarot (teachings that convey universal and natural laws and principles that are never outdated): Change the picture, and eventually you change the result. In the next section, I explain how one person did exactly this.

Geri's birthday gift

On the afternoon of her 42nd birthday, Geri got a surprise gift from her boss. Following the company-sponsored birthday cake and soft drinks, Geri opened her pay envelope and found a pink slip. Geri had been laid off. Immediately, her heart sank, and she felt like throwing up. Soon Geri felt furious about getting fired and awash with worries about her future. All this because of a pink slip of paper: What a powerful symbol.

Before knowing tarot, Geri would have seen only doom and gloom. But because she knew the power of tarot, she instead went home and pulled out her cards. She sat quietly and considered what she wanted to know about her work situation. After saying a short prayer, Geri laid out a simple five-card spread (which I show you how to do in Chapter 13).

Within a few minutes of looking at the cards, Geri began to see her work situation from the bigger picture. She thought, "My company has been downsizing for several months. It's crossed my mind that I could get laid off and should put out feelers for other jobs. I've been so bogged down working 12-hour days that I haven't had the time or energy to send out my resume or to phone friends in my field. Now I have a paid opportunity to do this. If I get into my old pattern of wallowing in pity, I can see myself falling into a deep depression. If I don't wallow and start doing what I know I've needed to do for awhile — being proactive — my future looks promising." Geri felt much better.

Speaking from experience

Like Geri, I work with the tarot to help myself become more proficient at reading or interpreting the picture-symbols in my life, changing the archetypes as I go. Time and again, the cards have gently yet firmly and safely guided me through life challenges: divorce, single parenting, remarriage, life in a blended family, the deaths of my parents and other loved ones, and even the maze of working in my unusual profession. The bottom line is that the tarot has helped raise my consciousness in innumerable ways and situations.

I don't work with the tarot to predict the future, but the tarot does help me co-create a future of conscious choice and avoid a future that is the result of following worn-out patterns that I'm honestly tired of repeating.

I read tarot so that I can see more in myself, others, and life situations than I perceive is present initially. The following saying in tarot-speak sums this up perfectly: "You make tomorrow by what you do today." If you're anything like me, Geri, and countless others, exploring the tarot holds something for you.

An individual interpretation

Ten people who look at the same work of art will have ten different interpretations of what they see. Even if you look at the same image two days in a row, you may interpret it differently each day. (I find this fascinating when I teach classes about the tarot.) This is because so many factors influence your interpretation. Your culture, family, schooling, profession, hobbies, and religious and spiritual training influence your perspective. You are also influenced by countless other factors:

- **Time of day.** Are you a morning or evening person?
- **Weather.** Are you feeling contracted by winter cold, or exhilarated by late spring sunshine?
- **Health.** Do you have PMS, or sore muscles from gardening, or have you just taken a rejuvenating nap?
- **Surroundings.** Is it quiet, or noisy? Do you like background music? (I prefer silence.) What scent, if any, is in the air? (The scent of hairspray wafting across the room makes me want to run, while musk makes me feel warm and sensual.)
- **State of mind and emotions.** Are you fearful, hurt, and angry? Or are you relaxed, open-minded, and empathetic?

Like art, the tarot is many things to many people. Don't try to force your interpretation of a certain image to match anyone else's, or even to match how you have interpreted it previously.

What Does Your Name Mean, Tarot?

Knowing the meaning of a new friend's name is interesting and insightful. For example, my blue-eyed, blond-haired, dark-skinned friend Aliyah, of Irish and Native American ancestry, astounds new friends when explaining the origins of her unusual name. Aliyah received her Hebrew name as a special birthday present from her spiritual teacher. Each time she speaks, writes, or hears *Aliyah*, she's reminded of her beloved teacher and her own spiritual practice. When Aliyah glowingly tells her story and explains the meaning of her name — "to step up to God" — friends get a pretty good idea of Aliyah's ideals and philosophy of life.

As you make friends with the tarot, you may want to know what its name means. The dictionary offers some interesting meanings, plus a bit of history.

Looking it up

According to Webster's Third International Dictionary, the word *tarot* has Middle French and Old Italian roots. Tarot is defined as "Any set of 22 playing cards consisting of a joker plus 21 cards depicting vices, virtues and elemental forces used in fortune-telling and as trump, a suit of cards that outrank other cards, in tarok, taroc, or tarocchi games." Tarok, taroc, or tarocchi is a card game that was developed in fourteenth-century Italy. The game was played with 78 cards, 22 of which were used as trumps. (The 22 trump cards are what we call the *major arcana* cards, which I discuss in detail in Chapter 7.)

For you sticklers on grammar, please note that the word *tarot* is capitalized only when you refer to a specific deck of cards, such as **The Light and Shadow Tarot.**

Acceptable pronunciations of tarot are:

TAHrow, as in arrow or marrow

TUHrow, as in furrow or burrow

TARrot, TarOH, and TAHrit are acceptable only around roofers, road pavers, and vegetables!

Creating anagrams

As a student in a Qabalistic mystery school (which I explain in Chapter 5), I was taught that the meaning of the word *tarot* is hidden within the word itself. Its meaning is a mystery that members of the school, or *initiates,* eventually decipher for themselves. The game of anagrams offers a fun and interesting way to decipher the meaning of the word. In the game, you use the letters of a word to make as many other words as possible.

Taking this game a step farther, you combine the meaning of the new words to understand the meaning of the word you started with. Playing this game with the word *tarot,* I came up with a deeper and more complete meaning than any dictionary offers.

Here's a listing of the anagrams I created from *tarot:* orat, tora, rota, art, tao, ro, and tar. (Try saying these words very quickly three times for one super tongue twister!)

- ✔ **Orat** is a Latin word for an oracle or speaker, someone through whom wisdom, hidden knowledge, and divine purposes are revealed.

- ✔ **Tora** is another form of the word *Torah,* the body of divine knowledge and law found in the ancient Hebrew scriptures. The Torah is the first five books of the Old Testament.

- ✔ **Rota** is the Latin word for *wheel,* giving us the ideas of rotation, cycles of change, and evolution — the laws of nature.

- ✔ **Art** is an appropriate anagram because the tarot is a set of pictures. It's also one of the hermetic arts and sciences — along with astrology, numerology, alchemy, and sacred geometry (see Chapter 4).

- ✔ **Tao** is a Mandarin Chinese word translated as "the way to eternal truth."

- ✔ **Ro** is Egyptian for "royal."

- ✔ **Tar** is believed to be an abbreviation for *Thoth,* the Egyptian messenger of the gods/goddesses/godhead who served as advisor to the king. Tar is the Egyptian counterpart of the Roman god Mercury and the Greek god Hermes. Tar is also interpreted to mean "road." And yes, tar is the black sticky stuff that you never want on your living room rug.

- ✔ **Ator** is an abbreviation for Hator, the Egyptian Goddess of Nature.

Putting it all together

Combining the meanings of these anagrams, I decided that the word *tarot* means the following:

> a set of pictures, acting as oracles, speakers, or messengers from the gods, goddesses, or godhead, that communicate a body of divine knowledge and purposes, eternal truths, and natural law that are a royal road or "way" to higher consciousness, also known as enlightenment.

As you see in the sidebar "Differing perspectives on the tarot," the tarot is a living, growing, constantly transforming, yet stable philosophy and system. (Yes, the tarot is filled with paradoxes.) By the time you finish reading this book, you may want to jot down what the tarot means to you.

Differing perspectives on the tarot

I emphasize throughout this book that the tarot takes on different meanings for different people. Following are some examples of what the tarot means to people I've met through the years:

Roger, the software engineer: "Each tarot card is like a file in my computer. I click on the card or file, and up pops the information I'm looking for."

Lorn, the Buddhist: "The tarot is the Western equivalent to the Tibetan Buddhist *tonkas,* highly detailed *mandala-like images* (designs symbolizing universal principles that bring personal wholeness and universal awareness) that put the Buddhist teachings into picture form."

Linda, the psychiatrist: "The tarot is a set of therapeutic picture symbols that link my clients to their subconscious mind and promote healing."

Heri, the shaman: "The tarot is a magic mirror through which I see past the world of matter into the world of spirits."

Claire, the second-grade teacher: "The tarot is a tool that helps to develop the whole brain."

Oggie, the witch: "The tarot is a 'natural religion' that honors a generic God."

Constance, the feminist: "The tarot is my way of connecting with the Goddess."

Nancy, the Hatha Yoga teacher: "I see the tarot as western Yoga — each card is a yogic teaching, *asana,* or posture."

Sammy, the nutritionist: "The tarot's 22 major arcana cards are the 22 amino acids."

The Jehovah's Witness (man at the door, name unknown): "The tarot is a tool of the devil that will prevent you from being saved with us on Judgment Day."

Lorna, the Sufi: "The tarot is another way of seeing the workings of the Beloved in my life."

Terri, the lesbian: "The tarot is the first spiritual system that showed me men have a female side."

Paul, the gay: "The tarot is a way I can connect with God without having to go to a church that tries to sanction who I make love with."

Tom, the ex-Mormon: "The tarot is a collection of holy scriptures in pictures."

The Jungian: "You and I are multi-faceted people. The tarot cards mirror aspects of our personalities that require contemplation and understanding."

Aaron, the *Kabbalist* (Jewish mystic): "The tarot is the ancient Hebrew alphabet in modern costumes and customs."

Elizabeth, the free-thinking iconoclast: "The tarot is a tool that helps me formulate a new image of my self and the world that matches my continuously changing belief system."

Matt, the *gnostic* (someone with personal knowledge of the impersonal): "The tarot is spiritual and mystical knowledge of my Self, the Divine, and of the order of the universe that's not associated with any type of religious dogma."

Chapter 2

Who Uses the Tarot and Why?

● ●

In This Chapter

▶ Predicting the future

▶ Communicating with spirits

▶ Supplementing therapy

▶ Taking tarot to the boardroom and classroom

● ●

*H*undreds of thousands (maybe even millions) of people are interested in and use the tarot. In this chapter, I show you that people who use tarot, like you, come from all walks of life. All age groups, races, and ethnic backgrounds are represented among tarot users. You probably pass tarot people on the street all the time but don't realize it! (They don't usually wear identifying marks, other than an occasional tee shirt, pendant, or earring showing a card that has special meaning for them.)

Despite what sensational newspaper coverage, TV shows, and B movies keep telling you, people who use tarot aren't all that unusual. Yes, every once in a while you hear about someone who is truly strange using tarot, such as Charles Manson, but those are the exceptions.

For the most part, tarot people are curious and intelligent, just like you. In the past, I've taught and consulted with pharmacists, jewelers, business executives, secretaries, teachers, software engineers, social workers, chemical dependency counselors, surfers, marathon runners, librarians, lawyers, doctors, court reporters, post office and court clerks, musicians, writers, dancers, actors, and on and on and on.

In more than 30 years of tarot work, I've had students and clients from ages 7 to 97. (One 95-year-old great, great grandmother, who had been doing card readings for more than 75 years, consulted me for a second opinion on a personal issue.) I've met with everyone from Hindu *sanyasins* (monks and nuns) to children of the rich and famous trying to find themselves.

In this chapter, I describe some of the groups of people who regularly use tarot cards and explain why the tarot is so useful to them. I start with some of the groups you probably already associate with the tarot, such as gypsies and psychics, and then I move to groups of people whose use of the tarot may come as a surprise to you.

Gypsy Fortune-Tellers, Psychics, and Mystics

I'm betting that one of the first images that comes to mind when you think of a gypsy fortune-teller is a dark-eyed man or woman, sitting in a dimly lit wooden wagon, laying out tarot cards on an embroidered scarf. There's a chance you're also thinking that the gypsy is a liar and a cheat.

I'm betting that one of the first images that comes to mind when you think of a psychic is a person with closed eyes, holding folded slips of paper, with questions written on them, over her "third eye." There's a chance you're also thinking the psychic is a fraud.

I'm betting that one of the first images that comes to mind when you think of a mystic is a half-dressed man with a long, white beard, sitting cross-legged, meditating in a cave. Or perhaps you think of a pale, emaciated woman, bleeding from *stigmata* — sores resembling the crucifixion wounds of Jesus. There's a good chance you're also thinking that the mystic cannot live in the everyday world.

Because these ideas are embedded in the *collective unconscious,* the collection of archetypes or models stored within the group mind of humanity, they are also most likely deeply embedded in your personal subconscious. In this section, I offer you some new ways to see these groups of people.

Gypsies: Beating a bad rap

Gypsy is a shortened form of the word *Egyptian.* Legend says that the tarot was given to the Egyptians in ancient times, and they, because of commerce, traveled the world sowing the tarot's wisdom.

We now know that the gypsies were nomadic people who probably originated in or near India. The gypsies did not necessarily develop the tarot, but they did help spread its reputation for "fortune-telling" wherever they traveled.

Gypsies usually adopt the religion of their country of residence, and they're traditionally sorcerers and necromancers. Because necromancers conjure up spirits of the dead to help them predict the future, gypsies gravitated to the tarot cards as a means of communicating this information.

Historically, the gypsies have been an exceptionally poor people, often earning their livings as metal workers, singers, dancers, musicians, horse dealers, auto mechanics, and of course, fortune-tellers. Because they are often underpaid and overworked, desperation drives some gypsies into unlawful activities, including giving faulty tarot readings. This behavior is part of the reason why the gypsies and tarot have gotten a bad rap. But it's important to realize that most tarot readers, including gypsies, are not trying to rip you off.

If you'd like to find out more about the gypsies, read *Bury Me Standing,* a superb book by cultural anthropologist Isabel Fonseca.

Psychics: Getting specific about the future

Psychics, sometimes called *sensitives,* also work with the tarot. Like the gypsy, the psychic taps into the unseen world of spirits. This world is comprised of humans who are in spirit form and lack bodies, divine spirits who never get bodies (such as angels), and the astral or spirit bodies of living humans. Some psychics also claim to contact the spirits of animals and plants.

Like the gypsy fortune-tellers, psychics use the tarot cards as a medium for expressing themselves to clients. Psychics channel information from the spirit world to you, and many psychics claim to have communication with the dead. They use the tarot as a vehicle for helping you see what they see. Most psychics give specific information, such as "You've been trying to get pregnant" or "When your girlfriend's father dies he's not going to leave the house to her."

Psychics advise in terms of good and bad, and they tell you what you should or shouldn't do. They also predict the future — for you and others. For instance, a psychic might say:

- "Don't quit your job for another six months, or you'll be sorry."
- "Put your money in the bank, and you'll be richer than if you invest it in real estate."
- "Your wife shouldn't drive your new car across the country, or else she'll have an accident."

If you're seeking this kind of information from the tarot, a psychic is for you.

Mystics: Communicating with divine spirits

The mystic also has access to the world of spirits in and out of physical form and the world of divine spirits who never take on physical form. But unlike a psychic, a mystic does a tarot reading from the world of divine spirits alone. Mystics don't believe that a spirit without a body knows more than a spirit with a body. Mystics use the tarot like a mirror, holding the cards up for you to look into and see yourself more clearly.

Mystics don't give advice in terms of good and bad. For the mystic, life is what you make of it; it's all in how you interpret life's pictures, or the tarot cards that are extensions of these pictures. Mystics give advice in terms of your spiritual development. For example, a mystic might say, "This is what your relationship with your mother looks like. Let's see how handling it is an opportunity for spiritual growth and wisdom." The mystic uses the tarot to point out universal principles that assist you in figuring out the mysteries of your life and in understanding the Great Mystery of Life.

Mystics use the tarot to empower you rather than themselves. Creating independent relationships with clients is their aim. Mystics also aim at consciously connecting you with your own higher soul, spirit, Self. They won't tell you exactly how to live your life, but they will make suggestions for living a life that is more spiritually attuned. They'll tell you about the future in terms of possibilities rather than sure things. For the mystic, much of the future is set in sand, not stone. If you're seeking this type of information from the tarot, a mystic is for you.

Using the Tarot in the Health Professions

I've taught and given tarot consultations to many health professionals. Numerous alternative postgraduate programs in psychology and the spiritual sciences offer courses in tarot. Many health and healing institutes offer courses in tarot as well.

I've also worked with psychologists, psychiatrists, and drug and alcohol counselors. The tarot is a new and potent way of getting information across to clients when more traditional methods fail.

Health practitioners aim to help their clients lead healthier and more well-balanced lives. It's wonderful finding out that many of these professionals are open to including the tarot as another way of achieving their goals.

Therapists: Tapping into the unconscious mind

Early in the twentieth century, cutting edge psychologist Carl Jung said that "the psychological mechanism for transforming energy — consciousness and life — is the symbol." Jung based his theory and practice of *Archetypal*

Psychotherapy on the tarot and the Qabalistic Tree of Life (see Chapter 15). Many Jungian therapists use the tarot in their practices today.

Non-Jungian therapists are using the tarot too. Much like the traditional Rorschach inkblot tests and the imagination-stimulating pictures of the Thematic Apperception Test (TAT), the tarot is commonly employed in accessing and evaluating the unconscious mind.

An increasing number of health professionals are doing therapeutic work that includes the tarot. Some therapists begin a session by letting a client look through the entire deck and select the cards that he or she likes best and least. The therapist then uses these cards as starting-points for the kind of guided association and fantasy–symbol work done in Gestalt therapy or psychosynthesis. Laying out tarot cards in a therapy session is a powerful way of assisting clients to actually look at their issues, as well as their possible solutions.

After other means had failed, one of my tarot students, who's also a psychologist, decided to spread out the cards with a client who was endangering himself and his family by refusing to take his seizure medication. When The Fool card turned up, followed by The Tower, the man laughed and said, "I guess I'd better think about getting back on my meds or I could be in big trouble."

Substance abuse counselors: Connecting tarot with the 12 steps

Some tarot students and clients are alcohol and drug counselors. I've also had students and clients who were ex-addicts and alcoholics, or who had started rehab after working with the tarot.

Because the tarot conveys the same universal principles found in the programs of Alcoholics Anonymous, Narcotics Anonymous, Emotions Anonymous, and Sex and Love Addicts Anonymous, drug and alcohol counselors welcome it.

The tarot cards and 12-step programs have something basic in common: Both systematically initiate you into higher levels of consciousness. Clients and students who have participated in 12-step programs often say things like, "That card reminds me of the first of the 12 steps, which is admitting that I'm powerless over a substance or person and that my life is unmanageable."

In the system of Ageless Wisdom that I associate with the tarot (see Chapter 5), the 12 steps correspond to the tarot's 7 steps of spiritual development. These steps are depicted by the last 7 cards of the tarot's major arcana — The Devil through The World cards. I see your questioning look, because you're wondering how 12 steps can fit into 7 cards. But I've found that several steps are covered in a single card. For example, The Star and Judgment cards illustrate the principles of the 11th step: "Seeking through prayer and meditation to improve conscious contact with God as we understand Her/Him, praying only for knowledge of His/Her will for us and the power to carry it out."

Taking Tarot into the Fortune 500

You'd be surprised to know how many businesses use the tarot in one way or another. In the last few years, some large corporations have begun using tarot as potent adjuncts in employee training programs and to assist in values clarification. Some businesses also hire tarot readers as entertainment at parties and celebrations.

A prominent British tarot reader recently told me about a psychic colleague who's "raking in the yen" doing tarot with members of large Japanese corporations. (In view of the present Japanese economy, I can't help wondering about the work he's doing.)

I have conducted tarot consultations for business people to help them with issues like hiring, firing, and interpersonal difficulties. I have also worked at many business parties and gatherings.

A few years ago, I received a phone message from a man requesting a tarot appointment. When I called him back, his voicemail mentioned his name and his position at a well-known Fortune 500 company. When we talked, I did my usual in-depth screening. After discovering that he really wanted someone to make predictions, I declined the job and referred him to a psychic.

Touching Students with the Tarot

Tarot is a great educational tool for children of all ages. In a nutshell, it's a right brain tool that facilitates whole brain learning. Traditional education is orientated to the left or linear brain, so children who are not linear thinkers have a difficult time learning. These children are ordinarily called *learning disabled*. As I explain in the following section, I discovered a new and exciting use for the tarot while working as a teacher's assistant in a local public school. A year later, I was teaching my method to several hundred elementary school teachers.

Improving reading skills

While assisting in my son's third grade classroom in the fall of 1978, I couldn't help but notice how many children were having problems reading. Out of the blue, I thought about having these children play with the tarot. After mustering my courage, I asked the teacher if I could try an experiment that would help the problem readers. Eager for whatever help she could get, the teacher agreed, and I plowed ahead.

The following week, I brought black-and-white, coloring-book style **Builders of the Adytum Tarot** cards to the class. While the children were enthusiastically coloring, I asked them to make up stories about what they thought their cards were about. I wrote out the stories in large print. When the children finished coloring, each one read back what he or she had said. The children and I had fun with this whole-brain adventure. By the end of the school year, each child had completed the entire major arcana, had a book of stories and pictures to bring home, and best of all, felt more confident about his or her reading ability.

The following year, I was invited to demonstrate this technique at a conference, sponsored by the County Office of Education, called "Right Brain/Left Brain Education for Teachers." Aside from a call from one ultra-conservative religious group threatening to boycott the conference because a woman doing tarot was listed among the presenters, it was a smashing success.

Helping youngsters express their feelings

I enjoy doing other kinds of tarot-related activities with young people as well. Generally, I find children less uptight and less self-conscious than adults when it comes to interacting with the cards.

How many times have you wracked your brain for ways to soothe an angry child or young adult? After you become comfortable with the tarot cards, try encouraging an upset youngster to pick out a few cards and tell you about the pictures. The tarot has a way of revealing hidden thoughts and feelings that may not otherwise come out.

If you use the tarot to communicate with kids, here are some guidelines you should consider:

- Let the child express his or her feelings.
- Repeat the child's words back to him or her: "You're feeling . . ."
- Refrain from offering judgments and opinions.
- Try having the child pick one or more cards that show how he or she sees the situation changing for the better.

If the child's pain and negativity persists, or if you believe the child is going to harm himself or someone else, seek professional counseling as soon as possible. But you may find that the tarot provides just the opportunity a child needs to express feelings that have been bottled up.

Appealing to All

At the beginning of this chapter, I provide a partial listing of the types of people who work with the tarot in one form or another. In this section, I want to share with you a short poem inspired by a 13-year-old girl who was a student in one of my summer tarot classes.

Do You Tarot?

Do you Tarot?

You are short, you are tall

You are big, you are small

You are young, old and in-between

You are yellow, red, brown, white and green

You work hard or just hang around

No matter how you look or what you do, doing tarot can be fun for you!

Grad Night Tarot

With the recent violence in schools throughout the United States, many educators are working to provide fun activities for students while ensuring their safety. For example, many high school Grad Night parties now feature discos, juice bars, and Las Vegas settings. Recently, I've been spicing things up in my part of the world with Grad Night Tarot. Not only are the grads lining up, but more and more teachers are joining in too. It's a fantastic chance to offer support, acknowledgement, and bits of sound advice at this important crossroads in a student's life.

If I live to be a hundred, I'll never forget one young graduate bursting into tears after turning over The Hanged Man card. He admitted that he'd been thinking about hanging himself because he felt so worried and anxious about doing well in college. (He was from a very poor family and was going to college on a scholarship.) After acknowledging his feelings, I offered him a different perspective of the card. I suggested that the card showed him taking a relaxing timeout after his 12 years of school before starting college in the fall. The card showed him the value of getting his mind out of the future and into the present moment. After he and I talked, the student willingly spoke with a school psychologist who was waiting to do some on-the-spot first aid.

Chapter 3

Let's Go Shopping!

1 love the words "let's go shopping." Who doesn't? Well, actually, my sweetie Bernard doesn't. He spends much of his day working indoors, so when he gets some free time he wants to be outside hiking, swimming, skiing, or relaxing. Bernard's idea of fun has little room for crowded parking lots and shopping malls. (I coax him with promises of treats before, during, and after shopping, but getting him out the door still isn't easy.)

Whether you're like Bernard or like me, this chapter shows you several ways of selecting and shopping for your tarot deck (or decks). Whether you want to browse through a store, leaf through a catalog, or surf the Internet, there are plenty of ways to find tarot decks that suit your personality and needs.

Strolling through Tarot Candy Land

When I first became interested in the tarot, a fortune-teller warned me, "It's back luck to buy your own tarot deck." Because I definitely didn't want bad luck, I waited to receive my first deck as a gift. Luckily, a good friend gave me the **Tarot of Marseilles** for Christmas in 1967.

As my interest in the tarot increased, I gave the fortune-teller's warning some deep thought. Slowly, the answer became clear: The tarot's wisdom, not the tarot cards themselves, is the gift that cannot be bought. This wisdom is given — or "gifted" — to you by your inner teacher as you're ready to receive it. This revelation freed me up to begin my tarot card collection, something that's both fun and beneficial to me and my students.

When I first became interested in the tarot (in the 1960s), only a few decks were available in the United States. Living between New York City and San Francisco, I was only able to find the Tarot of Marseilles, **Rider-Waite, Swiss Tarot**, **Church of Light**, and **Case** decks (all of which are still available). Oops, I almost forgot, the **Grand Etilla** deck was also available, but it's more of a fortune-telling or oracular deck than a genuine tarot.

In this section, I take you on a stroll through tarot candy land for small nibbles of the many delicious decks available to you. Whatever your taste, there's a tarot deck for you.

Decks, decks, and more decks

Tarot decks come in many shapes (round, square, rectangular) and sizes. My largest, **The William Blake Tarot**, measures 8½ inches by 5½ inches. My smallest, a tiny Rider-Waite Tarot, is only 1½ inches by ¾ of an inch!

Dozens of tarot decks are yours for the choosing, including decks based on subjects as varied as whimsy (**The Whimsical Tarot** and **Phantasmagoric Theater Tarot**), Russian history (**Russian Tarot of St. Petersburg**), and literature (the **Arthurian, Lord of the Rings,** and **Wonderland Tarot** decks).

You can still find copies of the tarot decks of antiquity, which I discuss in Chapter 4. The **Visconti-Sforza, Cary-Yale Visconti, Sola-Busca,** and Tarot of Marseilles shouldn't be missed.

If you're looking for more options of beautifully artistic, well-traveled, or out-of-this-world cards, read on.

The art of the matter

I know numerous people who don't study or read tarot but do collect decks solely for their artistic beauty. If you're a lover of art, consider the following:

- The **Tarot of the Cloisters,** inspired by thirteenth-century stained glass windows, is glorious.
- The **Sacred Rose Tarot** is influenced by Byzantine icons and the rose motif, symbol of Western iconography.
- Renaissance art depicting Greek and Roman deities appears in the **Renaissance Tarot.**
- The late-nineteenth-century Art Nouveau is shown in both the **Art Nouveau Tarot** and **Tarot Art Nouveau.**
- Art Deco is seen in Palladini's **Aquarian Tarot.**

✔ If you're drawn to surrealism, you'll like the **Haindl, Tarot of the Witches,** and **Navigators of the Mystic Sea** decks.

✔ The photographic realism of the **Vision Tarot** is pretty awesome, as is the postmodern **Tarot of the Imagination.**

✔ Fans of Salvador Dali should peruse the amazing **Dali Tarot,** and **The Bosch Tarot** is a compilation of the strange and imaginative paintings of Hieronymus Bosch.

Maybe you like collage? If so, the **Voyager Tarot** could be your deck of choice. Or, if goth is your passion, you may be drawn by the **Vampire Tarot.** Delight in the unusual? Check out the **Rohrig, Londa,** and **Cosmic** tarot decks.

Craving tapestries or marbleized papers? Amy Zerner's lovely award-winning tapestries in **The Zerner · Farber Tarot** should fill you up. The **Hudes Tarot** arranges ancient maps and star charts on marbleized paper. Or, if you can't resist gemstones and flowers, the **Tarot of Gemstones and Crystals** should hold your attention for hours.

A trip around the world

The tarot can help you explore the world and its many cultures:

✔ The Celtic wisdom traditions, mythology, and history are illustrated in the **Spiral** and **Sacred Circle** tarots.

✔ If you have a Welsh, Finnish, or Irish background, the **Tarot of Northern Shadows, Kelvala Tarot,** and **Faery Wicca Tarot** decks are calling your name.

✔ The **Napo** and **Tarot of the Trance** decks bring you the delightful flavors of Argentina and Mexico.

✔ The **Chinese** and **Ukiyo** tarot decks show ancient Chinese and Japanese living at its finest.

✔ The **African Tarot** highlights African-American symbolism in simple and colorful imagery.

✔ The unusual **Tarot of the Orishas** depicts Brazilian *Candomble,* a spiritualist religion originating in west central Africa, and the **Voodoo Tarot** provides a beguiling view of this fascinating tradition.

✔ **The Ancestral Path Tarot** illustrates the legends of cultures worldwide. Along similar lines is the **Cosmic Tribe Tarot.** My favorite in this genre is the **Tarot of the Ages,** the first deck showing the four primary racial groups (which is featured in the color insert of this book).

✔ The **Old English Tarot** gives you a wonderful taste of medieval England.

✔ Longing to return to ancient Egypt? Try the **Ibis Tarot's** Egyptian symbology. The **Egipcios Kier, Tarot of the Sphynx,** the **Ancient Egyptian Tarot,** and **Nefertari's Tarot** are also waiting to transport you back in time.

✔ The contemporary **Karma Tarot Deck** is based on life at Christiana, a creative community in Copenhagen.

Native American spirit

Several tarot decks depict Native American myth and culture:

✔ The **Santa Fe Tarot** has a Navajo theme.

✔ The **Tarot of the Southwest Sacred Tribes Deck** shows native peoples from all of the southwest.

✔ A glimpse of the **Medicine Woman Tarot** is sure to touch your heart.

✔ The **Native American Tarot** depicts tribes from the four corners of the United States (see the color insert of this book).

✔ If you're questing for answers, the **Vision Quest Tarot Deck** can help you find your way.

The feminine touch

If you're looking for a tarot that taps into the spirit of women, try the following:

✔ For you Goddess lovers, there's **The Goddess Tarot.**

✔ If you believe that women hold the key to wisdom, the **Mother Peace** and **Barbara Walker** tarots are for you.

✔ The **Gendron Tarot** offers a different take; the Great God(dess), along with animal companions, makes this deck quite an eyeful.

Out of this world

Looking for a heavenly deck? Try the following:

✔ If astrology is your fascination, perhaps the **Cagliostro** or **Crow's Magic Tarot** will bring you satisfaction.

✔ If you're a moon worshipper, **Tarot of the Moon Garden** may assist your practice.

✔ The **Master Tarot** aligns the tarot's wisdom with scenes from the life of Jesus Christ.

Special interests

If you've got a passion, chances are there's a tarot to match it. Just take a look at the following:

- ✔ **The Herbal Tarot** helps you become more familiar with the healing properties of herbs.

- ✔ My friend Rachel swoons over her dream man, James Bond, with the help of the **007 Tarot.**

- ✔ Angels, fairies, and gnomes anyone? **The Winged Spirit Tarot Deck, Angel Tarot Deck, The Fairy Tarot,** and **Tarot of the Gnomes** abound with these supernatural beings.

- ✔ Are you an animal lover like me? The **Dragon, Unicorn,** and **Wisdom of the Australian Animals** decks, as well as the marvelous **Tarot of the Cat People,** will make you feel right at home.

- ✔ Hang on to your pumpkin, there's the light-hearted **Halloween Tarot,** with bats and ghosts galore (see the color insert of this book). And speaking of holidays, one Valentine's Day I found the **Tarot of Love,** wrapped in silk and velvet, sitting on my doorstep.

- ✔ Is there a sports fan in your house? Why not get your honey the **Tarot of Baseball** to mark the beginning of spring training?

Qabalah cards

In Chapter 5, I discuss the Qabalah mystery school. If that chapter whets your appetite to explore this tradition further, look for **The Hermetic Tarot** (one of my loves), the **Tarot of the Sephiroth,** and **Thoth Tarot** (all are artistic wonders).

The **Oswald Wirth Tarot** shows the Hebrew letters given to each card by Eliphas Levi (see Chapter 5). There's also the **Golden Dawn Magical Tarot,** created by two high-ranking Golden Dawn members (see Chapter 4), and the **Golden Dawn Tarot,** based upon the works of the well-respected Dr. Israel Regardie. You might also delight in seeing **The Tarot of the Spirit, Witches Tarot,** or **The Tarot of Ceremonial Magik.**

A deck for all occasions

As you can see, there are tarot decks for almost all interests and occasions. Because of this variety, you can purchase or receive more than one deck. Here's how I came to receive a very special tarot deck.

After a long and luxurious life, Trooper, one of our family cats, passed on into cat heaven. Knowing my love of both the tarot and Trooper, my son Jonah sweetly gave me *Gatti Originali,* meaning **The Original Cats,** a fabulous miniature tarot deck from Milan, Italy. The deck is a marvelous testament to Trooper's 15 years of loud purring (he could almost be heard in the next room) while lying on our couch soaking up the California sunshine.

Habla Español? Parlez Vous Francais? Sprechen Sie Deutsch? Parla Italiano?

Numerous tarot decks are printed in languages other than English. The titles on cards in these decks may appear in Spanish, French, German, Italian, and even Dutch. Here's a listing of decks that are printed in multiple languages:

- The **Tarot of Marseilles** titles are in English and, appropriately, French.
- **The Crystal Tarots Deck** is titled in English, French, German, and Italian.
- **A Lo Scarabeo** tarot deck, based upon a Liguria-Piedmontese woodblock tarot from 1736, provides card titles and instructions in Spanish and English.
- The **Tarot of the Renaissance Deck** is printed in English, French, German, and Italian.
- The **Hanson-Roberts Deck** is available in English, French, German, Italian, and Spanish.
- The **Rider-Waite** comes in English, French, German, and Spanish, as well as a five-language edition deck of Dutch, English, French, German, and Italian.

Deciding on Your First Deck

When wearing my tarot teaching hat, people often ask me, "What deck should I get?" My answer is, "I honestly don't know what deck's right for you. What do you want to learn?" The usual response is, "I'm just starting out, and I want to know the basics."

Choosing a classic

If you're looking for the basics, starting with a classical tarot deck like the Rider-Waite is probably your best bet. (The Rider-Waite deck is featured in Chapters 7, 8, and 9.) Learning a classical tarot deck is like learning your ABCs; it prepares you for reading more difficult material. Like any art or science, after you learn your tarot fundamentals, you can pick up more abstract decks without getting confused and frustrated. Elementary meanings aren't as easy to see in some of the abstract decks.

A great deal is written about the Rider-Waite deck, giving you a good chance to check out numerous points of view — something quite helpful as you're getting to know the tarot. The Rider-Waite Tarot's original drawings were created by Pamela Colman Smith. The deck's overwhelming popularity has led to many modifications over the years, so it's now available in several different styles:

- The **Classical** or **Traditional Rider-Waite Tarot Deck,** in Pamela Colman Smith's original colors, is available in sizes ranging from pocket to giant.

- The **Albano-Waite,** also known as the "1968 psychedelic Waite," features "high" colors added by Frankie Albano.

- The **Universal Waite,** recolored by Mary Hanson-Roberts (who also created the **Hanson-Roberts Tarot**), has softer and somewhat luminous tones.

- The **Golden Rider Tarot** features the original deck's images done in brighter colors by Francois Tapernoux.

- The **Rider-Waite Deluxe Tarot Deck** has gilt edges and is specially packaged.

If you're a little shy about reading cards, you can try both the **Quick & Easy Tarot** version of the Waite Tarot and the **Starter Tarot Deck,** a Renaissance style tarot. Both decks have simple meanings printed on each card to help you get off to a fast and painless start. I discuss the specifics of tarot reading in Part III of this book.

Following your eyes, hands, and heart

When choosing a tarot deck, look for colors that your eyes love beholding. Also, it's important that your deck feels right in your hands. If you have small hands, a big deck could feel uncomfortable. Or, if you have big hands, a small deck could feel lost. Pick the deck you want, without being overly concerned about shuffling like a Las Vegas cardshark. (I show you several tried-and-true ways of mixing the cards in Chapter 11.) The bottom line is that you want a tarot deck you can wrap your heart around.

You may find yourself drawn to an exotic deck so strongly that you decide you don't want a classical deck, even though you know that the classic deck is the best way to learn. One solution is to get two decks: one for learning and another because you just love the deck.

Shopping for Your Deck

I certainly hope that I've whetted your appetite by describing the many different tarot decks available. Now, how do you get one (or two or three. . . . .)?

Hitting the bookstores

Although more and more bookstores are carrying tarot decks, their selections are limited. Because it's a place to buy books, chances are your *ordinary* bookstore stocks only a few basic tarot decks. If it's a larger store and/or there's a demand, the store may carry a couple of matching tarot deck and book sets.

Because the tarot is a spiritual or metaphysical tool, spiritual or metaphysical shops offer you the best selection of tarot decks. The stores should provide you with sample decks that you can see and touch before buying.

If stores don't have sample decks, you can end up buying a deck you don't like after you open it up at home. Then, you're stuck with the deck, because stores don't usually take tarot decks back. (Once the package is open, decks are considered "used.") So listen up, all of you bookstore owners out there: Wake up and greet your new customers! Investing in a good collection of sample tarot decks will almost certainly increase a store's business.

Cataloging

Do you enjoy lingering over breakfast with a good catalog? The most comprehensive tarot catalog is published by U.S. Games Systems, Inc. This beautiful, full-color, wonderfully detailed publication is guaranteed to please even the most finicky catalog shoppers. Order yours by calling 1-800-544-2637 or writing to U.S. Games Systems, Inc., 179 Ludlow Street, Stamford, CT 06902.

Llewellyn Worldwide, Ltd. has color photos and detailed descriptions of their authors' tarot decks in their *New Worlds of Mind and Spirit Magazine*. They also have a catalog, but as of this writing it doesn't have pictures of all their tarot decks. You can order the magazine or the catalog by calling 1-800-THE-MOON or writing to Llewellyn Worldwide, P.O. Box 64383, St. Paul, MN 55164-0383.

Inner Traditions, Bear, Inc. also has a catalog featuring several fine tarot decks. You can order a copy of the catalog by calling 1-877-246-8648 or writing to Inner Traditions, Bear, Inc. One Park Street, P.O. Box 388, Rochester, VT 05767.

Surfing the Net

If you love surfing the Internet, you can check out www.usgamesinc.com or www.llewellyn.com. You might also enter the keywords "tarot decks" into a search engine and see what appears on your screen.

Many tarot decks aren't available in stores or catalogs. Rather than selling their work to publishing companies, numerous artists choose to self-publish. Although time consuming, scanning the Internet for such gems is rewarding. One of my best finds to date is **The Healing Tarot** from www.bluewitch.com.

Chapter 4

History and Mystery: Where Does the Tarot Come From?

Much like the word *tarot* defies a single definition, the tarot's origins can't be pinned down to a single place and time. Because there's so much speculation and mystery around precisely when and where the tarot originated, it's interesting to explore the various possibilities.

Some people claim that the tarot emerged from the hieroglyphs, tablets, and scrolls of ancient Egypt, Greece, and Palestine. Others are certain that tarot is a byproduct of a fourteenth-century Italian card game tarok, later called *tarocchi*. Still other people claim that the tarot is a pictorial representation of an esoteric oral tradition arising out of the Middle East that managed to survive the Dark Ages and the Inquisition. Given that the tarot is many things to many people, chances are the tarot's chronological history will always remain an unsolvable mystery.

In this chapter, I offer you a brief introduction to the complex history of tarot. I present some theories about the tarot's origins, suggest how these various theories might all work together to give us some ideas about the tarot's power, and describe some of the oldest known tarot decks.

Place by Place

Because so many of the tarot's dates of origin are unknown or inexact, I won't try to create a chronology of how the tarot came to be. Instead, in this section I summarize various theories that place the origins of the tarot throughout the world.

Some prominent theories about the tarot's origins include the following:

- **Ancient Israel or Palestine.** One theory holds that the tarot came from the teachings of the *Essenes,* an ascetic sect living near the Dead Sea in ancient Palestine between about 200 B.C. and 100 A.D.

- **Greece.** Two theories place the possible origins of the tarot in Greece:

  - Some people think that the tarot may have come from the Greek philosopher Cebes who lived in the fifth century B.C. A student and friend of Socrates, Cebes designed a set of hieroglyphic figures in what is called the *Table of Cebes* that illustrated the creation of the world and the entire history of humanity.

  - Other people say that the tarot sprang from the ancient teachings of Hermes Trismegistus, the author of works on what we call the *hermetic arts and sciences* — tarot, astrology, numerology, alchemy, and sacred geometry. Legends say that Hermes Trismegistus gave the tarot to the gypsies because they were world travelers.

    Hermetic philosophy greatly influenced the metaphysical and occult thinking of the Middle Ages and Renaissance, especially Neoplatonism and Gnosticism. (Neoplatonism was a philosophical system developed in Alexandria, Egypt in the third century A.D. and revived during the Middle Ages and Renaissance. It was based on the doctrines of Plato and other Greek philosophers, combined with elements of Oriental and Judeo-Christian mysticism. Gnosticism was based on doctrines of certain early Christian and Jewish sects that valued personal inquiry into spiritual truth above faith.)

- **Egypt.** Several tarot theories focus on Egypt:

  - One theory holds that the tarot originated from Thoth, the Egyptian god of learning and communication, who is said to have created the tarot in *hieroglyphics,* the Egyptian language of picture symbols. (Many schools of thought propose that the tarot was an outgrowth of the Egyptian mystery schools, active many centuries before the birth of Christ.)

  - Egypt was a hotbed of esoteric learning until it became Christianized. In 390 A.D., the new Christian Roman Emperor Theodosius decided to destroy anything that was not Christian. Sadly, Theodosius ordered that the bathhouses and bakeries of Alexandria be set on fire by lighting the manuscripts from the Great Library. Some people claim that the tarot is a pictorial resurrection of the contents of the *Serapeum,* the part of the library containing the most precious and powerful books.

Just as Theodosius tried to wipe out whatever did not match his religious ideology, watch out if fearful people demand that you burn your tarot cards and books, telling you they're "tools of the devil." This has happened to me many times over my years of tarot practice.

- Another theory states that the tarot came from the *Bembine Tablet*, a work of sacred and instructional art from ancient Egypt that reappeared in mid-seventeenth-century Italy. Although the Bembine Tablet is lost, its various segments are said to have been engraved with the basic information appearing in the tarot — the signs of the zodiac, letters of the Egyptian alphabet, and symbols of the four elements.

✔ **Morocco.** The phoenix rises from the ashes! One legend states that during the burning of the Great Library in Alexandria in 390 A.D., a large group of priests working in the library joined together to save some of the manuscripts, which were in the form of scrolls, and carried them into distant monasteries. The legend also indicates that the scrolls remained hidden until they were translated into the universal language of pictures, the tarot, at a gathering in Fez, Morocco sometime in the eleventh century.

If this story about secretly hiding away sacred texts intrigues you, check out Umberto Eco's book or movie called *The Name of the Rose*.

✔ **Chaldea, Phoenicia, and Babylon.** Another theory holds that the tarot comes from the teachings of the ancient mystery schools of Chaldea, Phoenicia, and Babylon in the form of a "loose-leaf" picture book. Before the fifteenth century, books as we know them did not exist. The loose-leaf book consisted of individual pages of parchment that were either tied or rolled together (much like the scroll in the hand of The High Priestess tarot card, as you see in Chapter 7).

✔ **Arabia and Persia.** Some people say that the tarot has roots in both the Arabian mysteries (Moslem mysticism before the Sufis) and the secret doctrines of the Sufi dervishes (Moslem or Islamic mystics) of the late tenth and early eleventh centuries.

✔ **Jerusalem and Europe.** Another theory indicates that the tarot is an invention of the eleventh-century medieval European Knights Templar, founded by Hugh de Payens, who were believed to have been initiated into the mystery schools of the Near East while crusading in the Holy Land. The Templars brought this "forbidden wisdom" back to Europe when they returned from the crusades.

The Knights Templar, alchemists, and later the Rosicrucians (a fraternity of religious mystics originating in Germany in the fifteenth century) supposedly converted their knowledge into ordinary playing cards, a form recognized only by another student of the same group, so they could avoid the cards' destruction and their own persecution. If you read about the history of the Templars, you'll find that their plan didn't work. In addition to having their personal properties confiscated and being thrown into jail and tortured, many Templars were murdered. But this theory does explain why certain cards were *veiled,* or drawn as something other than what they genuinely were. You can find examples of veiled cards in Part II, where I give an overview of the major arcana.

✔ **Italy and Spain.** Some people say that tarot cards were designed to conceal and protect certain spiritual teachings and to keep practitioners safe during the Inquisition of the fourteenth and fifteenth centuries. These teachings were considered heresies, and the people who believed in them were considered heretics.

I mention earlier in the chapter that some people believe that the tarot came from the unusual card game tarok, or *tarocchi,* a forerunner of bridge, developed in Italy in the fourteenth century. This game is played with the regular 56-card deck, with the addition of the 22 tarot cards as trumps or high cards.

✔ **Germany.** Another theory says that the tarot sprang from the first Rosicrucians, a secret fraternity of religious mystics originating in Germany in the fifteenth century. It's been speculated that the tarot is the book of universal knowledge, which the Rosicrucians claim as part of their body of knowledge.

Mystical principles are often conveyed by suggestions rather than directives. The *Rota Mundi,* or Wheel of the World, is a term frequently used in the early writings of the Fraternity of the Rosy Cross (also known as the Rosicrucian Order). If you rearrange the letters of the Latin word *rota,* you get a phonetic representation of the word tarot. *Rota* suggests not only the cyclical nature of the universe and evolution of human consciousness; it hints at the tarot's role in these processes.

✔ **Europe.** Some people believe that the tarot is a symbolic expression of the basic tenets of eighteenth-century Freemasonry, an international secret fraternity similar to the Rosicrucians. The founder of Freemasonry, Cagliostro, was trained in the Arabian, Egyptian, and Persian mystery schools and was well appraised of the doctrines of the Rosicrucians and Knights Templar.

✔ **England.** Two theories indicate that the tarot's origins are in England:

- Some people think that the tarot is an outgrowth of the system of Enochian Magic developed by the philosopher and advisor to Elizabeth I, John Dee, in sixteenth-century England. I explain Enochian Magic in Chapter 5.

- Some people believe that the modern tarot comes from the teachings of the Order of the Golden Dawn (OGD), founded in London in the late eighteenth century. OGD was the first open, or publicly accessible, order or fraternity in the Western mystery school tradition in more than 1600 years. The teachings of OGD are said to have been based on the principles of Rosicrucianism and Freemasonry.

Stringing the Theories Together

I'm the first to admit that these theories are all over the place — literally. Yet after much thought and meditation, I started thinking that all the theories regarding the tarot's origins are like beads on a string. Individually, they are only beads, but together they form a necklace. I strung these theories together using the following principles:

- First, I believe that humans are all connected. The scientific theory of *Morphic Resonance* has proven that when a new idea or way of behaving dawns on you, you can be pretty certain that the same idea or way of behaving will eventually dawn on me.

  Here's another way of looking at this theory: As I indicate in Chapter 1, humanity is connected on a psychic level through the collective unconscious. The collective unconscious is like a bank containing all human memories and history from the beginning of time. You and I continually deposit and withdraw ideas — such as the idea of making tarot cards — from this bank. When you or I make a deposit in this bank, anyone who's on our wavelength can withdraw that same idea.

- Second, the tarot is related to the Western mystery school tradition, which I discuss in Chapter 5. In certain branches of this tradition, each member is charged with coloring or creating his or her own tarot deck. Needless to say this was, and still is, a powerful method of assimilating the tarot's teachings. This concept is verified by dozens of contemporary tarot decks, each expressing the artist's particular slant on the cards.

After stringing these ideas together, I came to the conclusion that the various groups mentioned in the previous list of theories had each developed the tarot in a form harmonious with their intellectual, cultural, and spiritual personalities — in scrolls, glyphs, hieroglyphs, tablets, loose-leaf picture books, or playing cards.

All we can say for certain is that the tarot originated somewhere in antiquity; whether it was Western Europe or the Middle or Near East is a matter of speculation. Differing theories regarding the tarot's origins emerged because the tarot kept appearing in different parts of the world, and various people wanted to assimilate its teachings.

Taroting through Time

After the darkness of the Middle Ages came the light of the Renaissance. The artistic and intellectual freedom and rebirth of Renaissance Europe led to the creation of many tarot decks, and those that have survived are described in this section. Many decks were commissioned works of art, while others were purely personal expressions. You'll notice that many decks bear the name of the artist, the artist's patron, or the person directing the deck's creation. Occasionally, when one person is the artist and another either the patron or director, the deck will be called by both names.

Older decks were created in oil paint or tempera. Some, like the **Visconti-Sforza,** come from the same artistic tradition as the illuminated manuscripts, decorated with gold leaf and paints sometimes made from precious gems. (The *illuminated manuscripts* were copies of old texts created during the dark ages by monks who were said to have been in a state of awe and reverence for the Holy Spirit.) Rather than being created by monks for Church libraries, as were the illuminated manuscripts, these tarots were created by artists for the rich, royal, famous and, in some instances, infamous. Other tarots, such as the fifteenth-century **Boiardo** and **Sola-Busca** decks, were produced in woodcuts and copper engravings. Italian card makers later developed a reinforcing technique: The print typically had its back glued to a second rectangle of paper generous enough to wrap around the edges of the print and form a frame for the image on the front.

With the passage of time and introduction of computer technology, fewer and fewer decks are being hand painted. Today, tarot decks are done in a black-and-white coloring book style that you can color yourself, or in collage, or with computer graphics programs. The **Daughters of the Moon, Dalai,** and **Gendron** tarots exemplify these styles. These changes make the creation of your personal tarot deck more likely than ever before.

I am not a tarot historian. In the sections that follow, I cover what I think are the most important and interesting decks of the centuries. If this introduction sparks your interest in a greater exploration of these and other decks, look at Stuart Kaplan's excellent *The Encyclopedia of Tarot,* Volumes I, II, and III. You might also consult *A Wicked Pack of Cards* by Decker, Depaulis, and Dummett.

Decks of antiquity

Aside from the Templar Deck, which disappeared along with the Knights Templar, the early tarot decks seem to have been commissioned by the elite to note special occasions and to honor and immortalize members of the commissioning family or other prominent people.

For example, the Visconti-Sforza deck was created to commemorate a marriage between members of the Visconti and Sforza families. Some people say that the bride and groom are represented by the couple shown on The Lovers card (see Chapter 7).

Early tarot cards show images as varied as Alexander the Great, King Midas, beggars, caricatures of reigning tyrants, living popes, the devil hungrily devouring his victims, a priest-like hermit wearing rosary beads, a Tower card with a figure suggesting the Roman Emperor Nero fiddling in the foreground as the tower burns behind him, and a crowned serpent swallowing a person.

No known books exist that explain the spiritual and philosophical meaning behind the early tarot decks. The decks listed in the following sections all originated in Western Europe. Although several late-twentieth-century decks are Chinese, Indian, and Japanese in style, none of the ancient decks seem to have come from Asia (but occasionally a bit of Hindu influence appears).

Twelfth century

The Knights Templar Tarot. Although it's widely believed that the Knights Templar brought the tarot to Europe during the Crusades, there's no existing copy of the Templar deck. A few years ago, a psychic told me that the Templar deck would reappear during the first part of the new millennium. I guess I'll have to wait and see!

Fourteenth century

The Gringonneur Tarot. Jacquemin Gringonneur painted three packs of cards for Charles VI of France in 1392. History books call King Charles both Charles the Mad and Charles the Well Beloved. Charles VI suffered from recurrent seizures and bouts of mental illness, yet was also believed to have been a mystic. Many people think that the cards were a form of occupational therapy for the afflicted monarch.

One of the most interesting features of this deck is The Moon card. The card shows two astrologers measuring the planetary configurations with astrological compasses and a book that maps the heavens. People used to think that 17 Gringonneur cards survived as a hand-painted tarot in the Bibliothèque Nationale (National Library) in Paris. However, Gringonneur's cards are now thought to have been ordinary playing cards, and the Bibliothèque's illuminated tarot is believed to have been painted in Italy in about 1470. In any event, this might be just the excuse you need to head off to Paris!

Fifteenth century

Visconti-Sforza Tarot. Around 1430, the last Visconti Duke of Milan, Fillipi Visconti, commissioned the artist Bonifacio Bembo to create three tarot decks. The three decks are usually termed the Visconti-Sforza Tarots, but individually they are known as **The Bergamo** (part of which is now housed at the Pierpont-Morgan Library Collection in New York and part at Bergamo, Italy); **The Brambilla** (housed at the Brera Gallery in Milan); and **The Visconti de Modrone** (which is included in the Cary Collection at Yale University Library in New Haven, Connecticut). This last deck is also called the **Cary-Yale Visconti.** It's an unusual tarot because its major arcana depicts the virtues of Faith, Hope, and Charity. A fifteenth-century Italian tarot painted by an unidentified artist is also included in the Cary Collection.

The Mantegna Tarot. This engraved Italian deck is said by some to have been designed by the artists Baldini or Botticelli. Although it's called the Mantegna Tarot, the original designs for the cards can't be attributed to the artist Mantegna or his pupils. Some historical texts identify the chief artist as simply "the Master." Art experts consider this tarot to be one of the finest examples of fifteenth-century Italian printmaking.

This deck's 50 cards appear in five groupings: Conditions of Man, Apollo and the Muses, Liberal Arts, Virtues and Cosmic Principles, and the Ten Firmaments of the Universe.

The Geofroy Tarot. Only 38 cards remain from this mid-fifteenth-century French woodcut-style tarot deck, created by Catelin Geofroy. It's one of the earliest decks to number the major arcana in the style of the Tarot de Marseille (described in the "Eighteenth century" section). You can see these cards at the Museum fur Kunsthandwerk, in Frankfurt, Germany.

The Boiardo Tarot. The wood-engraved Boiardo Tarot, a partial edition of which is said to reside in a private collection in Switzerland, was created in the late fifteenth century. After The Fool card, the Boiardo cards are named for emotions and experiences such as Disdain, Chance, Wisdom, Patience, Error, Deception, Modesty, Peril, and Labor. Despite having been produced by woodcut, which would have made mass production easy, these cards are rare.

The Sola-Busca Tarot. The Sola-Busca Tarot is named for the family that acquired it. The most outstanding feature of this tarot is that, unlike other decks that show only groups of suit symbols, the Sola-Busca shows full pictures.

Queen Catherine de'Medici

The French Queen Catherine de' Medici — granddaughter and daughter of the great art patrons of the Italian Renaissance, Cosimo and Lorenzo de' Medici — had Nostradamus as her personal astrologer. Because of her love of the arts and occult, there's an excellent chance that Queen Catherine owned a pack of tarot cards.

The Dürer Tarot. German painter and engraver Albrecht Dürer drew adaptations of 21 of the so-called Mantegna cards in the late fifteenth century. These are part of the Sloane Collection at the Museum of London in England. High tea or a stroll around Piccadilly Circus, anyone?

Sixteenth century

The Hebreo Tarot. One of the most significant tarots from Bologna, Italy is the woodcut deck by Agnolo Hebreo. The deck is represented by a single surviving card, showing an especially fierce devil devouring his victims. This card is now housed in the British Museum in London, England.

Hebreo's tarot would have been called a *tarocchino,* a "little tarot," which is characteristic of Bologna. This shortened deck omits some of the *pips,* or number cards, of the four suits.

Seventeenth century

The Colonna Tarot. The artist who created the Colonna Tarot is thought to have been related to the Colonna family of Rome. The Italian word *colonna* means "column," and some of these cards are imprinted with a column. Only two fragmented sheets of these cards are known to exist. They can be seen at the British Museum in London.

The Mitelli Tarot or Tarocchine di Mitelli. This deck by engraver Guiseppi Mitelli is a mid-seventeenth-century variation on the Tarocchini of Bologna. This deck has two Popes and two Emperors but lacks the Empress and Popess typical of most Italian tarots. (The Popess, or Female Pope, was the forerunner of today's High Priestess.)

Jacques Vieville Tarot. This woodcut deck of 78 cards is named for its Parisian maker. This tarot shows an interesting departure from tarot decks to date. The Tower card is called The Lightning and depicts a lightning-struck tree instead of the traditional building. In this feature, the Vieville tarot provides a transition to a pattern typical in Belgian tarots. A complete Vieville Tarot is in the Bibliothèque Nationale in Paris. You now have another reason to go to France.

Eighteenth century

In Bologna in the 1700s, the local *tarocchino* underwent a further change. Four cards (usually the Juggler, Popess, Empress, and Emperor) were replaced out of respect for the Pope, who ruled Bologna and the surrounding territory. The four new cards depicted armed Moors, exotic warriors from Islam.

Vandenborre Tarot. These Swiss cards were designed by F.I. Vandenborre of Brussels, Belgium. The deck's most distinguishing characteristics are Bacus (Bacchus, the god of wine) irreverently replacing the Pope, and a multi-eyed Devil card, which suggests a Hindu influence. Both designs are unique to Belgian tarot cards.

By studying a deck's style, you can trace its origins back to a particular region. For example, distinctive patterns are associated with Ferrara, Marseille, and Belgium. But it is also possible that specific details and the order of the major arcana cards depend upon the artist.

The Conver Tarot de Marseilles. This mid-eighteenth-century French woodcut by Nicholas Conver was published by Paul Marteau in 1949 and has become widely used today. Some experts believe that the Marseille tarot shows the correct numbers of the major arcana. (I explain the numbering of the major arcana in Chapter 6.) An edition of this deck is housed at the Bibliothèque Nationale in Paris.

The Etteilla Tarot. In 1789, the Parisian cartomancer Etteilla published an esoteric tarot in which he rearranged and redesigned the major arcana cards. Originally called the Grand Etteilla, this deck has been reprinted by B.P. Grimaud and others today.

Nineteenth century

The Mlle. Lenormand Cards. Various fortune-telling or *oracular* cards published in the nineteenth century were named for Marie Anne Lenormand, soothsayer for Napoleon. These were not tarots, but were decks of 36 cards that had the French suits of clubs, hearts, spades, and diamonds, along with other artwork from that time period.

Twentieth century

The Papus Tarot. This deck is based on the writings of the French occultist Gerard Papus and was designed by Gabriel Goulinat. Although it's a French deck, Hebrew, French, Sanskrit, and Egyptian hieroglyphics appear on this 1909 Egyptian-styled tarot.

The Waite or Rider-Waite Tarot Deck. The medieval art on these cards was created by costume designer Pamela Colman Smith, under the direction of Arthur Edward Waite. This world-famous tarot deck was published by Rider and Company in London, England in 1910. The deck is sometimes called the Waite-Smith or Smith-Waite Tarot.

Aleister Crowley

Aleister Crowley, one of the head teachers of the Order of the Golden Dawn, was a brilliant and eccentric occultist. Crowley wore many faces ranging from poet, mountaineer, yogi, philosopher, and practitioner of magic to egomaniac, womanizer, misogynist, drug user, and abuser. His critics called him depraved, while his friends said he was only doing publicly what other people were doing privately.

Church of Light Tarot. This black and white Egyptian-style tarot was originated by its namesake esoteric group and written about by Elbert Benjamine, who wrote under the name of C.C. Zain. These cards have Hebrew and Sanskrit letters, planetary symbols, and astrological signs with their correlating constellations. The drawings are smaller than those on your average playing cards — I spent most of a winter straining my eyes while I enjoyed coloring in these cards.

J.A. Knapp Tarot. This deck was created in 1929 under the direction of the world-renowned occult philosopher and artist Manley Palmer Hall. Each major arcana card has a Hebrew letter on it.

The Thoth Deck. The exquisite art in this deck was created by Lady Frieda Harris, under the intermittent direction of Aleister Crowley. Theoretically, this deck should be called the Crowley-Harris or Harris-Crowley Tarot. Instead, it is named for the Egyptian god, Thoth, who is the counterpart to the Greek and Roman messengers of the gods, Hermes and Mercury. The name suggests that the tarot brings messages from on high. Because of Crowley's sometimes infamous reputation, the deck is most often known as "Crowley's deck." Three cards are renamed in this tarot: Strength is named Lust; Justice is named Adjustment; and Judgment is named The Aeon.

Most modern decks are based upon the elementary design and numbering system of the Waite or Thoth tarots. Again, more about numbering in Chapter 6.

The Case Tarot Deck. The classical black-and-white art in this deck was designed by Jessie Burns Parke, under the direction of Paul Foster Case. You would think this deck would be named the Parke-Case or Case-Parke Tarot. Case insisted that Parke's name appear on The Hermit card and her monogram appear in the lower right-hand corner of the other cards. Because Parke felt "privileged to be as acting as Case's hands," she asked that the deck not include her name. This deck, complete with Hebrew lettering, was specifically designed for the Builders of the Adytum, a modern Qabalistic mystery school.

Looking at the Tarot Today

There are presently hundreds of tarot decks based on everything from Fairy tales **(The Inner Child Tarot)** and witches **(The Witches Tarot)** to herbalism **(The Herbal Tarot)** and baseball **(Tarot of Baseball)**. In Chapter 3, I delve into contemporary decks that you can purchase.

With the birth of each new tarot deck, it's evident that the hand-detailed tarot cards from antiquity, and those created in the traditional style of the Rider-Waite deck, are becoming a thing of the past. Today's tarot decks tend to be modern or ultramodern in the style and/or the medium in which they're created. Many tarot decks are the products of computer programs, photography, or the old (but recently regenerated) medium of collage. **The Sacred Circle Tarot**, **Vision Tarot,** and **Voyager Tarot** decks exemplify these mediums. I know of several tarot teachers who hold weekend tarot card-making workshops featuring collage. There's even a trippy **Glow-in-the-Dark Tarot Deck** — a version of the classic Rider-Waite Tarot Deck's 22 major arcana cards in luminous ink.

The first truly modern tarot deck is **The New Tarot, The Tarot For the Aquarian Age**, by John Cooke and Rosalind Sharpe. Appearing in 1968, its artwork is vividly colored and modernist. The titles of these cards were changed from the classical Fool, Magician, High Priestess, and so on to the Nameless One, Changer, and Mother. I recall immediately putting this deck on hold at the local metaphysical bookstore until I cashed my next paycheck. This deck is presently out of print.

Next came **Morgan's Tarot** by Morgan Robbins (formerly known as James Morrison) and Darshan Chorpash. This 1969 "psychedelic style," black-and-white, hand-drawn, 87-card tarot deck (that you can color if you'd like) definitely blew my mind. Morgan's Tarot is a complete departure from the traditional 78-card format, not only in the number of cards in the deck but also in their style and names. Cards have handwritten names such as "Freak," "Far Out," "No trips without a tripper," and "I come from a different planet."

I spent an afternoon with the brilliant and highly imaginative Morgan (who preferred being called by his last name) in the early 1970s. While sipping our espresso, we talked about many things; but the one that stands out in my mind was Morgan's prediction that his deck would eventually revolutionize the tarot. In my opinion, it has. Morgan's tarot paved the way for other *oracular* decks — decks that function like the tarot but are not arranged in the traditional major and minor arcana-card style. This highly innovative deck is still available.

Chapter 5

The Tarot and the Mystery School Tradition

As a teacher and practitioner of tarot for more than 30 years, my vision of the tarot has room for almost everyone's take on it. For example, a Sufi believes that the tarot is another way of seeing the workings of the Beloved in his or her life. Pagans view the tarot as a natural religion honoring a generic god. Psychologists conceive of the tarot as a set of therapeutic picture symbols linking people to their subconscious minds to promote healing. Of course, some people think of the tarot solely as a means for telling the future, wielding power over others, and/or conjuring up demons — I definitely have reservations in these departments. For me, the tarot is first and foremost a depiction of the teachings of what is called the *mystery school tradition*.

This chapter is a mystery school primer. After you read it, you may feel impassioned about joining a mystery school, or you may want to run as far away from the mystery school tradition as you can, but I want to at least give you enough information so you can make your own decision.

In this chapter, I first explain what a mystery school is and how it differs from other schools. Next, I introduce you to one specific mystery school tradition called *Qabalah*. I show you the connections between the mystery schools, Qabalah, and the tarot before offering a quick history lesson so you can understand how long tarot has been part of the mystery school tradition.

Not every tarot professional agrees that the tarot emerged from the mystery school tradition. The tarot's connection with the mystery schools has been a subject of hot debate within the tarot community for generations. As you read this chapter, you may agree with the mating of the two or think the whole debate is a lot of hooey, but I hope you'll at least give the subject some thought!

Demystifying the Mystery School

Mystery schools have been around for hundreds — possibly thousands — of years. They are places where students, or *initiates,* receive esoteric teachings: teachings that are secret or private rather than publicly disclosed.

Mystery schools convey what is called *Ageless Wisdom* — teachings that convey universal and natural laws and principles that are never outdated. For example, one simple teaching of Ageless Wisdom is that change is unavoidable and constant. Just as summer follows springtime, you've been born and you will die. Members of mystery schools are encouraged to "think big."

The name *mystery school* reflects the fact that the schools' teachings are always mysteries that each member unravels in his or her own way and time. This means that you understand the teachings in your way, and I understand the teachings in mine. Both ways are perfect for who you and I are. The bottom line is that understanding is a matter of personal evolution.

The mystery school experience

The present-day experience of a mystery school can include one-on-one work with a teacher and the teachings, group classes or seminars, and lessons done through written correspondence. A few groups even work over the Internet.

Most mystery schools have external measures of your progress called, yes, "grades" (A is the highest and D is the lowest), but the greatest measure of progress is noticing changes in your awareness — thinking and behaving with increasing amounts of clarity and love. While learning is life-long, formal mystery school participation is optional. Graduation is enlightenment or cosmic consciousness.

Open and closed mystery schools

Two types of mystery schools exist: open and closed. The existence of each type generally depends upon the religious, social, and political climate of the day.

A closed mystery school is a secret or esoteric society that preserves and protects its teachings and its members from harassment in times of religious, social, or political intolerance and persecution. During such time periods, mystery school teachings are often called heresies, and the schools' members heretics, because the schools' teachings do not support what is preached by the church and legislated by the state.

The other type of mystery school is an *open public order*. (The word *order* is a synonym for a mystery school.) Open public orders surface when the world is more tolerant of individual differences. An open order looks like any church or temple, and anyone can join it. In recent years, the world has become increasingly accepting of the type of thinking encouraged by the mystery schools, so more of these schools are available to the general public. My writing this book on the tarot is living proof of this fact.

Mystery school guidelines

In my experience, mystery school teachings don't tell you exactly what to do and how to do it. It's assumed that you have a sound mind and a basic sense of right and wrong. The teacher provides you with guidelines or clues that help you develop a relationship with your own inner teacher or intuition.

The mystery school guidelines take the form of universal and natural laws and principles, or *Ageless Wisdom*. The laws and principles help reveal who and what you really are, and how you and the universe operate. Using these guidelines, you become skilled at solving the mysteries of your life, and you grow spiritually. One of the biggest mysteries of the mystery school is how, when, and where you will apply the teachings to figure out the mysteries of life for yourself.

Following is a listing of mystery school guidelines:

- No one knows what's best for another person; ultimately, only you know what's best for you.
- You are offered suggestions, not directives.
- You, the initiate, develop in your own way and time.
- What's right for one person is not right for everyone.
- What works for you in one situation might not work in all situations.
- The mystery school offers you guiding principles, not formulas.
- Much of the learning involved in a mystery school takes place by testing and trying — applying the guiding principles to life situations, seeing what results, and learning from it.

- The mystery school encourages you to love and accept yourself exactly as you are, so that you can know the spiritual being you are at heart.

- The mystery school guides you to think big by considering yourself, others, and conditions from the big (impersonal) as well as from the little (personal) point of view.

- If you're willing to take responsibility for yourself and aren't looking for someone to run your life (or, as my friend Laurie says, "take out your karma"), the mystery school is for you.

Looking for a Mystery School?

There are many types of mystery schools, and not all of them work with the tarot. Some of the bona fide mystery schools that work with the tarot are:

- Builders of the Adytum
- Fraternity of Hidden Light
- Hermetic Order of the Golden Dawn
- Philosophical Research Society
- The Santa Cruz School for Tarot & Qabalah Study
- Servants of the Light
- Thelemic Order of the Golden Dawn

Contact information may be found by searching the Internet and spiritually oriented bookstores and magazines.

Connecting with Qabalah

When a mystery school tradition uses the tarot as a vehicle for communicating its teachings, it's known as a Qabalistic mystery school. The word *Qabalistic* is derived from the word *Qabalah,* which refers to a set of mystical teachings and practices that emphasizes the core truths shared by the world's great religious and spiritual traditions, and bridges the gap between Eastern and Western spirituality.

Qabalah is a Hebrew word meaning "to receive" and "from mouth to ear," which indicates that Qabalah is an oral and aural tradition: You receive its teachings and then tell other people about them. Qabalists believe the Qabalah is sent from on high — from the Godhead or divine spirits and angels.

There are two other common spellings of the word Qabalah: Kabbalah and Cabala. Each spelling conveys a slightly different meaning. Obviously, I spell Qabalah with the letter Q. But after 30 years of working with students from varying backgrounds, plus training in Yoga, Buddhism, and other Eastern traditions, I have also renamed the tradition. I call it *Universal Qabalah*.

The teachings of Universal Qabalah are non-sexist, non-racist, and non-homophobic. The teachings unite Judeo-Christian mysticism with the hermetic arts and sciences — tarot, astrology, alchemy, numerology, and sacred geometry.

Universal Qabalah crosses all sorts of barriers by embracing the essential principles of Hinduism, Buddhism, Sufism, and Shamanism, to name a few. Clearly, the Universal Qabalah is a nondenominational and inclusive system.

Qabalists call the Qabalah a "pathless path" because, like any true mystery school or *order,* the Qabalah offers you guidelines for living instead of exact formulas. Again, these guidelines are known as *Ageless Wisdom.* For example, the most important thing I've learned from Qabalah is to strive to see, hear, smell, taste, and feel divinity in all people, in all places, and at all times.

Some people call Qabalah "do-it-yourself divinity" and "the Yoga of the West." Qabalah is a spiritual path that can help you connect with your soul, spirit, or Self. Qabalah raises your level of awareness so you're able to see your daily work, responsibilities, and pleasures as part of your spiritual practice. Chapters 8 and 9 on the tarot's minor arcana clarify this idea by depicting scenes from everyday life.

Linking the Tarot and the Mystery School

I was trained in a Qabalistic mystery school, and now I'm responsible for stewarding a mystery school. Consequently, I'll always see the tarot as a pictorial representation of the teachings of the mystery school tradition.

I believe that the tarot illustrates universal and natural laws, truths, and principles — Ageless Wisdom — in the language of picture symbols. The marriage of the tarot with the mystery school tradition is based on this premise: Mystics know that if you meditate on a symbol with enough intention, the meaning of that symbol will be revealed to you.

In the mystery school tradition, the tarot cards are called *keys;* they are clues that open the doors to higher consciousness. The tarot's archetypal images are a type of shorthand that trains your mind to key into metaphysical and mystical principles. These principles elevate your level of awareness so that you're able to read the pictures of your life with increasing clarity and live a more fulfilling life.

For years, I romanticized the idea of being initiated into a mystery school. I thought initiation was about being led blindfolded into a room filled with the scents of myrrh and frankincense, to the drone of magical formulas and mystical verses that would automatically raise my level of consciousness. My experience has shown me quite another picture. While mystery school initiation includes this ritual, the application of Ageless Wisdom to solve the mysteries of daily life is much more important.

Making the Historical Connection

In the following sections, I give you a brief introduction to some ways in which the tarot might be connected to the mystery school tradition in general (schools such as the Egyptian and Greek mystery schools that taught other systems besides Qabalah) and to the Qabalistic mystery schools in particular (those using the Qabalah and its pictorial representation, the tarot, as their sole teaching mediums). I'm hoping this basic background helps you understand why I think the tarot is linked to these traditions.

There is a difference between a mystery school and a Qabalistic mystery school. The Egyptian and other mystery schools taught Qabalah along with other systems. The Qabalistic mystery schools taught only Qabalah.

The tarot's tie to the mysteries

Following are examples of some of the people who have drawn connections between the tarot and the mystery school tradition:

- ✔ **Antoine Court de Geblin,** an eighteenth-century French occultist and scholar, was one of the first modern authorities on the tarot. Some people say he was the first person to link the mystery school tradition with the tarot. de Geblin proposed that the tarot originated in Egypt and was used in sacred initiation rites into the ancient Egyptian mysteries (likely one of the first mystery schools) and priesthood. Like the ancient Greek philosopher Cebes (see Chapter 4), de Geblin believed that the tarot illustrates the creation of the world and the entire history of humanity.

Moses and the mystery schools

It has been speculated that Moses, raised as Egyptian nobility, received training in the Egyptian mysteries, which included Qabalah.

Some Qabalists say he used the Qabalistic teachings to help lead the Hebrew people during their years in the desert.

- ✔ **Paul Christian,** a French librarian, became interested in the occult while renovating libraries after the social and political upheavals of the late eighteenth century. His clean-up work inspired him to become a writer and a spokesperson for a French secret society. Christian's 1870 book *The History and Practice of Magic* tells of a supposed initiation to the Egyptian mysteries. During this rite, oversized versions of the tarot's 22 major arcana cards were lined up in a great chamber. As the initiate walked before each card, the initiator described its symbolism. Sounds like quite a stroll!

- ✔ **Edouard Schure,** a nineteenth-century French writer and occultist, shared information similar to Paul Christian's. In a chapter of *The Great Initiates,* which discusses initiation into the hermetic mysteries, Schure alludes to the same ceremony.

- ✔ **Gerard Papus,** a doctor and philosopher living in France in the late nineteenth and early twentieth centuries, wrote that the tarot represents sacred rites that occurred in the depths of the pyramids. He also claims that the tarot springs from the *Tetragrammaton,* the sacred four-letter Hebrew name of the Most High God.

The tarot and the Qabalah

Following are examples of some of the people who have drawn connections between the tarot and the Qabalah:

- ✔ **John Dee,** an Elizabethan philosopher and advisor to Elizabeth I, subscribed to the ideas of cutting edge hermetic/Qabalistic philosophers and humanists. Along with Edward Kelly, Dee developed the system of Enochian Magic (see the sidebar in this chapter), which was later expanded by MacGregor Mathers of the Order of the Golden Dawn (who is discussed later in this section).

Enochian Magic

Practitioners of Enochian Magic believe that Enoch, the son of Cain and father of Methuselah, was "translated," or brought to heaven without natural death (Genesis 5:18–24). Assuming the heavenly form of the archangel Metatron, he's believed to be the personification of the Most High (Exodus 23:21) and, according to Qabalistic writings, the primary communicator of the Qabalah (and hence the tarot) to humanity. For further information, check out the *Ethiopic Book of Enoch* and *Secrets of Enoch*. If all this piques your interest, check out the recently published **Enochian Tarot,** which consists of 88 cards (10 more than a traditional tarot deck).

- ✔ **Eliphas Levi,** a nineteenth-century French priest, was the first person to *openly* link the tarot to the Jewish Kabbalah. Levi believed that if you're imprisoned with nothing but the tarot, you can unlock the great secrets of life and the mysteries of the universe. You can see Levi's system in the **Oswald Wirth Tarot**.

- ✔ **Doctors Wescott, Woodford, and Woodman** founded the Order of the Golden Dawn (OGD), the first *open* order in the modern Western mystery school tradition, in l886. The teachings and protocol of OGD are based on a book from the ancient Rosicrucian order (see Chapter 4), which was discovered in a used bookstore. Unusual, but strange things certainly happen in tarot land!

- ✔ **Samuel Liddel "MacGregor" Mathers** was the head teacher of the OGD, which emphasized the Qabalistic Tarot and Qabalistic Tree of Life (see Chapter 15). Membership in the OGD included the famous and infamous: brilliant mystic and writer Dion Fortune; spiritual psychologist and author Israel Regardie; poet William Butler Yeats; Irish politico Maude Gonne; and occultists, Qabalistic philosophers, and writers Aleister Crowley, Arthur Edward Waite, and Paul Foster Case.

- ✔ **P.D. Ouspensky,** an early-twentieth-century Russian mystic and Sufi (Moslem mystic), suggested a connection between the tarot and the hermetic/Qabalistic philosophers and humanists. Ouspensky proposed that the tarot is a tool for conveying unity — depicting the interactions between divinity and humanity and the workings of universal and natural laws and principles in symbols.

The OGD legacy

The Waite and Thoth tarot decks (see Chapter 4) came out of the Order of the Golden Dawn. Both Arthur Edward Waite and Aleister Crowley served as teachers at different times in OGD's history. My teacher, Paul Foster Case, was Arthur Edward Waite's student and successor.

Case broke away from the OGD when misuse and misunderstanding of its teachings caused it to fall apart. Rather than live by the principles of Ageless Wisdom, which are *completely* non-competitive, members got involved in the no-win game of trying to "one-up" each other

spiritually. The attitude of "I'm more evolved than you are and therefore have more rights and power" was a complete contradiction of the mystery schools' tenants. Ah, the human soul and its evolutionary journey!

Following the sunset of the OGD in 1900, Case founded a new open order — The Builders of the Adytum, which opened in Los Angeles in 1904. With the help of Jessie Burns Parke, Case created **The Case Tarot Deck.** Because Case was Waite's student, their decks are similar.

Part II

Pick a Card, Any Card: A Guided Tour Through the Tarot Deck

The 5th Wave By Rich Tennant

"This deck was designed by Coco Chanel in the '50's. That's why the queens all carry small quilted handbags."

In this part . . .

Part II starts off by giving you suggestions for interpreting the meanings of tarot cards and by sharing some of the idiosyncrasies among various decks, such as card placement and numbering. Starting with Chapter 7, I take you on a card-by-card guided tour through a deck, showing you what each card looks like and suggesting concepts and questions related to each card.

Chapter 6

A Magic Mirror: Preparing for the Tarot's Possibilities

. . . .

In This Chapter

▶ Relying on intuition and common sense

▶ Looking beyond black-and-white meanings

▶ Understanding card reversals

▶ Observing the dance between Strength and Justice

. . . .

*T*his chapter is your warm-up before you start the full-on exercise of reading tarot cards. It's geared to get you loose and focused while preparing you for the workout of running the full course of the 78-card tarot deck. If you choose, you can skip the preliminaries and dash into Chapters 7, 8, and 9, which introduce you to the cards themselves. But you could end up with some pulled muscles, strains, and sprains.

In this chapter, I offer some things to consider as you're looking at tarot cards. You might call this a prerequisite course before you take Card Interpretation 101.

To start, I discuss the way I approach my own interpretations of cards, including *neutralizing* their meanings by interpreting cards with the understanding that nothing in life is all black or all white. Next, I explain card *reversals* — the change in meaning that occurs when a tarot card appears with its *up* side *down*. Finally, I describe some common variations among tarot decks, so if the deck you use isn't ordered exactly the same as the deck I describe in Chapters 7, 8, and 9, you'll understand why.

I could just throw you into the middle of a tarot spread and say "read," but you'd probably get sweaty palms and not have a very rewarding experience. So in this chapter, I begin laying a step-by-step foundation for reading and interpreting cards.

Getting Ready to Read

The tarot is a magic mirror that helps you look at both your personal and higher soul, spirit, Self. (I capitalize the term *Self* to show that it refers to the divinity that lives within you, me, and all living beings.)

Before you look into the mirror of tarot, I encourage you to consider what you expect to find. Many books about tarot offer very specific interpretations of the meaning of each card. I don't do that in this book, but I do offer something that I consider more valuable: a model for determining meaning for yourself.

Reconciling positives and negatives

Living in a world divided into good and bad, positive and negative, you and I have been taught to think in polarized terms. For this reason, you may expect that certain tarot cards always carry positive meanings, while others are always negative. But like life, no tarot card is either all good or all bad. A card's meaning depends on how you see and act on what the card suggests.

I'm not suggesting that good and evil don't exist; they certainly do. What I'm saying is that life is a combination of light and dark, or positive and negative energies. Within every positive or negative experience lies the potential of perceiving and experiencing its opposite. It requires work to overcome years of setting good and bad, positive and negative against one another, but that's exactly what I encourage you to do in order to experience the true power of the tarot.

As I discuss in Chapter 1, how you interpret or "read" life and its picture symbols determines their meaning. Add to this fact the idea that life is neither all black nor all white, and you get the following guideline for interpreting cards:

> If the meanings of the picture symbols of your life depend on how you read them, and the tarot cards are picture symbols of life, and life is shades of gray, then the cards can be interpreted in shades of gray, too.

Amber's approach to interpreting

This is not your typical tarot book, and what you read in Chapters 7, 8, and 9 may seem vastly different from what you expect to find in the chapters that focus on each card in a tarot deck. In this section, I explain the basic model that I use for approaching the interpretation of a card.

Following are some of the most important guidelines I follow when reading a tarot card:

✔ Because I believe in the self-reflective qualities of the tarot so completely, I use the term *you* in my interpretations. However, a card may apply to another person in your life. Keep in mind that the tarot is not so much about understanding other people as it is about understanding yourself.

✔ I phrase each card's interpretation in the present tense, but interpretations can be changed into the past or future tense as needed. The position of a card in a tarot spread and its relationship to neighboring cards can help you determine whether it most likely applies to the past, present, or future. I discuss this point in detail in Chapter 13.

✔ People are generally more open to receiving suggestions than directives. For this reason, I phrase interpretations in the form of questions instead of definite statements. Doing so allows room for the possibility of changes in you, others, and situations.

Much of your life is not set in stone, but in sand. Forming questions with words such as "might you," "could you," "are you," or "this suggests" creates room for this important fact of life.

Recognizing the role of memory

Interpreting or reading tarot cards is a matter of *your* response to the image presented. As I explain in Chapter 1, how you respond to or read the situations, picture symbols, or archetypes of daily life is based on factors such as your own and others' experiences in similar situations and your present state of mind and health.

Because I'm linked with a Qabalistic mystery school, I believe that the five Qabalistic principles of memory influence how you read cards. These principles are:

✔ **Similarity:** You tend to remember things that are similar to what you know and have experienced.

✔ **Contrast:** You tend to remember things that contrast with or stand out from what you know and have experienced.

✔ **Feelings:** You tend to remember things that bring up strong feelings such as love, anger, hatred, and sorrow.

✔ **Recency:** You tend to remember events that are closer in time to the present (unless your short-term memory is shot).

✔ **Frequency:** You tend to remember something that's repeated.

So much of what we say and do is done from memory, and tarot interpretation is no exception. Everyone uses all five types of recollection. An important aspect of interpreting the tarot is the recognition of how your interpretations often reflect your memories rather than your conscious thought. Because of this, it's beneficial to ask yourself if what you're calling up is completely relevant to the card before you — or if it is an initial recollection or reaction that could benefit from a more careful investigation. Following is an example of how this might play out.

Although Josie has numerous ideas for writing children's books, she feels that she's uncreative. After looking through the university extension catalog, Josie impulsively signs up for a class that is focused on writing children's literature. But the night before the class starts, Josie feels nervous and considers backing out of it. Josie decides to take out her tarot cards and ask, "How can I deal with feeling uncreative as I begin taking this creative writing class?"

Josie turns over the Seven of Cups. The card, which is shown and interpreted in Chapter 8, immediately confirms what Josie already believes about herself: "My mind's filled with lots of ideas, but I can't seem to write anything worthwhile."

The tarot cards were designed to help readers see pictures (and life situations) from new angles. If Josie would spend a little more time contemplating the card, her mind might start opening to these new perspectives.

Before deciding that the story is over, Josie reviews the questions under the Seven of Cups in Chapter 8. The following questions jump out at her: "Are you suddenly realizing that every dream has limitations?", "Are you learning about the power of creative imagination?", and "What might you release to gain the focus and energy required for manifesting your desire?"

Looking at the card a while longer, Josie starts seeing and thinking differently. (Shamans call this process *shape shifting*.) "All those cups! I have so many ideas, my energies are all over the place. If I can zero in on *one* idea and develop it, I might get somewhere. The other ideas aren't going to run away. I can use them for other stories. And instead of being so caught up in criticizing what I'm going to write before I even write it, which inhibits me, I can just start playing with words — and playing, and playing, and playing. Doing this, I'm likely to improve." Voilà, Josie has changed her perspective *and* answered her question in a more full-bodied, conscious, and less reactive way!

Wrestling with the Meaning of Reversals

Unlike the double-sided images on regular playing cards, the pictures on tarot cards have definite upright and reversed views. The difference between an upright and reversed view is obvious; when you look at a card, its picture is either right-side-up or upside-down.

Whether a card turns up upright or reversed depends on how you mix and shuffle the deck. (I describe different methods of shuffling in Chapter 11.) The way you interpret a reversed card depends on how much you know about the meaning of reversals, and how much common sense and sensitivity you apply to your interpretation.

Interpreting in black and white

Many tarot books tell you that when a card falls right-side-up, its meaning is positive, and when the card is reversed, its meaning is negative. For example, **The Two of Cups** card in the Rider-Waite deck shows two young people promising themselves to one another. The magical Caduceus of Hermes rises over their cups with a lion's head between its wings (see Figure 6-1).

Many books would tell you that the upright meaning of this card is mutual cooperation, a harmonious partnership, the beginning of a new friendship or love relationship, or a blessed union. The reversed meaning would be the end of a friendship, love, or partnership; a lack of cooperation; disharmony; or star-crossed lovers.

Figure 6-1:
The Two of Cups card from the Rider-Waite deck, upright and reversed.

Shifting into neutral

Interpreting reversed cards is a matter of mixing intuition with a good dash of common sense. To arrive at an interpretation, I recommend that you take into consideration three things, in addition to the meaning of the card itself:

- ✔ Your question (the question you are hoping the tarot reading will help you answer)
- ✔ The cards surrounding the reversed card
- ✔ The position that the card falls in (past, present, future)

I discuss these points in some detail in Chapter 13, but I mention them now so that you're prepared the first time you encounter a reversed card. Trust me, as surely as you're reading these words, soon you're going to be looking at a card and wondering, "What happens if *this* card turns up reversed?"

The tarot's Ageless Wisdom (its universal principles) explains that the difference between things diametrically opposed to one another, such as night and day, hot and cold, or East and West, is a matter of *degree*. Night stops being night when the sun begins rising. Boiling water becomes warm when cold water is mixed in. Every set of opposites can be reconciled or neutralized. This concept has taken me away from giving tarot cards polarized (upright and reversed) meanings and shifted my interpretations into neutral.

If I encounter a reversed Two of Cups card, for example, I might be prompted to ask some of the following questions: Are you enjoying mutual cooperation? Might you be resolving a dispute with your business partner? Are you feeling that a friendship might be turning into love? Is it possible you're attracted to someone for both spiritual and physical reasons?

Guidelines for interpreting reversals

When you encounter a reversed card, you can combine what you discover about that card in Chapter 7, 8, or 9 with the following guidelines to arrive at a meaningful interpretation:

- ✔ A reversal may suggest that your energy is blocked or closed off, either consciously or unconsciously.
- ✔ A reversal can tell you that the upright meaning of a card has already happened.
- ✔ A reversal may indicate that you're procrastinating, resisting, or denying something.

✔ A reversal can show that you're holding down — either consciously suppressing or unconsciously repressing — a need or desire to do something important. It can also show that you are controlling a destructive impulse.

✔ A reversal may be a turning point — an opportunity for you to bring the qualities of the card into more conscious expression.

✔ A reversal may suggest the benefit of stretching out and learning or trying something new. Instead of being fearful or lazy, the reversal encourages you to do what you're having others do for you.

✔ A reversal could show that it's time for inner verses outer work — a time for self-reflection or reviewing, revising, or reevaluating a situation or plan rather than taking action.

✔ A reversal suggests that things might just not go as planned. Stay flexible and allow for the unexpected!

✔ A reversal may represent the inner, private part of you — internal qualities that aren't understood by or apparent to others. For instance, if a reversed king comes up, that may mean that although people perceive you as passive or lacking assertiveness, you're aware that you're seen in this way but are consciously choosing to show this quiet and actively receptive side of your personality.

Depending on its position in a spread, the reversal of a card that is traditionally externally oriented — for example, a knight, king, or the Five of Wands — can show the value of assuming a less active role (such as leaving space for others to step up) or the importance of being more participatory.

The reversal of a traditionally internally oriented card — for example, a page, a queen, or the Four of Cups — can show the value of assuming a more active role (stepping up and claiming your power) or the importance of being even less involved than you're tending to be.

✔ A reversal can indicate pressure, building under the surface, that's going to keep building until you either act or explode.

✔ A reversal may suggest your potential for a new awareness or beginning.

✔ Because the card is actually upside down, it may depict mental, emotional, or spiritual instability. Perhaps you're making changes in these areas, or perhaps you want to make changes before they're made for you.

✔ The meanings of all cards are shades of gray, yet there's the tendency to label some cards positive and others negative. Reversals tend to bring out the negative side of a positive card or the positive side of a negative card. For example, if you encounter The Sun card reversed, you might consider whether you're expending too much energy, courting burnout and exhaustion. The Devil card reversed might prompt you to ask whether you are confronting your innate attraction to self-destructive relationships.

Differences between Tarot Decks

Tarot decks differ from one to another. The names and order of the major arcana cards (see Chapter 7), the minor arcana cards (see Chapter 8), and the court cards (see Chapter 9) often vary.

For example, as I explain in Chapter 7, the major arcana cards generally begin with The Fool and end with The World. However, in a few decks The Fool is the last card rather than the first. Because the 22 cards that make up the major arcana represent the continuing journey from spirit to matter and matter to spirit, this change of position is of little consequence.

The most puzzling and consistent of all variations has to do with the eighth and eleventh cards. In some decks, the eighth card is called Strength, or something similar such as La Force, and the eleventh card is Justice, La Justice, or Adjustment. Yet in other decks, the cards' positions are reversed: Justice occupies the eighth position and Strength the eleventh.

I hear you asking, "So what's up with eight and eleven? What's the *right* way to order these cards?" I wish I could provide you with a simple answer. Like so many other aspects of the mysterious tarot, this question has many answers.

Truthfully, this question has been a subject of debate — sometimes quite hot and heavy — among tarot teachers and practitioners for as long as I can remember. It's up to you to pick the system you feel comfortable with (much like picking out your own tarot deck). I offer the following sections — summaries of the most widely discussed points of view in this debate — to help you decide which system you prefer.

Justice before Strength

People who prefer Justice in the eighth spot and Strength in the eleventh believe that the correct ordering for the tarot cards appears in the Visconti-Sforza Tarot, dating from 1430. The Tarot of Marseilles, from the mid-eighteenth century, is the most well-known deck after the Sforza. This deck mimics the arrangement of the Sforza deck.

Strength before Justice

People who prefer Strength in the eighth spot and Justice in the eleventh say that the correct ordering of the tarot cards appears in the Waite (or Rider-Waite) Tarot published in 1910. The mystery school tradition, of which

Arthur Edward Waite was a member, proposes that blinds were put on the earlier cards, reversing the order of Strength and Justice.

In the mystery school tradition, *blinding* — purposefully withholding or obscuring information, or giving misinformation — occurs when a teacher wants you to go through the process of deciphering certain mysteries for yourself. The astute student is enticed by the subtle or gross inconsistency of the blind and, instead of taking it at face value, decides to verify it. Solving the mystery involves making contact with your inner teacher, which in my opinion is a very worthwhile endeavor.

The concept of blinding connects with one of the primary principles of the mystery schools: If you're *ready* to see the truth, you see it. If you aren't, you remain blind to it, even if it's right in front of you.

Limbo land

There's no right or wrong way to order the cards in a tarot deck. The question of the ordering of Strength and Justice has been in limbo land for generations and will probably remain there ad infinitum. The further back you go into tarot history, the more variations and inconsistencies you find. Tarot people have finally agreed to disagree, so there's no absolute ordering of the first 22 tarot cards.

Chapter 7

Hitting the Big Time: The 22 Major Arcana Cards

In This Chapter

▶ Defining the major arcana

▶ Discovering principles connecting the cards

▶ Interpreting individual cards

*I*f you've been reading this book straight through from Chapter 1, then your patience is about to pay off! It's time to dive into the tarot deck, card by card. In this chapter, I explain the *major arcana* or *trumps,* the first 22 cards in the tarot deck. I explore the origins of the words *arcana* and *trump,* and then I show you how the major arcana, like the tarot itself, represents different things to different people. Finally, I introduce you to each major arcana card, one by one.

You're about to embark on one of the simplest ways of making friends with the tarot: dividing the deck into three parts, beginning with the 22 major arcana cards, and then moving into the 56 minor arcana cards, which are comprised of 40 number or *pip* cards and 16 court or royalty cards. (I cover the two groups of minor arcana cards in Chapters 8 and 9.)

When it came time to select the deck for showing you the tarot, I felt stuck — there are so many wonderful decks to choose from! Deciding to take a break from the various tarots parading through my mind's eye, I took part of an afternoon off and went for a walk by the ocean. By the time the sun disappeared into the Pacific, it was clear that the **Rider-Waite Tarot Deck** would serve both of us best.

I chose to present the tarot to you through the Rider-Waite deck because it's a classic, meaning it will *never* go out of style. In certain tarot spreads, there's a card for the "possible future," and I'm thinking about yours. If the tarot intrigues you (and I assume it does or you wouldn't be reading this book), there's more written about the Waite deck than any other. For my non-English speaking friends, this deck is printed in multiple languages: English, French, German, and Spanish, plus a five-language edition of Dutch, English, French, German, and Italian. Pretty impressive!

I must admit that, had this section of the book been printed in color, I'd have chosen my favorite deck, **The Albano-Waite.** This boldly colored variation of the Rider-Waite was done in 1968 by Frankie Albano and recently reprinted by U.S. Games Systems. I'm amazed to say that I'm wearing out my third vintage pack of these cards. Much to my surprise, each time I wear a deck out, another just seems to come my way! (The tarot's angels are certainly looking after me.)

So clean off your glasses or drop those contacts into solution and turn on the light over your head so that it shines directly onto the pages of this book. Now you're ready to begin looking at the pictures in your life in some new and, I hope, insightful and transformational ways.

Defining the Major Arcana

What is the major arcana? It's time to dust off what my third-grade teacher, Miss Rose, said would "always be a trusted friend," the dictionary.

The word *arcana* is a fascinating one. *Arcana* is the plural of *arcanum,* which stems from the Latin word *arcanus,* meaning "closed" and "secret." Arcana also originates from the French word *arca,* meaning "chest, box, container, or ark."

Both *arcana* and *arcanum* mean "the mystery of mysteries," the ultimate secret behind the hermetic arts and sciences — tarot, astrology, numerology, alchemy, and sacred geometry. Additional definitions for these words are "secret or mysterious knowledge or information known only to the initiate" and "an extract of the vital nature of something, a powerful elixir or medicine" (the alchemist's "elixir of life"). Whew!

Simply put, *arcana* refers to a chest or container of sacred secrets. Adding the word *major* lets you know that the *major arcana* is an important container of sacred secrets.

In tarot, the word *arcana* refers to an entire grouping of cards, whether it's the 22 major or 56 minor arcana cards. The word *arcanum* is used when you refer to one specific card, such as the Wheel of Fortune or Five of Cups.

Just as Noah's ark was a container for its precious cargo, each tarot card or group of tarot cards is a container for its precious cargo: the sacred secrets of life depicting who and what you really are and how you and the universe operate.

The major arcana cards are also known as _major trumps_. In card games, trump cards are cards of a suit that outrank all others. (Many people say that your name is your fate and fortune. Perhaps the name Trump has provided "the Donald" with some of his motivation?) The word _trump_ originates from the word _triumph_, meaning "a public celebration or spectacular pageant."

The mad and mystical Charles VI of France is thought to have been the owner of one of the first known tarot decks. King Charles was a known lover of pageants and passion plays. This got me thinking that his cards — thought of as his therapeutic tools and a source of diversion — were a portable pageant or passion play that reminded the long-suffering king of the triumph of the human spirit over adversity.

Preparing to read major arcana cards

Now that you know how to define _major arcana,_ you can take the next step and prepare yourself for interpreting what the major arcana cards mean. Before I introduce the individual cards, here are some general thoughts to keep in mind about the major arcana:

- The major arcana illustrates, in picture form, the path that anyone on _any_ spiritual path develops or evolves through to higher consciousness. This is one reason the tarot can be a powerful adjunct to whatever spiritual path you may already be following.

- The major arcana shows the story of human development — the fool's journey. (I discuss this more in Chapter 17.) You can relate to this in terms of one or multiple lifetimes.

- Spiritual psychologists associate each major arcana card with specific archetypes — ways of thinking, feeling, and behaving that humans revert to when triggered by particular internal and external conditions.

- The major arcana is a full-on depiction of universal and natural laws and principles, plus the spiritual development that results from living by them.

- The major arcana is a filing cabinet of spiritual and mystical wisdom. Think of it like a computer file. Soon you'll be "clicking on" certain symbols, and information will be appearing on the screen of your mind.

- Mystics believe that the 22 major arcana cards are pictorial elaborations of the 22 letters of the Hebrew alphabet, induced from meditations on these letters.

- The 22 major arcana cards represent the foundational principles of the manifest universe called the "cube of space," described in the Hebrews'

Sepher Yetzirah, or "Book of Creation," and used by Qabalists down through the ages. True to geometry, this cube has 22 dimensions: 12 sides, 6 faces, 3 axes, and 1 center. Each dimension corresponds to one of the 22 letters of the Hebrew alphabet and a major arcana card.

✔ Qabalists think of the major arcana cards as "keys" to the door of higher consciousness.

✔ The major arcana cards comprise 22 of the 32 paths on the Qabalistic Tree of Life (see Chapter 15). Each card illustrates the personal experiences and learning you have when moving from one level of awareness, or sphere of the Tree of Life, to another.

Pulling the race card

Before we take another step, it's time to pull the race card. There was a time when the King of Cups referred *only* to a light-eyed, fair-skinned male, and Queen of Pentacles was a dark-eyed, olive-skinned female. During this time, there wasn't an African, Oriental, East Indian, or Native American anywhere in sight in a tarot deck. I'm using the Rider-Waite Tarot Deck in this book because it illustrates the basics like no other deck, but I'll be the first to say it lacks ethnic diversity.

Fortunately, more and more tarot decks are depicting people of color — and rightly so. I've colored in my own personal tarot cards showing people of all races, and I continuously encourage my students to do likewise.

Because the cards reflect aspects of yourself, if you're not Caucasian, you could have some difficulty relating to the cards on the pages ahead. What to do? Become an artist of course! Before multi-racial decks were available, I pulled out my crayons and added various skin tones — including a few greens and blues — to my Rider-Waite deck. You may find yourself doing likewise. (Also, check out the cards in the color insert in this book. Some of these decks reflect racial diversity, particularly the Tarot of the Ages.)

Touring the Cards

Before you explore each of the major arcana cards, I encourage you to visit Chapter 6 if you haven't yet done so. If you have read Chapter 6 already, please keep in mind the information I share in the section called "Amber's approach to interpreting." It goes a long way toward explaining what you find in the following interpretations of each major arcana card.

Interpreting or reading the cards is a matter of your response to the image presented. How you and I respond to or "read" the situations, pictures, symbols, or archetypes of daily life is based on factors such as your experiences in similar situations, collective influences (such as cultural and collective myths), and your present state of mind, emotions, and health.

In Chapter 1, I explain that there are two types of archetypes or concepts — personal and impersonal (universal). Personal archetypes are based on your particular experiences, while impersonal or universal archetypes are based on the experiences of humanity as a whole. (In regard to the Qabalistic tarot, impersonal or universal archetypes represent universal and natural laws and principles shared by all of the world's spiritual and religious traditions.) When interpreting tarot cards, it is best to consider both the personal and impersonal archetypes.

The personal transformation that can result from tarot reading stems from becoming aware of your personal archetypes, then aligning them with impersonal or universal archetypes. This practice involves seeing the big in the little or the infinite in the finite.

Remember, life is a set of picture symbols. When we change our worn-out associations with these pictures, we change ourselves and, inadvertently, the world around us! The standards of beauty exemplify this phenomena — allowing for what was once considered unbeautiful by a group to become beautiful (and vice versa).

As you review the following interpretations, please remember that I'm trying to give you the essence of each card. If you find yourself thinking that there must be more to each card than what I'm presenting, you are absolutely correct! There are an infinite number of meanings for each card and symbol.

This is an introductory tarot book. Instead of interpreting all the symbols in each card, I touch upon those that I think might be the most helpful to your understanding. These interpretations, based on Qabalistic mystery school teachings, follow the words "Universal archetype." The remaining meanings, those in question form, result from considering the card as a whole.

There's much to be gained from learning about the meanings of each symbol on a tarot card. Many good books offer you this type of interpretation. *Jung and the Tarot* (Weiser, Inc.) by Sallie Nichols, *The Tarot* (Builders of the Adytum) by Paul Foster Case, and my book *Living the Tarot* (Wordsworth Editions, Ltd.) are three books recommended by many tarot teachers.

The Fool

Universal archetype: The sun behind the fool suggests the one divine spirit filling all of creation with life. The fool steps off the cliff: The soul is about to take on a new body and lifetime. The divine child is sent from high above to bring spiritual upliftment to humanity. The fool is the universal life-giving principle called *super-consciousness,* the changeless reality that expresses itself through continuous change.

- Are you suddenly feeling adventurous?

- Is it time for you to follow your inner promptings instead of the expectations and promptings of others?

- Are you perceiving yourself as a beginner in some area: career, relationship, love, self-care?

- What uncharted area of your life are you moving to explore?

- Have you unexpectedly seen yourself or a life situation from the bigger point of view?

- Do you sense "spirit" pushing and pulling you towards your destiny?

- Are you feeling as if you're being guided through life?

- Could others be judging your carefree behavior as foolish?

- What benefit does a little foolishness have the potential of bringing you?

- Who is taking advantage of your lack of experience or knowledge?

- What precipice or unknown set of circumstances are you fearlessly going over?

- Where are you needing to take a leap of faith?

- Might you benefit from paying more attention to your intuition and less attention to your rational mind?

THE MAGICIAN.

The Magician

Universal archetype: The magician's hand gestures communicate the ancient hermetic axiom, "As above, so below; as below, so above." Each human personality or ego is a vehicle, medium, or channel through which the one divine spirit manifests itself. The magician is your *conscious* awareness of yourself as an individual. His wand indicates the parts that intention and attention serve in bringing your desires into form. The four tools on his table symbolize the four-fold process of creation: inspiration (wand), imagination (cup), discrimination (sword), and manifestation (pentacle). (These tools are discussed in Chapter 8.)

- How might you notice and experience more magic in your day-to-day life?

- Might you reduce a lot of stress by living more in the present?

- What are you desiring to manifest?

- What situation requires your undivided attention?

- Are you having difficulty focusing your attention?

- Could you benefit from improving your communication?

- Are you able to appreciate and accept your own or another's personality?

- What change are you resisting or surrendering to?

- What's making you feel distracted and restless?

- What area of your life is calling for change?

- Is your thinking muddled?

- Are you feeling like a message-bearer?

- Are you underestimating your ability to learn new things?

- What goal are you manifesting by concentrating your attention?

- What tools are at hand?

- Are you aware of your higher Self coming through your personality?

- Do you know that you have the perfect body and personality for doing your spiritual work?

The High Priestess

Universal archetype: The priestess represents complete neutrality, as she is sitting between the pillars of the positive and negative polarities. Her scroll suggests that she carries a record of all that's occurred to you and the human race. The receptivity of the priestess is your *personal subconscious* and the *collective unconscious* rolled into one.

- How could you benefit from being neutral?

- Are you prone to living in the past?

- Are you involuntarily receiving the feelings or thoughts of others?

- What are you reacting to?

- What memories/dreams are resurfacing?

- What habit is being reactivated?

- What is your intuition telling you?

- Have you been too impressionable?

- Where might receptivity prove helpful?

- What could you gain from self-reflection?

- Are your instincts aroused?

- Do you have otherworldly experiences?

- What situation is being neutralized?

- Are you feeling independent, virginal, or incorruptible?

- Are you being true to your Self?

- Have you glimpsed beyond the veil of physical reality?

- What feelings or memories are you blocking?

- Where might a passive attitude be harmful?

- What subconscious pattern are you becoming aware of?

- Are you suddenly experiencing that your subconscious reflects what your conscious mind pays attention to?

- Is your psychic sensitivity increasing?

- Are you trying to see into the future?

THE EMPRESS.

The Empress

Universal archetype: The lush surroundings suggest that the empress is both mother nature and the maternal or nurturing part of you. Her pregnant body implies she's filled with the desire to bring her children, symbolizing her passions, into form. The empress is your creative imagination — when filled with the desire to create something, you should be willing to nurture and nourish it along to birth and afterwards. If you don't do this, it dies or remains in the realm of wishes and fantasies. She is also the Divine Mother, known as Understanding, on the Qabalistic Tree of life.

- Does the relationship with your mother or other women in your life need repairing?

- What are you mothering?

- Do you need some loving care?

- Are you feeling sensual?

- How are you ruling your queendom?

- Are you feeling fertile, or are you feeling out of creative juice?

- What dreams are you planting?

- What seeds are bearing fruit?

- What are you wishing to get pregnant with, give birth to, or abort?

- Are you in touch with your heart's desire?

- Are you experiencing the amazing power of your creative imagination?

- How are you imagining your future?

- What creative endeavor are you (or do you want to be) involved in?

- How might you rekindle your creativity?

- What or whom do you feel protective towards?

- Whom are you punishing by withholding affection?

- What needs more or less nurturing in your life?

- What needs a creative touch?

- Do you want better female role models?

- Might you benefit from spending more time in nature?

- How are you preserving the environment?

- Are you developing a relationship with your female side?

THE EMPEROR.

The Emperor

Universal archetype: The emperor holds a globe in his left hand, symbolizing how he innately watches over — lovingly rules and regulates — the world his counterpart, the empress, has brought into existence. His long white beard suggests the "Ancient of Days," the Divine Father, known as Wisdom on the Qabalistic Tree of Life. The emperor is the part of you that's observant, reasonable, organized, and disciplined, intimating that without these qualities, creativity is short-circuited and doesn't bear fruit.

- Does your relationship with your father or other men in your life need repairing?

- What are you fathering?

- Who has overpowered you?

- What power struggle are you experiencing?

- Might you benefit from better rules and regulations?

- What rules or regulations are you rebelling against?

- Do you want to be more self-regulating?

- Might you benefit from being more organized?

- Is it time to take charge?

- Are you being assertive or aggressive?

- What requires your loving protection?

- Might you benefit from opening your mind to seeing from many views?

- What would you gain from taking courses in leadership training?

- Do you experience difficulty in dealing with authority figures?

- Might you need to be more or less reasonable?

- Why are your putting reason aside?

- Have you been too analytical in your thinking?

- What project would benefit from your organizational abilities?

- Do you want better male role models?

- What needs overseeing and discipline?

- Are you developing a relationship with your male side?

The Hierophant

Universal archetype: Like the high priestess, the hierophant sits between twin pillars signifying neutrality. This symbolism is so important that it's reiterated in his being seated over the black-and-white tiled floor. Asking for inner guidance and then being open to receiving it — no matter what the guidance may be — is the principle signified by the monks (the conscious and subconscious parts of you) kneeling at the hierophant's feet. The hierophant's hand signals "be still and listen," telling you to listen to the truth within *your* heart of hearts.

- What higher authority are you tuning into?

- What authority have you defied?

- Might it be worthwhile to put aside what you think you know in order to *really* know?

- How could you benefit from being still and listening before acting?

- Is religion turning you off or on?

- Are you thinking about taking a teacher?

- What wise counsel have you received from a respected authority?

- Do you realize that the ultimate teacher lives within you?

- What truth are you seeking (or do you already possess)?

- Are you embracing a new spirituality?

- How could you be better at listening to yourself or others?

- What are you doing for others rather than for yourself?

- Do you know that you're the final authority on what's right or wrong for you?

- What's stopping you from heeding the truth?

- Are you more Self-possessed, or possessed by others?

- Are you craving new forms of religion or spirituality?

- Are you in tune with your intuition or inner teacher?

The Lovers

Universal archetype: The archangel Raphael, "Healer of the Most High," raises his hands in blessing, suggesting the wholeness resulting from women embracing their maleness and men embracing their femaleness. The card's similarity to the Garden of Eden signifies that self-awareness, awareness of yourself as an individual (*self-consciousness*), is the first step to enlightenment. The man looks at the woman, suggesting how your personality tends to turn to your subconscious for its responses. The woman looking at Raphael intimates that self-love and acceptance are necessary for loving relationships. The card hints that relationships have a reciprocal quality that leads to self-healing. Whether communications originate from yourself or others, they are catalysts that can raise your consciousness and the consciousness of others.

- What's bringing you greater self love?

- Is a new love entering your life?

- Are you aware that disliking the opposite sex alienates you from the other side of yourself and from divinity?

- How are you making friends with or healing the male and/or female part of yourself?

- Is less neediness and more self-reliance improving your relationships?

- Are you realizing that self-love is a prerequisite for successful relationships?

- Are the feeling and thinking parts of yourself being synthesized?

- Do you feel blessed knowing that there are no mistakes, only lessons to be learned?

- What might you gain or lose from standing naked with your feelings?

- Are you aware that your soul mate is who you are with, not some ideal person?

- What are you desiring to experience, despite its consequences?

- Do you feel drawn to loving someone of the same sex?

- Might a temporary separation from a loved one help heal your relationship?

The Chariot

Universal archetype: The chariot symbolizes the human body or vehicle in which you take your spiritual journey through life. The water in the background shows that the charioteer must leave home, or what is familiar, to find your higher soul, spirit, Self. The charioteer is under the impression that he directs his life, but the star-studded canopy overhead hints that divinity has precedence over all. His standing above and between the black-and-white sphinxes suggests that the charioteer is learning to view success and failure as two sides of the same coin of Self-knowledge.

- What are you moving towards or away from and why?

- How are you being a spiritual warrior?

- What are you reluctant to leave?

- Are you feeling pulled in two directions at once?

- How might you rise above a polarized situation?

- Do you find that you take whoever you are wherever you go?

- What are you feeling overly attached to or wishing to avoid?

- What inner tensions and contradictions are you struggling to maintain control over?

- How could you feel more at home while traveling?

- In what defeat/victory is there a potential victory/defeat?

- In what arena of life are you enjoying a triumph?

- Are you feeling impatient with your spiritual evolution?

- Are you understanding that you can only control your thoughts and actions?

- How might your passions be commanding you, rather than you commanding them?

- In what ways might self-discipline be rewarding?

- Are you experiencing more self-trust and acceptance?

Strength

Universal archetype: A woman dressed in white, the symbol of the pure hearted and evolved part of you, lovingly approaches the wild beast, the bestial or unevolved part of you. The creature responds by licking her hand. Strength suggests what it takes to embrace yourself fully. Everyone has a beast, or immature qualities, within us. The card suggests that befriending, owning, and/or acknowledging these parts of you makes you a complete person. This doesn't mean that we let the beast run wild; it means that the mature part of you lovingly, yet firmly, guides it.

- What lion are you handling or fleeing from?

- Might a roaring lion be lying in wait within you?

- Have you gotten in touch with a desire to be wild?

- What feelings are you trying to shut down?

- How might you go about taming a beast?

- When is your sensitivity a strength or a weakness?

- When is your strength a weakness or a strength?

- Who or what are you taming with tough love?

- Is not facing a raging lion making you feel like a hero or coward?

- Is an experience of inner strength making you feel the need to be less forceful?

- Could it be time to befriend the beast within yourself or within another person?

- How could you make amends for being beastly towards yourself or another person?

- How would gentleness help a potentially dangerous situation?

- Where are you being called upon to walk your talk?

- How could directing unconditional love to all parts of your personality change your life?

The Hermit

Universal archetype: The hermit stands on a mountaintop, intimating that he has an objective or wise view of what's happening in the world below. He willingly holds a lantern in his right or conscious hand, suggesting that he's cognizant of being a bearer of the light of wisdom and understanding in the darkness of confusion and ignorance. The wand in his left or subconscious hand implies that he's assimilated his life experiences and serves as an inspiration to others. In addition to encouraging those traversing the mountain to higher consciousness, his presence states that help, if sought, is always available.

- What soul guidance are you following?

- What mountain are you climbing?

- Are you seeking the light of hope during a dark time?

- Might someone or something be that light for you?

- Is there some way you can shine your light without being attached to whether or not others can see it?

- Could you enjoy withdrawing from the world?

- Why are you resisting your need to be a hermit for awhile?

- What tools or teachings are close at hand?

- Might you feel old and wise, although you're young in years?

- Do you feel comfortable or uncomfortable being alone with yourself?

- What overview or interconnection have you suddenly seen?

- Are you concerned about fitting into the world?

- Are you alone without feeling lonely?

- What lesson are you assimilating?

- What wisdom are you sharing with the world?

- Are you finally realizing that there are as many paths to higher consciousness as there are people?

- Might you want to serve those less fortunate than yourself?

Wheel of Fortune

Universal archetype: Four winged guardians surround the wheel, indicating that all fortune comes from on high. The undulating serpent of knowledge suggests that life's ups and downs bring the potential of knowing your Self more fully. The jackal-headed guardian of the underworld, Anubis, on whom the wheel seems to rest, reminds you that although dark times are a natural part of the life cycle, divinity is always traveling with you. A sphinx, guardian of the mysteries, sits outside the wheel, watching creation cycle through its stages of birth, life, death, and rebirth — the wheels within wheels. The guardian's placement, above the wheel, suggests the development of *witness consciousness,* a state bearing calm and perspective in the midst of life running its course.

- Are you increasingly aware that every action creates a response somewhere in time?

- What cycle are you completing or beginning?

- What opportunity is at hand?

- Just when you felt you were getting the hang of something, did it change?

- Might you benefit from stepping outside of a situation, to watch and wait rather than participate?

- What moment are you seizing?

- Have you thought about getting help handling your mental and emotional ups and downs?

- What unfortunate or fortunate circumstances have the potential of turning around?

- Are you experiencing the repercussions of some action?

- Are you fighting the movement of life's wheel?

- Why are you resistant to being where you are?

- How could you be more aligned with the changes at hand?

- What action are you being rewarded for?

- What is coming full circle?

- How are you remaining centered during times of upheaval?

- Are you becoming more accepting of life's ups and downs?

- In what ways is life making you a better person?

Justice

Universal archetype: Like the priestess and hierophant, justice sits between twin pillars suggesting neutrality and a well-balanced perspective. Holding scales in her right hand and the sword of discernment in her left, justice weighs out or calculates the possible results of her actions before taking them. After deciding that she's willing to take responsibility for what might ensue, she acts with the faith that her chosen course of action will balance out in time. Justice's outstretched foot shows she's always ready to act, helping to rebalance and modify a seemingly set cycle of events.

- Are you taking responsibility for your actions?
- What justice are you seeking?
- What seemingly unjust situation is working out justly?
- What imbalances are you correcting?
- What action could you take to mitigate the effects of a harmful act?
- What situation would it help to weigh the pros and cons of thoroughly?
- How is pain compelling you to change your behavior?
- What injustice is upsetting you?
- How might your present actions rectify a past injustice?
- Are you wielding the sword of justice to protect yourself or another?
- What unfairness are you obsessing about?
- What are you having difficulty adjusting to?
- Are you experiencing a period of adjustment?
- What's throwing you off balance?
- How is another person's lack of equilibrium affecting you or your environment?
- What might you do to rebalance yourself?
- Have you gone too far in trying to right a past wrong?
- What experience is restoring your faith in the idea that life has a way of working out for the best?

THE HANGED MAN.

The Hanged Man

Universal archetype: Comfortably suspended from a tree shaped like the Hebrew letter *tav* (the letter of the World or Universe card), the hanged man has temporarily stepped out of ordinary time and into eternal time. His pose suggests the practice of adding a universal perspective to your earthly one. His halo and white hair indicate he's passed through wisdom's door. Despite being tied, the hanged man hangs freely, suggesting that an expansive attitude towards life's restrictions has the potential to free you. The hanged man's legs point to heaven, symbolizing our true roots.

- What reversal are you experiencing?

- What's got you hung up?

- What beliefs are you suspending?

- Do you need to honor your Self by doing something unconventional?

- Is something restricting yet freeing you?

- Are you transitioning from one state of consciousness to another?

- How is your perspective shifting?

- Is your most important attachment the one to higher consciousness?

- Is it worthwhile to take time for self-reflection?

- Are you putting your plans on hold for a while?

- Why are you behaving like a martyr?

- Might you listen to your Self although it's telling you to do what's contrary to what you want to do?

- How might you create stability in the midst of instability?

- What sacrifices are you making?

- Where might relinquishing control be valuable?

- What truth are you surrendering to?

- What are you afraid of losing by reversing your views?

- What important issue is now unimportant due to a change in your perspective?

Death

Universal archetype: Death rides a horse that represents an elevation in status, symbolizing how death is a consciousness-raising experience — you leave your personal consciousness behind to see yourself and your actions objectively. All fall at death's feet, a reminder that whatever is born eventually dies. The sun rising in the east between two towers signifies that death is as much a part of the life cycle as the sun's rising and setting. Death's integral connection with life — it being part of the natural flow of life — is also shown by the water in the card's background, the stream of life first seen flowing out of the robe of the high priestess.

- What worn-out behaviors are you holding on to?

- What are you afraid of letting go of?

- What dream is dying an untimely death?

- Are you feeling stuck?

- Are you experiencing a spiritual rebirth?

- What desires are falling away?

- Why do you resist growing up?

- Have you survived a near death experience?

- What part of you is being transformed or eliminated?

- Might you be dealing with the passing of someone near and dear?

- What worn-out ways of thinking or relating are you being forced to drop?

- Are you contemplating the idea that death is a natural continuation of your soul's development?

- What or who are you mourning?

- Are you becoming less attached or more attached to your body as you age?

- What little deaths are you noticing daily?

- Do you fear dying more than death?

- What death are you denying?

- Is a life-threatening illness increasing your appreciation of life?

- How might death bring renewal?

Temperance

Universal archetype: The archangel Michael stands with one foot on the water and the other on land, suggesting that a spiritual foundation supports your daily life and your worldly growth and development support your spiritual growth. This is again seen by the water flowing between the angel's two cups, mixing the seemingly contradictory elements of spirit above and matter below. The rainbow overhead promises that you will be completely successful in spiritual work you undertake in this lifetime.

- Do you feel protected by your guardian angel?
- What aspect of your personality is being purified and refined?
- What are you feeling excited about?
- What desire is being dampened?
- What aspects of your personality are being unified?
- Have you been wrestling with a drug, alcohol, food, or other addiction?
- What combination of people in your life is or isn't working out?
- What new combination needs to be made?
- How might you consolidate your energies?
- Could you be going from the frying pan into the fire?
- What opposing forces are being reconciled?
- Are you seeking or experiencing contact with your higher Self?
- What guidance are you gratefully receiving?
- Who's angering you?
- Is it time to put your philosophy into practice?
- Do you feel like you're undergoing "trial by fire"?
- Are you in a potentially volatile situation?
- How are life's stresses and strains spiritualizing your life?
- Are spiritual teachings giving you needed support?
- What test are you failing or passing?

THE DEVIL .

The Devil

Universal archetype: The archangel Uriel, meaning "Light or Shadow of the Most High," perches on his throne. In Hebrew, numbers translate into letters and vise versa. Using this system, the card number for The Devil, number 15, becomes the word *Jah,* one of the many names for divinity. Uriel's hand gesture symbolizes the value of looking past superficial appearances to the one spirit within all. The devil's white beard hints that he is the shadow of the Most High, bringing you to terms with your shadow — your immaturities. If divinity can have a shadow, so can you! Accepting your humanness enables you to lift off the chains of self-hatred. The loose-fitting chains around the humans, stemming from the devil's throne, imply that the same power that appears to be restricting you is freeing you! The card's similarity to The Lovers suggests that going through hell creates a passion for freedom.

- Do you feel like you're living in hell?
- Are you being plagued by shame and guilt?
- Are you feeling a little devilish?
- Do you feel imprisoned by the material world?
- What are you choosing to remain ignorant or narrow-minded about?
- What lie are you propagating by refusing to look past its surface?
- Why are you living in denial?
- Are you afraid of seeing yourself more truthfully?
- How are you seeking release from mental bondage?
- Do you feel powerless over your sexual urges?
- Who or what are you trying to exert undue influence over?
- Might you be purposefully harming another?
- Who or what are you blaming for your shortcomings?
- Are you behaving like an ass?
- Could it be valuable to go with your instincts once in a while?
- When was the last time you laughed at your humanness?
- How might you acknowledge and make friends with the "dark" or unevolved, unloved side of yourself?

THE TOWER.

The Tower

Universal archetype: Because the Tower of Babel was built on the false premise that humanity could surpass divine power, divinity struck it down. When you and I are too proud or unaware to let go of excessively egotistical and/or erroneous ideas (or "towers"), lightning, a universal symbol for divine intervention, helps lighten our load or enlighten us. The crown, falling people, and eroded foundation show conceptions, built upon human versus divine principles, being dislodged by universal wisdom and understanding.

- Are you feeling that you're about to explode or come unglued?

- Is your life falling apart?

- How are you handling your anger or the anger being directed at you?

- Do you really believe that you're better than everyone else?

- What needs restructuring?

- What old and unsafe structure has fallen?

- How have you been isolating yourself?

- What warning signs are you closing your eyes to?

- Are you or someone close to you having a breakdown?

- What explosive situation are you dealing with?

- What have your words or actions destroyed?

- Do you feel like you're getting hit upside the head?

- What ego-crushing defeat are you experiencing?

- Are you getting a dose of humility?

- How are you overstepping your boundaries?

- Are you being put in your place?

- Who is acting out?

- What natural disaster or accident has befallen you or your environment?

- Are you in shock?

- What must crumble in order for a better structure to be built?

The Star

Universal archetype: A naked woman on bended knee pours water onto the land and into the water while gazing meditatively into the rippling pool, symbol of the magical waters of universal consciousness. Both water and earth support her, suggesting that when you seek spiritual reference points on which to base your life, they appear. While meditation and prayer, stirring the pool of the universal mind, provide proof of divinity's existence, the physical world offers the same experience when perceived with senses that have been spiritualized by prayer and meditation — those intent upon seeing, hearing, feeling, tasting, touching, and smelling divinity in all.

- Are you shining like a star?

- When are you going to start starring in your own life?

- What hope might you see in a dark situation?

- What is getting stripped away?

- How is your conscience guiding you?

- What are you wishing or praying will occur?

- What are you seeking to know, no matter what it reveals?

- Why are you down on your knees asking for guidance and direction?

- Is your interest in spirituality activated?

- How are you integrating your insights from prayer and meditation into your daily life?

- What truth do you put first in life?

- Is your life getting reshaped by spiritual practice?

- Are your sensory perceptions clearer?

- Are you ready for self-reflection?

- How are you standing naked with your higher Self?

- Are you being more honest about what you need and who you are?

- What inspirations are you receiving?

- Are you saying "no" to others and "yes" to your Self?

THE MOON.

The Moon

Universal archetype: A crayfish eases out of a pool, symbolizing the great ocean or womb of life from which all originates. A wolf and dog bay at the moon, and all phases of the moon are visible. These symbols show that as you travel the highway to higher consciousness (the path heading to the distant mountains), you must evolve through all states of consciousness — nothing can be skipped.

- What life cycle is ebbing or flowing?

- Where do you see your abilities waxing or waning?

- What path are you about to traverse?

- Are you needing to blend the tame and wild parts of yourself?

- Do you feel like you're heading into the unknown?

- How have you been deceiving yourself or another?

- Are you understanding that all events in your life are part of your spiritual journey?

- Might you count your blessings?

- Do you feel alone?

- Are you finding that the spiritual path has many twists and turns?

- How might you emerge from a descent into overwhelming emotions and feelings?

- What old wound is healing or festering?

- Could you be ready to forgive yourself or another?

- What changes do you find your spiritual practice bringing you?

- Is a psychic sideshow distracting you from your spiritual work?

- What past hurt have you been harboring too long?

- What fears require handling so that you may progress on your path?

The Sun

Universal archetype: The sun beams down as a child, wearing a feather (as does the fool), rides bareback on a horse. In addition to showing the raising of awareness, riding a horse without a saddle or bridle symbolizes the child's complete mastery over his animalistic instincts, first seen in the Strength card. The wall in the card's background states that great obstacles have been overcome, and as a result, the "child within" has been healed.

- Is your heart opening to yourself or another?

- Are you feeling optimistic or pessimistic?

- What might you be overdoing?

- Could you be heading for burnout?

- What's filling you with vitality?

- Is your health being restored, or is it in jeopardy?

- How are you sharing light and love?

- What happiness are you enjoying?

- What wall have your overcome?

- What are you basking in?

- What plan is getting reenergized?

- Could you be more open-minded and tolerant towards others?

- Are you relishing the beauties of life?

- Are you suffering from a lack of sunshine?

- What accomplishment are you celebrating?

- How is your energy and enthusiasm helping or hindering you or others?

- What resources are being stored for a rainy day?

- Are you sensing the divine light in all?

- How are you creating a happier, healthier, more enjoyable life for yourself and others?

- How might you bring energy to a situation without negating the efforts of others?

Judgement

Universal archetype: The archangel Gabriel, "Messenger of the Most High," sends out an awakening call to those who can hear it. People rise out of their coffin-like boxes, or dead self-limiting constructs, into limitlessness. Stepping out of temporal reality into eternal reality, you experience life. You and others are exactly as they should be — blamelessness and compassion reign supreme. This change of perspective is like switching from watching a movie on a small screen to a big screen — suddenly a larger picture becomes visible.

- Are you hearing the call to higher consciousness?

- How might you benefit from withholding judgment?

- What judgment has been handed down?

- What are you repenting for?

- How are your freeing yourself from unnecessary self-judgment?

- What truth are you hearing or unwilling to hear?

- Is your ability to give or receive constructive criticism improving?

- Are you blowing your horn too long and too loud?

- What worldly concerns are you experiencing release from?

- What rite of passage or transformation are you experiencing?

- What glimpse of the eternal are you seeing?

- What time pressure is lifting?

- Is your time sense changing?

- Are you realizing that you have forever to complete your spiritual work?

- What dead way of thinking or behaving are you rising above?

- Are you listening more to your Self and less to others?

- Are you feeling liberated from the judgments of others?

- Are you part of a group effort for social, political, or environmental change?

The World

Universal archetype: The woman, or "dancer" as she's sometimes called, stands on air, symbolizing that the spirit supports her endeavors. The card is called both The World and Universe. By honoring your worldly obligations and responsibilities, you master worldly life and gain spiritual freedom, shown by the victory wreath. The four winged guardians surrounding the Wheel of Fortune appear again, suggesting that by serving the powers that they represent, they are now at her service. She's a magician or master of transformation in its most complete sense — someone able to step into cosmic consciousness at will.

- Why are you dancing on air?

- What project are you signing off on?

- Are you celebrating a long-awaited event?

- Why are you straining to experience cosmic consciousness?

- Is the practical application of spiritual teachings increasing your self-esteem and mastery of life?

- How are you transmitting cosmic energy?

- How are self-discipline and flexibility freeing you in the midst of heavy responsibilities?

- Where and how are you letting go and letting God/dess?

- What liberation are you discovering within the limitations of your daily life?

- Why are you no longer feeling tied down?

- What is taking superhuman effort to complete?

- Are you successfully reparenting yourself?

- Are you experiencing self-actualization?

- How is a mixture of love, hard work, and unattachment liberating you?

- Where are you being called to play both male and female roles in life?

- How is the fulfillment of your day-to-day responsibilities honoring your spiritual obligations?

Chapter 8

Certainly Not the Minor Leagues: The Minor Arcana Number Cards

In Chapter 7, I explain that the tarot's major arcana is an important container of sacred secrets, depicting universal and natural laws and principles plus the spiritual development that results from living by these laws and principles. Despite what its name might suggest, the *minor arcana,* consisting of 56 cards, is not an unimportant container of sacred secrets. The minor arcana cards illustrate the practical application and integration of the major arcana's laws and principles into daily life.

In this chapter, I give you an overview of the four tarot suits and their corresponding tools. Before I get to the individual cards, I walk you through some basic information about how the four minor arcana suits correspond with nature's four elements (fire, water, air, and earth), the four Hebrew letters that represent the name of the Most High, the four processes of creation, and the four bodily humors. Finally, I guide you through each of the 40 number or *pip* cards. (Yes, you're correct. I did say there are a total of 56 cards in the minor arcana. I cover the last 16 cards, the court or royalty cards, in Chapter 9.)

Number cards and the pips

The number cards in the minor arcana are sometimes called *pip* cards or *pips.* The name hints at the different types of artwork appearing on the cards. The word *pip* means "a dot" (so *pips* means "many dots") and refers to a unit of numerical value on dice or dominoes.

The minor arcanas of some tarot decks show only arrangements of tools to match the number of the card, such as six cups or swords. These cards are often referred to as *pips.* Other decks, including the one featured in this chapter, feature full illustrations on the number cards.

Suit Yourself

Before delving into anything unfamiliar, I want to show you how the tarot's minor arcana compares with something very familiar — your standard playing cards. Like playing cards, the minor arcana cards are divided into four suits, also called *tools*. The four suits, or tools, of the tarot's minor arcana are traditionally called wands, cups, swords, and pentacles. (For you grammarians, the suits are capitalized only when they refer to a specific card, such as the Ten of Cups.)

If it helps you to think in these terms, you can match playing cards and tarot cards like so:

> clubs = wands
>
> hearts = cups
>
> spades = swords
>
> diamonds = pentacles

Your introduction to the minor arcana would not be complete without knowing where the names of the four suits originated. The names for suits came out of the Middle Ages and represent classes of people. The wands are staffs or cudgels, weapons of the peasantry, and they represent agriculture. The cups, or sacred vessels, signify the clergy. The swords stand for the soldiers or warriors. The pentacles, or money, symbolize the merchants.

Like the cards of the major arcana, those of the four suits (or tools) are called by a variety of names. Some interesting variations include:

- **Wands:** batons, pipes, spears, staves, rods, staffs, imps
- **Cups:** chalices, grails, vessels, cauldrons, ghosts
- **Swords:** crystals, blades, epees, bats
- **Pentacles:** coins, stars, shields, discs, stones, worlds, pumpkins

No matter what the system or deck you choose to work with calls the suits, you can still apply the information in this chapter to your readings.

Place Your Order Here!

The four minor arcana suits correspond to Mother Nature's four elements: fire, water, air, and earth. The associations between suits and elements are as follows:

wands = fire

cups = water

swords = air

pentacles = earth

Like the major arcana, there's more than one way to order these elements and their corresponding tarot suits and tools. The two primary ways of ordering the cards are according to density and according to direction.

Ordering the minor arcana by density

You can order the elements and their corresponding suits according to their physical density or weight. In this order, earth (pentacles) is naturally the heaviest and lowest, and air (swords) is the lightest and highest. A tarot deck ordered by density features the suits in this order: swords, cups, wands, pentacles.

Ordering the minor arcana by direction

You can also order the elements according to the direction the elements move in — up, down, or horizontally. Here, fire (wands) occupies the highest place because it rises. Because of its weight, earth (pentacles) pulls downwards. Water (cups) is also heavy but can extend itself horizontally. Air (swords) rises and extends. Only fire moves upwards naturally. A tarot deck ordered by direction features the suits in this order: wands, cups, swords, pentacles.

The order of the four suits and elements is not haphazard. The order comes from deciding to sequence the elements according to their weight or the direction in which they move. Both models are completely acceptable and workable. Ultimately, you pick the model that works best for you.

In this book, I order the minor arcana cards according to the *direction* of their movement, making fire the highest and first element and wands the first suit. I've chosen this route for your benefit, because more decks begin with the element of fire and suit of wands than with the element of air and suit of swords.

Connecting the Suits with Four Magic Letters

Now for a bit of magic. My sequencing of the four suits also fits together with the Hebrew *Tetragrammaton,* the four-lettered name of the Most High: Yod, Heh, Vav, Heh. (You may have seen this name represented as *Yahweh.*) This section explains the connections between the four suits, their corresponding elements, and the Tetragrammaton.

As if that weren't enough, the Qabalistic tradition (see Chapter 15) teaches that the Tetragrammaton represents the magical four-fold process of creation and its four corresponding levels, or worlds, of creation: archetypes (or model ideas), creative possibilities, formation/mental formulation, and physical manifestation. In this section and the next, I show you how this four-fold process unites with the Tetragrammaton, the elements, and the minor arcana suits. I know this may seem a little overwhelming, but stick with me! The rewards of seeing these connections are well worth a little effort.

The Tetragrammaton offers you a spiritual yet practical way of understanding the basics of each of the four suits — how they function individually and fit together in a sensible whole.

The Hebrew alphabet is called the *flame alphabet,* because every Hebrew letter is a variation of the letter *yod* (ʼ), which is associated with fire and the radiant universal energy. Because of its association with fire, *yod* is linked with the suit of wands in the minor arcana.

Yod means "open hand." The letter itself actually resembles a spark, and it represents the radiant universal energy coming (from on high) through you, sparking the process of creation. The wand represents you receiving an inspiration and then setting your intention upon attaining that particular something. ("I'm going to wave my magic wand and create a . . .") *Yod* and the suit of wands represent the first step of the four-fold creation process — the ideation of an archetype or model.

The Hebrew letter *heh* (ה) is associated with water and, therefore, the suit of cups. *Heh* means "window." The light from the spark enters the window. If you reverse the Hebrew letter, *heh* looks like a cup or womb waiting to be filled or impregnated with the flow of creative possibilities and the feelings they evoke. The cup represents you imagining and fantasizing about the various forms your particular "something" may take. ("It's going to be heart-shaped, square, or oblong.") Just as water takes the shape of whatever it is poured into, your imagination takes the shape of what your mind thinks. *Heh* and the suit of cups represent the second step of the four-fold creation process — imaging the various forms an archetype or model might take.

The Hebrew letter *vav* (ו) is associated with air and, therefore, the suit of swords. *Vav* means "hook or link." Swords cut things into pieces. A sword also cuts through, and away, excess material. If I ever make my own tarot deck, I'm going to substitute scissors for swords; scissors are a more contemporary and less violent association with the creative process than the sword. *Vav* and the suit of swords represent the third step of the four-fold creation process — selecting a form for the archetype or model.

The sword links, or hooks up, the world of creative possibilities with the world of manifest form. The sword represents you mentally analyzing, examining, reformulating, planning out, and creating a pattern for what's being created. As the world of formation, it's committing you to the form your particular "something" is going to take. ("It's going to be a round cake with pink icing, not an oblong with yellow frosting.")

Finally, the Hebrew letter *heh* (ה) is also associated with the earth and, therefore, the suit of pentacles. Heh means "window." Windows close and open. Upright, this letter looks like an overturned cup or container. Stretching this idea, you get a birth canal manifesting what's been gestating in the womb above. The pentacle represents you doing the physical work involved in bringing your clearly established form into the world. It's buying the ingredients for your cake, then mixing, baking, frosting it, and cleaning up the kitchen. (Of course, you get to lick the spoons and bowls!) *Heh* and the suit of pentacles represent the fourth step of the four-fold creation process — the physical work that goes into bringing the archetype or model into tangible form.

Amber's New Car: The Four Suits in Action!

The experience with my car, Bella, shows you the four suits and the four-fold process of creation in action.

One morning after an exceptionally heavy night of rain, I went out to start Bella, my mechanically reliable yet externally worn-down 14-year-old car. Not entirely to my surprise, I found that she'd taken on nearly six inches of water.

The sight of my various belongings floating about in the soppy mess sparked me with the inspiration to get a new car. The sparking of the idea of a new car equals the **wand** suit and the first process of creation, the imagining of an archetype.

Then the fantasies started flowing. I started imagining all the cars I'd *love* to own, from a vintage coral-and-cream T-bird to a new apple green Volkswagen Beetle. My desiring and dreaming equals the **cup** and the second process of creation, the emergence of creative possibilities.

I would dream and dream, yet still no car appeared. I was stuck in indecisiveness. I had to settle down and look at things such as what size car I needed, whether to get a standard shift or automatic, and my budget. Careful examination helped me decide what kind of car I actually needed and plan out how to get it. This process is equal to the **sword** suit and the third step of creation, the mental formation or patterning of the exact thing I wanted. After doing this, I was better able to link the super-physical worlds of ideas and imagination to the physical world of manifestation.

Next, I went shopping, test drove some cars, and went through the fun of bargaining with the dealership. Finally, I drove home with my nearly new, gold colored Toyota station wagon, which fits my driving needs perfectly. Shopping, buying the car, and bringing it home equals the **pentacle** suit and the fourth process of creation, the manifestation of the thing I had been envisioning.

Ha Ha Ha Ha! Linking the Humors and Suits

So far we've seen how the suits match up with the elements, the letters of the Tetragrammaton, and the four processes of creation. Think we're done with our game of fours? Not quite! In this section, I make one more connection with the suits before we turn our attention to each card of the minor arcana.

Humor is not only something that makes you laugh; it's also a state of mind, mood, and spirit. For example, you've probably heard someone say "He's in surprisingly good humor today."

In medieval times, people believed that a person's humor was dependent on four bodily fluids: blood, black bile, choler, and phlegm. The predominance of one of these humors was thought to determine your character and general health. If you were sanguine, people believed that you had an excess of blood. If you were melancholy (like Hamlet), you had an excess of black bile. If you were choleric (quick-tempered), choler dominated your humors, and if you were phlegmatic (calm or sluggish), phlegm was dominant.

Just as the four elements, letters of the Tetragrammaton, and processes of creation are associated with the suits of the minor arcana, so are the four humors. The suits and humors are matched as follows:

✔ **Wands:** sanguine, a passionate disposition

✔ **Cups:** melancholic, disposed to emotional fluctuations

✔ **Swords:** choleric, an irritable disposition

✔ **Pentacles:** phlegmatic, a calm sluggish temperament

Putting It All Together

I've already covered a lot of ground in this chapter, and it seems only fair to give you a tool for remembering all the connections I've made so far. I do just that in Table 8-1, and I also add some information about associations made with the four suits of the minor arcana. Earmark this page — I hope you return to it many, many times!

Table 8-1	Attributes of the Tarot's Four Suits			
Suit:	**Wands**	**Cups**	**Swords**	**Pentacles**
element	fire	water	air	earth
Hebrew letter	*yod*	*heh*	*vav*	*heh*
creative process	archetypes	creative possibilities	formation	physical manifestation
humor	sanguine	melancholic	choleric	phlegmatic
function	inspiration	imagination	discrimination	manifestation
colors	red	blue	yellow	green
direction	south	west	east	north
season	spring	summer	fall	winter
strengths	insight	love	truth-seeking	stability
weaknesses	egocentric	over-emotional	judgmental	inflexible
countries	southern	occidental	oriental	northern
psychological function	intuition	feeling	thinking	sensing
archangel	Michael	Gabriel	Raphael	Uriel

As you view the cards in the following section, keep these things in mind:

✔ Wands (fire) explore your spiritual self — inspirations, intuition, ideas, flashes of insight, influxes of spiritual energy, willpower, and enthusiasm.

✔ Cups (water) explore your emotional and imaginative self — emotional responses, reactions, and impulses; feelings; psychic and emotional sensitivity; dreams; fantasies; passions and desires; impressionability; and creative self-expression.

> ✔ Swords (air) explore your mental, thinking self — analyzing, arguing, examining, discerning, detaching and eliminating, truth-seeking, decision-making, reasoning, planning, patterning, and communicating.
>
> ✔ Pentacles (earth) explore your physical self — health, money, work, service, products, resources, instincts, environmentalism, physical acts, and activities.

Psychologist Carl Jung linked the four ways in which your personality functions with the four elements and the four tarot suits: intuition/fire/wands; feeling/water/cups; thinking/air/swords; and sensing/earth/pentacles. Jung taught that much like the four elements make up the physical world, the four functions of personality are the ways through which your spiritual self incorporates its life experiences.

Interpreting the Minor Arcana

Before you explore each of the minor arcana cards, I encourage you to visit Chapter 6 if you haven't yet done so. If you have read Chapter 6 already, please keep in mind the information I share in the section called "Amber's approach to interpreting." It goes a long way toward explaining what you find in the following interpretations of each minor arcana card.

Although most tarot systems link universal archetypes only to the tarot's major arcana, time and training has helped me see these archetypes in the minor arcana cards as well. The symbolic interpretations of each card, which follow the words "Universal archetype," are based upon universal principles gleaned from meditation on the ten spheres of the Qabalistic Tree of Life (see Chapter 15).

Interpreting, or reading, the cards is a matter of your response to the image presented. As I explain in previous chapters, how you and I respond to or read the situations, picture symbols, or archetypes of daily life are based on such factors as your own experiences in similar situations, your present state of mind and health, and your willingness to see things from a new perspective.

All the people in the minor arcana are extensions of The Magician, a symbol of the human personality (see Chapter 7).

Ace of Wands

Universal archetype: A wand — symbolizing divine inspiration and will and the element of fire, and signifying vitality — is held by a hand reaching out of a cloud, the world of unseen yet very real forces. An extension of your pointing finger, the wand suggests the value of paying attention to what's going on in front of you right now. It also indicates the importance of being mindful or conscious of your intentions — why you're thinking, saying, and doing what you are. Each wand in the suit is leafing out, suggesting that it's bursting with life.

- What power is at hand?

- What new opportunity is being handed down or over to you?

- What ideas are sparking or activating you?

- Are you becoming more willful?

- What situation is showing you the meaning of the words "thy will, not my will"?

- Are you waiting for the impetus to get moving?

- What's finally off to a good start?

- Are you experiencing an influx of creative energy?

- What idea is either taking off or unable to get off the ground?

- How is your power being usurped?

- What do you feel afire with?

- Are you thinking that the life force is against you?

- Do you recognize that you're being disempowered by a power greater than yourself?

- What spiritual insight or inspiration is exciting you?

- Is some insight initiating you into greater spiritual awareness?

- Whom have you overwhelmed with a show of power?

- How are you handling your new potency or impotency?

- What situation might be out of hand?

ACE ☙ CUPS.

Ace of Cups

Universal archetype: A cup, symbol of receptivity and containment, and the element of water, signifying feelings and imagination, extend from a hand reaching out of a cloud. Whatever is poured into a cup or vessel takes its shape. Water, also symbolizing the universal creative substance from which the manifest world comes, flows into the water below, fertilizing the world. Received by each human imagination, this substance takes the shape of the vessel or personality it enters. A dove, symbol of the Holy Spirit, holds an offering over the cup. It suggests that no feeling or imagining in this world is truly personal; all comes from on high and can be seen as the host or body of divinity.

- What dream has the potential of getting fulfilled?

- Are you receiving or needing spiritual nourishment and fortification?

- What fullness are you appreciating or not appreciating?

- Are your or another's emotions flowing like water?

- Is your heart opening up to yourself or another?

- What's filling you up to overflowing?

- Are you discovering your heart's desire?

- How are you contributing to your unhappiness, displeasure, and lack of fulfillment?

- What receptivity are you experiencing?

- Is it a time of destructive, yet constructive, emotional upheaval?

- Are you feeling filled with the Spirit?

- Are you feeling pregnant with possibilities?

- What pleasure(s) are you enjoying or would you like to enjoy?

- Are messages coming through your dreams, fantasies, and meditations?

- What higher love is entering your life?

- In what area are you being called on to give, as well as receive?

- Are you feeling empty and in need of replenishment?

- How might you refill your cup?

- Do you believe that love makes the world go 'round?

ACE of SWORDS.

Ace of Swords

Universal archetype: A sword — symbolizing cutting apart, elimination, formation, and the element of air, and signifying analytical thinking and planning — is topped with a crown of power and grasped by a hand coming from the clouds. The sword shapes the ideas and imaginings coming from on high into the mental patterns or matrices after which physical forms are made.

- What truth is at hand?

- How might you develop your analytical skills?

- What are you comfortable or uncomfortable taking charge of?

- Is it time to cut away what's extraneous and get down to essentials?

- What power could be used for help or harm?

- What conquest seems possible/impossible?

- What ideas could use refining?

- Who is exploiting you, or what are you exploiting?

- What choice are you being asked to make?

- Do you have too much or not enough power?

- Are you defending or protecting the truth or administering justice?

- What plan needs more thought?

- What needs prioritizing?

- Is mental clarity emerging from mental chaos?

- How are you discerning fact from fiction?

- Why are you having difficulty focusing your mind?

- Is surgery needed for proper healing?

- Is some decision calling out to be faced and made?

- What could you use help figuring out?

- What might it be best to dispose of?

- What kind of adversity are you experiencing?

Ace of Pentacles

Universal archetype: A pentacle — symbol of the manifest world, all in it, and the element of earth, and signifying solid forms — is cradled in an outstretched hand coming from a cloud. It floats above a garden much like the one appearing in The Magician card. In the center of the pentacle is a pentagram. This five-pointed star has a head, arms, and legs and symbolizes humanity as "keepers of the Garden of Eden" (planet earth). The pentagram also symbolizes magic — the magic of bringing heaven to earth and earth to heaven. No doubt, everything on earth is spirit temporarily frozen in form.

- What material attainment or reward is in your hand?
- Are you beginning a job or moving into a new environment?
- Are you feeling materially blessed?
- Might you benefit from sharing your resources with others?
- Are you wanting better pay for your work?
- Who might benefit by not relying on you for money?
- Are you understanding that physical things are spiritual ideas with clothes on?
- What seeds are you planting?
- Are you experiencing health problems?
- How are you handling or not handling your finances?
- Are you enjoying or overindulging your body and senses?
- Is some financial or work situation getting out of hand?
- What opportunities for business, security, or better health are you considering?
- How is material success corrupting you or another?
- Do your body and environment deserve better care?
- Are you overly attached to your belongings?
- What does having "enough" mean to you?
- What needs or doesn't need your care?
- In what ways are or aren't you prospering?

Two of Wands

Universal archetype: Holding a globe in one hand and a wand in the other, a man surveys the environment. Another wand is secured in a ring on the wall. Intention leads to attention. He's contemplating the wisdom of initiating a project and where in the world to do so. The wand in the ring shows that he's also considering the wisdom of turning his attention inward. It's been said that the card shows Alexander the Great's unhappiness in the midst of conquering the world. The card asks, "What brings true and lasting satisfaction?"

- After all you've accomplished, do you still need the thrill of a challenge?

- Is it wise to step into or out of the world?

- What would you like to achieve?

- What are you on the brink of doing?

- What signal are you waiting for?

- What conflicting ideas can be synthesized?

- What change are you seeking?

- What opportunity for growth are you seeing?

- What challenge might be drawing you out of your comfort zone?

- Have you been comfortable long enough?

- Why are you feeling restless?

- Are you directing so much energy out that you're neglecting your inner needs?

- What's your backup plan?

- How does it feel having the world in the palm of your hand?

- Would you like to do some traveling?

- Are you having doubts about traveling with others?

- Are you contemplating your impetus for adventure thoroughly?

- Might you benefit from stepping back and letting your intuition be your guide?

Two of Cups

Universal archetype: A young man and woman are pledging their cups to one another. The symbols not only suggest the possibilities of intimacy with another person; they also suggest your *animus* and *anima* — your inner male and female and/or conscious and subconscious parts — getting acquainted. This results in intimacy with oneself. The Caduceus of Hermes, symbol of healing and renewal, rises overhead, indicating the wisdom and restoration resulting from such an interaction.

- Is the reconciliation of differing views at hand?

- What dreams or nightmares is your relationship mirroring?

- Is marriage or spiritual union in or out of your plans?

- Are you having your first harmonious relationship with yourself or another?

- Are you getting more in touch with your feelings?

- Do you feel married to your Self?

- Are you feeling attracted to an old friend?

- What are you lovingly sharing?

- Might you be fearing or experiencing a broken relationship?

- Is love motivating you to make healthy compromises?

- Are you compromising too much?

- Might you be experiencing a union of opposites?

- Are you open or closed to giving or receiving love and affection?

- Are you sharing or unwilling to share intimate feelings?

- Do you feel vulnerable?

- What old wounds are healing through your present relationship?

- Do you love yourself as much as you love another?

- What are you projecting onto another?

- Are you feeling forced to choose between yourself and another?

Two of Swords

Universal archetype: A blindfolded woman balancing two crossed swords sits with her back turned to the water. Some say she's at a crossroads. Does she go the way of the world or the way of the spirit? Or, can she do both? Internal analysis and planning preclude external action. In order to act wisely she turns away from excessive emotions, the water, and other distractions to seek equilibrium. The card is seen as a reminder of the principle of Ageless Wisdom that states, "Equilibrium is the basis of the Great Work!"

- What decision needs to be made?

- Why are you choosing not to choose?

- What truce are you calling?

- What could you be blinding yourself to?

- How is indecisiveness working in your favor or working against you?

- What are you buying time for?

- Is extreme emotion hindering your ability or another's ability to make rational choices?

- What crossroads or turning point are you at?

- What feelings are worth putting behind you?

- Do you need to separate yourself from someone or something?

- Is your inner vision being activated?

- Why are you hesitant about acting?

- What balance are you seeking to maintain?

- How is procrastination affecting you?

- What would you rather not see?

- Is your habit of withdrawing from others or the world a mode of self-care that you wish to reevaluate?

- Might shifting into neutral in the midst of conflicting demands prove helpful?

- Could you clear your mind and relieve yourself of external pressures or influences by meditating?

Two of Pentacles

Universal archetype: A young person balances two pentacles (symbols of physical work and items) connected by an infinity sign. She's learning the spiritual value of physical work, seeing the infinite in finite life (what Qabalists term "the big in the little"). Boats riding the waves in the card's background suggest that every human vessel is subject to physical change; wisdom lies in remaining balanced in the midst of life's ups and downs. Acknowledging that physical things and situations are tools aiding spiritual growth can bring equanimity.

- What circumstances are you weighing?

- How are you managing to juggle your daily responsibilities?

- Do you think you're about to drop the ball?

- Are you attempting to balance conflicting demands?

- Do you need time for rest and relaxation?

- Are you preoccupied with money matters?

- Do you feel like you're doing more than your share of the work?

- Are you contemplating a change of lifestyle or career?

- Are you recognizing that material obligations are spiritual in essence?

- Must you choose between two things you want to do?

- Are you being pulled in more than one direction at once?

- Are your physical energies spread too thin?

- Are you experiencing difficulty in taking proper care of your home, family, work, and body?

- Are you feeling anxious about the uncertainties of daily living?

- Are you feeling torn between physical pleasures — the joy of eating everything you desire and the joy of having better physical health?

Three of Wands

Universal archetype: A mature man lean-ing on a wand looks out from the cliff's edge overlooking a sea dotted with ships. Two wands are planted in the foreground. The ships at sea suggest that his ideas and inspirations have been launched. Now it's time to decide whether to increase his chances for success by turning to the assistance that's available, the two waiting wands, or continue going it alone. Some-where along the line, all successful people understand the importance of assistance.

- Is a visionary insight giving you fore-sight into the future?

- How are your past experiences behind you and supporting you?

- What do you envision yourself achieving?

- What idea or project are you launching?

- Who's helping you put your plans into effect?

- Are you too proud to accept assistance?

- Are you feeling that the power and force for a long-planned achievement is with you?

- What gains are you or were you expect-ing to realize?

- What delays are over?

- What are you putting behind you?

- Are you considering a reinvolvement after some time out?

- Do you feel optimistic, pessimistic, or neutral about the future?

- Where are you focusing (or having diffi-culty focusing) your attention?

- Are you spending too much time talking about ideas, rather than gathering the energy to carry them out?

- Why are you feeling frustrated or blocked?

- What do you have (or want to have) dominion over?

- Are you lacking the willpower to follow through?

Three of Cups

Universal archetype: Three young women offer cups, filled with creative possibilities, to one another and the powers that be. The number three connotes a creative endeavor — the coming together of two forces to bring a new element into being. Feelings of mutual understanding, agreement, love, hopefulness, and thanksgiving permeate the image.

- Do you desire or need to celebrate life?
- What creation might you offer for blessing?
- Do you recognize the spirit behind your achievement?
- Are you wishing for or experiencing rich rewards?
- Are you sharing the fruits of your labors?
- What hospitality might you extend or withdraw?
- Is it time to touch base with or dodge friends and family?
- Might you or another benefit from invoking divinity or the nature spirits before starting a project?
- Are you experiencing an emotional or spiritual opening?
- Is a synthesis of creative energies taking place?
- Are you enjoying love and communication between family and friends?
- Could you be reaping what you've sown?
- Would you benefit from working with others toward a common goal?
- Are you enjoying or avoiding a meeting of hearts?
- What experience are you sharing?
- What friendships are enduring through good times and bad?
- What friendships are being outgrown?
- Are you requesting spiritual guidance?
- Are you giving thanks where they are due?

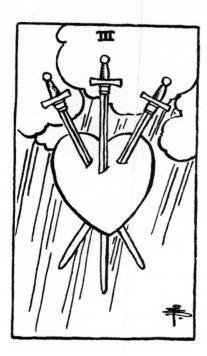

Three of Swords

Universal archetype: Three swords pierce a heart; rain falls from the clouds above. Yes, there is pain and suffering. Suffering is part and parcel of life. Relief, or rain, comes from mourning and crying. It also comes from wanting to figure out (symbolized by the mentally oriented swords) why you are suffering and what you may be thinking and/or doing that's keeping you in this state. The heart also suggests that release from pain can come from searching your heart to understand what you're attached to achieving or averse to doing.

- What anguish are you feeling?

- Are you purposefully or accidentally inflicting pain on someone?

- Is understanding or mental clarity emerging from a distressing situation?

- What cloud has a silver lining?

- Are you feeling betrayed?

- What must you do, despite the sorrow it brings?

- Is your pain clearing up?

- What suffering must you or another endure a little longer?

- What has pierced your heart?

- Is pain making you face reality?

- What might mend your heart?

- What truth is helping to heal your pain?

- What valuable lesson lies in your heart-breaking situation?

- What are you unable to see about the situation at hand?

- Might you need help through a difficult time?

- Are you able to be analytical about or detached from a trauma?

- What buried pain is affecting your life?

- Are you ready to see how you're responsible for your situation?

- What must you get off your chest so that you don't become ill?

- How are you releasing your pain?

Three of Pentacles

Universal archetype: A sculptor is commissioned to work in a monastery. The three upraised pentacles carved into the structure imply that his work is an expression of his spiritual ideals. The document suggests that an understanding between the artist and his two patrons has been reached. The artist's high level of skill and the fact that he's receiving recognition and financial compensation in return for his efforts are signified by his raised position.

- Do you love your work?

- What are you dedicated to producing?

- Are you receiving or needing support or recognition at your job?

- Is your productivity blocked?

- Might working more cooperatively with others improve your product?

- Are there opportunities for further development, or are you at a dead-end job?

- What service are you doing or wanting to do for others?

- Are you receiving or needing to give constructive criticism?

- What job are you mastering?

- What practical skill might it be worthwhile to learn?

- Are you desiring to live up to your own or another's high standards?

- Might you need to set higher or lower work standards for yourself or others?

- Who is unable to appreciate your artistry or perfectionism?

- What job are you over- or under-qualified for?

- Are you developing patience (or are you in need of patience) when training others?

- Does work function like a meditation or spiritual path?

- Are you a workaholic?

- Are you in the wrong line of work?

- Do you need a vacation?

Four of Wands

Universal archetype: Four wands support a garland and two dancing women uplift bouquets, suggesting celebration. An old manor dominates the card's background, suggesting tradition. The image symbolizes the value of coming together to honor old traditions, rites, and rituals as well as the worth of creating new ones.

- Why are you feeling joyous or optimistic?

- How are you helping to build a better world?

- Are you counting your blessings?

- Are you feeling inspired to put down roots and be more stable?

- What traditional or nontraditional project are you involved in?

- Are you celebrating what you've helped put together?

- Are you planning or canceling a marriage or commitment ceremony?

- What group are you no longer a part of?

- Are you feeling like an outsider?

- Is illness making you less able to participate in life?

- How might you get into the swing of things?

- Are you feeling the need to bring more rituals or ceremonies into your life?

- What are you commemorating?

- Might another's expectations be inhibiting your enthusiasm?

- What bounty are you sharing in?

- Are you breaking with tradition or family to honor your own needs?

- While following your inclinations, are you mindful not to throw the baby out with the bath water?

Four of Cups

Universal archetype: A young man sits under a tree contemplating three cups on the grass. A hand issuing from a cloud offers him another cup. The man's arms are crossed, suggesting that despite external pressures, he is withdrawing to follow his inner promptings rather than those of others. The continuing presentation of the cups of creative possibilities show the importance of allowing time for things to unfold. Patiently waiting for the proper thing to present itself and trusting that one's intuition will signal the time for movement is implicit.

- Why are you closed off from external input? What are you rejecting?

- Are you scared or waiting for a better offer?

- Are you waiting for a vision or revision?

- What feelings are you closed off from and why?

- Are you going inside before acting?

- What aren't you recognizing?

- Do you want to come out of your shell?

- What's being offered to you?

- Can you see that your wish is being granted?

- Why are you holding back?

- Are you enduring criticism because you're sitting back watching things unfold?

- What or who are you distancing yourself from?

- Are you tired of what the world is offering?

- Are you depressed or coming out of a depression?

- Are you feeling defensive or letting down your defenses?

- Might meditation help you achieve detachment?

- Are you seeking inner peace?

- Are you reevaluating your feelings?

- What are you dreaming about?

- Why are you feeling apathetic?

- What opportunity are you about to seize?

Four of Swords

Universal archetype: The image of the body resting in the foreground presents a contrast to the vivid scene going on outside the window. The image suggests someone who's "all thought out" and indicates the value of having mercy on oneself by temporarily retreating from the world so that all one has to do is "be." Swords are associated with mental formation and formulation. There are times when mental formulation is best preceded by letting go of one's preconceptions in order for new ideas to enter. This is the Qabalistic principle of "dissolve et coagula" — praying for and meditating on receiving a new or renewed mindset.

- How might you gather your composure before a stressful event?

- What are you retreating from?

- What concerns do you need to temporarily lay aside?

- Are you being advised to withdraw from your usual activities in order to improve your health and affect healing?

- Could you be dealing with another's ill health?

- Do you need regeneration in order to move forward more effectively?

- Are others making it difficult for you to turn inward?

- Why are you afraid to slow down after running so hard and fast?

- Could you be opting for (or are you being forced into) early retirement?

- Might you benefit from contemplating your plans rather than acting on them as they stand?

- Who is being ostracized?

- Is your introspection a way of avoiding obligations?

- Are you recouping your mental clarity?

- Are you afraid that someone or something might interrupt your quiet?

- Are you waiting for someone to rescue you?

- Are you in touch with your Self?

Four of Pentacles

Universal archetype: Because the pentacles, symbols of the physical world, are on this man's head and heart and under his feet, the image suggests a preoccupation with worldly matters and perhaps the need to hold on to what he's earned. The man's position — stationed outside the city — implies that he must take care of himself before he can take care of others. There's also the possibility that he's considering assisting those less fortunate.

- Do you fear that someone or something will take what you're working so hard for?

- What security are you clinging to?

- How might material possessions be alienating you from your Self or others?

- Is your financial situation together, or is it falling apart?

- What might make you feel secure in a constantly changing world?

- How could you be abusing your position or power?

- Might you be learning the importance of caring for yourself before others?

- What possessions are you gaining or losing?

- What does "having enough" mean to you?

- Are you being miserly?

- Are you taking what isn't yours?

- What are you protecting or defending?

- Does a past experience make you worry about taking financial risks?

- Are you constantly thinking about money or possessions?

- Could you be obsessed with providing for others?

- Are you realizing that your greatest possession is your health?

- Are you placing too much emphasis on material security and not enough on the source that everything comes from?

Five of Wands

Universal archetype: Five men brandish wands, suggesting that the game of life is in progress. People going in different directions signifies diverse opinions, divided attention, conflicting interests, and/or how each person is performing a special function within the group. One person seems to be trying to call the group to order. If there's to be some type of concerted action, personal interests need to be put aside so the group's intention can be carried out.

- Are you involved in a contest, disagreement, or dispute? What game are you playing (or what game are you reluctant to play)? Are you or others playing fairly?

- What competing idea are you trying to get across?

- What truth are you inspired to stand up for?

- What dispute could be resolved amicably?

- What ego struggles are occurring or being resolved?

- What's requiring reorganization?

- Where is leadership needed or being fought against?

- Are you fighting a worthwhile battle?

- Are you facing adversity courageously?

- What contest of wills are you participating in?

- Are you seeking to impose your will on others?

- What are you learning from healthy competition?

- Do you need to assert yourself or pull back?

- How might you benefit from checking out another's ideas?

- What struggle is taking a toll on you?

- Do you channel your aggressive energies into contact sports?

- What rules are falling away?

- Why can't you reach a compromise?

- Might opposing forces come together around a common goal?

Five of Cups

Universal archetype: A cloaked woman looks sideways at three overturned cups; two others stand upright behind her. The image suggests that in order to turn to the two cups behind her (the creative possibilities or life that awaits her), she must first mourn what's been lost, the three overturned cups. The card also depicts someone stuck in loss, depression, sorrow, and anger who needs help turning her/his life around.

- Are you facing or avoiding a terrible loss? Who or what is disappointing you?

- What are you having difficulty releasing?

- What plan is being disrupted?

- What's depressing you?

- Are you harboring bitterness and resentment?

- Could your depression be anger turned inward?

- What loss are you unable to come to terms with?

- Is it time to get help dealing with your feelings?

- Why are you cloaked in negativity?

- What are you blaming or punishing yourself for?

- What truth could you be turning away from?

- Are you mourning, or have you finished mourning?

- What are you learning from your pain and suffering?

- What or whom did you take for granted until it was gone?

- How might you get on with life and appreciate what you have, rather than continuing to dwell on what's no longer possible?

- What trauma or abuse are you confronting or needing to confront?

- Is there an alternative to what you've lost waiting for you to recognize it?

Five of Swords

Universal archetype: Actions create reactions. A man looks disdainfully after two retreating men. Their swords lie upon the ground. He carries two raised swords in his left hand, and another sword in his right hand points downwards. All things change; he's temporarily wielding power over others. If vengeance motivates the actions of the man in the foreground, he may look like a winner but really isn't. If others (the men in the background) refuse to fight for what they don't believe in, they may not look like winners but really are.

- What mind games are you playing?

- Are you parting ways with friends, family, or business associates?

- Might you disarm another with truth?

- Do you realize that when you win unfairly you're a loser?

- Are you retreating because what you're fighting over isn't worthwhile?

- Are you feeling attacked?

- Where are you or another being divisive?

- Are you feeling superior to others?

- Why are you feeling shame, humiliation, defeat, or despair?

- Whom have you taken down, and at what price?

- Are you aware that you're already paying for the pain you're inflicting?

- Is your self-esteem damaged?

- Might you be so concerned about winning that you don't care how you do it and what results from it?

- Who are you getting even with, or who is getting even with you?

- Whom are you bullying, or who is bullying you?

- Are you feeling cowardly?

- What dispute are you losing?

- Whom have you eliminated and at what cost?

- Who is threatening you, or whom are you threatening?

Five of Pentacles

Universal archetype: Two impoverished people, perhaps related, trudge through snow and cold. A window with panes of five pentacles shines above. Physical hardship and destitution permeate the image. The shining window above suggests the spiritual development that can come from dealing with physical handicaps and deprivation. The window also suggests that these people have been born into these circumstances to balance their past actions or karma. An older interpretation of the card refers to the people as *mendicants,* a now defunct order of friars composed of physically handicapped people who begged for their living.

- Why are you living like an outcast?

- What light might you be missing in the darkness?

- Are you being independent rather than taking assistance with conditions you can't honor?

- What material loss are you experiencing — your job, family, home, money?

- What comforts are you choosing to do without?

- Although you're materially poor, are you feeling spiritually rich?

- What inner light is available to guide you through difficult times?

- What might be crippling you or another?

- Who are you assisting in times of ill health or economic difficulties?

- Who might you ask for help?

- Are you or another too proud to accept assistance?

- Who could you be disempowering with help?

- Are you dealing with a physical handicap?

- Are you unskilled with finances?

- Are you playing at poverty/slumming?

- Might you be too lazy to take care of yourself?

- Are you emerging from hard times?

- Are you learning compassion for those less fortunate than yourself?

Six of Wands

Universal archetype: A wand-carrying crowd walks alongside a laureled man honorably seated on a horse. The rider holds an adorned wand, showing that he's realized a goal through intention and attention and is being venerated as a hero or leader. The group's admiration, support, and agreement have helped place him in this position; losing this consensus might mean him losing his position (at least externally). This scene can be likened to Jesus entering Jerusalem with everyone welcoming him as the Messiah.

- Whom or what are you rallying around?
- What position or responsibility are you assuming?
- What type of leadership is being expected of you?
- Are you anxious about others' expectations?
- Is your spiritual awareness being raised?
- What recognition are you receiving (or do you desire to receive)?
- Who represents your cause or interests?
- What rewards are you receiving?
- What moral victory are you enjoying?
- Are you becoming aware that success is a team effort?
- How could you be more responsive to others' needs?
- Are you experiencing a defeatist attitude?
- Do you have unrealistic expectations?
- Are you up for a promotion?
- Has someone obtained the position you wanted?
- What ideals are moving you?
- Are you feeling superior/inferior to others?
- Are you feeling rightfully proud, or are you lacking humility?
- Are your self-esteem and confidence getting boosted?
- Are you more focused on your status than on the job ahead?
- Is success taking longer than anticipated?
- What behavior are you modeling?

Six of Cups

Universal archetype: Children stand in a garden, their cups filled with flowers or beautiful feelings or fantasies. The card suggests an idyllic childhood in which one feels unconditional love and support, a state many people never experience. The man standing watchfully in the background suggests a principle of Ageless Wisdom: We are all children of divinity watched over and loved by our divine parents in ways our physical parents were unable to do.

- What love is entering or reentering your life?

- Are you an incurable romantic?

- Do you love nostalgia?

- Are you living in past dreams and fantasies?

- What gift is your higher Self offering you?

- Are you experiencing emotional give and take?

- Might a traumatic childhood be causing you or another to resist growing up?

- Are you cleaning up old family issues?

- Are you healing your inner child?

- Is a relationship moving into a new phase?

- Have you been reminiscing about the "good old days"?

- What friend or family member are you responsible for?

- Is your love of home, family, and traditional values causing conflict?

- Are children or childlike pleasures becoming increasingly important?

- Who is offering you, or who are you offering, friendship and love?

- Do you feel loved and protected?

- Is your focus on the past keeping you from living in the present?

- What broken relationships are undergoing repair?

- Are you or another clinging to worn-out customs or beliefs?

Six of Swords

Universal archetype: A ferryman carries passengers to the other shore. The plans for the journey have been well thought out, symbolized by the six balanced swords stuck in the boat. The passengers' backs are turned, suggesting faith in the unseen. The ferryman (our invisible higher soul, spirit, Self) guides the seated figures (our personality and body) to another life experience and/or level of consciousness.

- Are you moving into a more peaceful time or environment?

- Are you detached from your tumultuous past?

- Do you believe that your higher Self is carrying you to safety?

- Whom are you offering refuge to, or who is offering you refuge?

- Might proceeding with your plans relieve your anxiety?

- What plans are unexpectedly delayed?

- Who is assisting you?

- What are you fleeing?

- What do you think you're heading toward?

- Might this be a good time to retreat?

- Who's scheduled to visit?

- What necessary service are you performing?

- Are you changing direction based on clear thinking or emotionality?

- What or whom could your mindset be cutting you off from?

- What tension is being released?

- Is your suffering or another's suffering almost at an end?

- What or who do you think you're escaping?

- Do you realize that there are always problems to be solved?

- Do you feel like you're heading into exile?

- Are you considering renouncing your citizenship, or are you dealing with immigration issues?

Six of Pentacles

Universal archetype: A well-dressed man weighs money in a pair of scales, distributing it to those in need. Six pentacles float in the air, suggesting that although the money comes through the man, the impulse to give it comes from on high. The man with the scales (our higher soul, spirit, Self) gives the kneeling recipients (each of us) the physical conditions (body, environment, and so on) we need to grow spiritually, whether we are aware of it or not.

- What are you receiving by giving?
- What are you giving by receiving?
- What business transaction is occurring?
- What resources are you sharing or in need of?
- What gift has turned against you?
- Who's supporting your work?
- Who are you mentoring?
- Have you considered giving anonymously?
- What guilt are you allaying with gifts?
- Who is taking advantage of your generosity, or vice versa?
- Are you biting the hand that feeds you?
- Might you be more charitable?
- Who are you bribing, or who is bribing you?
- Are you giving or receiving too much?
- Do you place enough value on your product or talents?
- Are you too proud to take a needed handout?
- Is money putting you or another in a powerful position?
- Do you pay your workers enough?
- Do you give others what they need, rather than what you want to give them?
- Who is the true giver of everything?
- Are you receiving or not receiving the financial aid you applied for?

Seven of Wands

Universal archetype: A man on a craggy cliff brandishes a wand; six others come up from below. This man shows the courage and inner certainty to separate himself and/or his thinking from the group, the wands beneath him. Although he is being subjected to flak for following his ideals, he appears intent upon holding his ground despite being threatened.

- Whom or what are you separating yourself from?

- What ideas are you rising above?

- How are you taking your power?

- Are you feeling threatened by, or are you threatening to, others?

- What are you required to stay on top of?

- Who's all talk and no action?

- Why might you marshal your energies?

- Might you need to hold your ground or give in?

- How are you standing up for your ideas and beliefs?

- Are you energized for the long haul?

- Are you holding your own or might you ask for help?

- What opposition are you confronting or retreating from?

- What has the potential to overwhelm you?

- What or who are you empowered to protect?

- What unwanted input is assaulting you?

- Are you feeling more defensive than necessary?

- What problems are you handling or fleeing?

- What obstacles are you overcoming, or what obstacles are overcoming you?

- How are you receiving conflicting ideas?

- Are you lacking assertiveness?

- What advantage do you have?

Seven of Cups

Universal archetype: Cups filled with visions, especially those with other-worldly possibilities, arise from the clouds in front of a shadowy figure. Cups signify creative imagination. It appears that a whole array of creative possibilities have been conjured up, suggesting that this person has a potent imagination. Whether the energy to bring everything that's been dreamed up into being is present, and/or whether the ability to select one or two possibilities to focus in on exists, are the hidden challenges presented by the image.

- Are you being asked to make difficult choices?

- Might you be experiencing conflicting emotions and uncertainty?

- Are you suddenly realizing that every dream has limitations?

- Are you learning about the power of creative imagination?

- What might be causing your confusion?

- Are you having dreams or visions?

- Are you feeling unsettled by a flood of psychic phenomena?

- Could you be on sensory overload?

- What reality are you avoiding by living in fantasyland?

- What dreams could become reality?

- Might you benefit from reviewing your priorities?

- What might you release to gain the focus and energy required for manifesting your desire?

- Are mind-altering drugs helping you achieve altered states of consciousness?

- Are your meditations motivating you to seek things of spiritual value?

- What are you missing by keeping your head in the clouds?

- Are you more concerned about what you don't have than with what you do have?

- What situation are you viewing unrealistically?

Seven of Swords

Universal archetype: A man is in the process of carrying off five swords as two others remain stuck in the ground before three decorated tents, suggesting exotic possibilities. In the process of taking something from the world of creative possibilities into reality, a plan must be made. Formulating a plan, certain possibilities must be eliminated or left behind. Because the man looks back while moving forward, the image suggests he is leaving some possibilities behind, but not without some reservation.

- Might you be achieving only partial success?

- Why are you acting alone?

- Why are you taking what isn't yours?

- Why are you looking back while moving forward?

- What information are you carrying from place to place?

- Are you feeling emotionally detached from the results of an action?

- Might you be concealing your thoughts?

- What are you giving up or choosing to leave behind?

- What are you sorting through and eliminating?

- What plan are you carrying out?

- Are you not as confident as you seem?

- Are you acting with or without consent?

- Could you be breaking an agreement?

- Is your inner Self compelling your actions?

- What calculated risk are you taking or resisting?

- Why might you be throwing caution to the wind?

- Could some caution be worthwhile?

- What do you think you're getting away with?

- Is something catching up with you?

- What might you gain or lose from securing help?

- What's stopping you from finishing the job?

Seven of Pentacles

Universal archetype: A man gazes intently at seven pentacles, or material world things, attached to greenery while resting on his hoe. Perhaps he vacillates between surrender to what is and anxiety about what will be. Things are clearly out of his hands, as seen by his pose. The plants will mature in their time, not his. It appears that he's done as much as he can to bring fruit from the plant; now nature must work her magic.

- Are you reviewing your life?
- What cycle is nearly complete?
- Do you appreciate what you've accomplished?
- Are you overly attached to a specific outcome?
- What's growing through hard work?
- Where might you let go and let nature take its course?
- What project is delayed?
- Do you feel trusting or anxious about an investment?
- Are you requiring patience?
- What skill do you desire to learn?
- Is your physical energy low?
- Are you being lazy?
- How might you get reenergized and nourished?
- Are you waiting for something important to happen?
- What's growing or not growing from your hard labor?
- What's flourishing without your help?
- Are you realizing that you can't do anything but wait?
- Are you ready to reap what you've sown?
- What facet of your life needs cultivation?
- Are you contemplating a job change?
- Why are you feeling bored?
- Do you desire to live closer to nature?
- What are you learning from your mistakes?

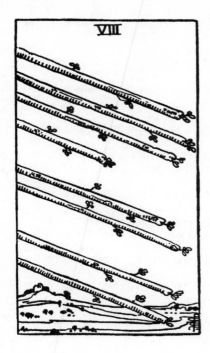

Eight of Wands

Universal archetype: Eight wands, symbols of inspiration, fly swiftly through open space. The wands can be seen as falling to earth or rising from it. Falling wands would indicate that when you sincerely seek messages or inspiration and insights from on high, they come. Rising wands would indicate that you then become the vehicle for launching messages or inspiration and insights out into the world. A certain amount of non-attachment is required for both tasks.

- Who or what's got you excited and energized?

- Where are you off to or coming from?

- Is everything up in the air?

- What's being put into motion or delayed?

- What's heading your way?

- Are you rushing into something?

- Are you always on the go and too busy?

- What end is near, or what end is nowhere in sight?

- Do you feel "grounded," like you're coming down to earth?

- Are you feeling fidgety, impatient, or uneasy?

- Do you feel like you're spinning your wheels or wasting time and energy?

- What new direction are you being inspired to follow?

- Is your energy level building, or is it high, too high, or ebbing?

- What's unexpectedly accelerating?

- What could be demanding all your attention?

- What or who is prompting you to move too fast?

- What idea is taking off? Is the way opening up before you?

- Are you flooded with ideas and inspiration?

- Are you doing or trying to do too many things at once?

- Are you concerned about keeping up?

- What's coming full circle?

Eight of Cups

Universal archetype: Leaning on a wand, a man walks away from eight cups filled with imaginings, dreams, and/or feelings, and heads towards higher ground. The image suggests he's turned away from an emotionally loaded situation to seek an overview in the hills beyond. Taking this "time out" has the potential to clear his mind and enable him to sort things through more effectively.

- What emotions are you taking time out from?

- What are you putting off or passing up?

- What are you desiring to detach yourself from?

- What cycle is completing or beginning?

- Are you seeking increased self-awareness, spiritual perspective, or a vision?

- Is someone walking away from you?

- Could you be turning your back on something you want but don't need?

- What are you leaving or returning to?

- What feelings are activating your change of behavior?

- What is sufficiently or insufficiently handled?

- What's drawing you closer?

- Is it time to walk away from or follow your feelings?

- Are you seeking answers to questions like "Who am I and what do I want from life?"

- What attachment is keeping you from moving on? Are you afraid of the unknown?

- What can't presently be resolved?

- What habits are you putting behind you?

- Are you feeling that you deserve more than you have?

- Might you benefit from retreat and self-reflection?

Eight of Swords

Universal archetype: A woman, bound and blindfolded, finds her way through a fence and gateway of eight swords. Although she might not actually know it, the structure in the background suggests that she's already traveled a great distance. Her vision and movements are limited, yet her insight, intention, and mental stamina are leading her through what seems to be the last leg of her journey to freedom.

- How could looking inside help you see more clearly what's going on outside?

- What have you almost broken free of?

- Are mental constructs keeping you imprisoned?

- What's preventing you from asserting yourself?

- Are you exiting or entering mandatory confinement?

- How are you finding freedom through limitation?

- Are you aware or unaware of options open to you? Is intuition guiding you?

- What trial are you courageously passing through?

- Might you benefit from being less or more patient?

- What are you blinding yourself to?

- Might you be experiencing shame and humiliation?

- Do you think that you don't fit in?

- What mental strain are you under?

- How might you be responsible for your position?

- What prevents you from seeing your way?

- What is trapping or oppressing you?

- Must you choose between undesirable situations?

- Is your mind closed to new perceptions?

- Although your restriction is unpleasant, is it familiar?

- How might you release yourself from your self-imposed prison?

Eight of Pentacles

Universal archetype: Pentacles are the culmination of the creative process. An artisan working in stone exhibits his finished products, the eight pentacles. The image suggests that "practice makes perfect." Meditatively centered on each piece of work, the scene suggests the focus (wands), passion and imagination (cups), mental discipline (swords), and physical energy and perseverance (pentacles) required to perfect a skill.

- What are you finishing?

- Are you due for a raise or promotion?

- What new skill might increase your income?

- Are you feeling energized, tired, or lazy?

- Are you completing or beginning school or a training course?

- What are you perfecting?

- Are you skilled with your hands?

- Do you realize that practice makes perfect?

- Are you setting a good example?

- How might your daily work be a spiritual practice?

- What's absorbing your attention, time, and energy?

- Are you underemployed or unemployed?

- What meaningful work are you doing or seeking?

- Are you desiring a new job or career?

- Do you enjoy your work, or have you not found work you enjoy?

- Do you care about the work you do?

- Do you enjoy being productive?

- Is work, or your boss, too demanding?

- Are you overly attached to what you do, and do you tend towards workaholism?

- Are you earning as you learn?

- Are you finding that money doesn't always come from work, but from your attitude toward working?

Nine of Wands

Universal archetype: While remaining watchful, a warrior-like man holding a wand steps away from eight others wands. Having already done battle, indicated by his bandaged head, the look on his face suggests he's got the idea that he may be in another combative situation. Only time will tell whether this is true or not. Choosing to remain on alert, he's both attentive to and intent upon handling whatever might await him.

- Do you need to protect or defend yourself or others?

- Would you welcome assistance?

- Could you be exhausting yourself by constantly being on alert?

- What are you readying yourself for?

- Is opposition lurking?

- What might be sneaking up on you?

- Are you looking for an argument?

- Are you feeling self-confident?

- Whom are you feeling less or more important than?

- Are you open or closed to compromising or calling a truce with the opposition?

- What are you handling alone?

- Are you so used to overextending yourself that you don't consider asking for help?

- Is getting support easy or difficult?

- Are you standing your ground?

- Why are your defenses up or down?

- Is a strong constitution and self-confidence helping you through difficult times?

- What are you battling with?

- What fight are you stepping away from or into?

- What's fortifying you in the face of adversity?

- Might you be overwhelmed?

- Are you prepared to face anything?

- Do you trust your own abilities?

Nine of Cups

Universal archetype: A satiated looking man seems to have had his fill of the cups from the table in the background. Nine cups, symbolizing desires and creative possibilities, are behind him. The image suggests he feels confident that what he wants will be forthcoming. The table is draped, hinting that what will *actually* emerge from beneath the cloth remains a mystery. Although this man has done his best, he would do well to remember that what actually appears will be a reflection of his level of development.

- What are you in control of?
- What thoughts or feelings are you sitting on?
- What are you accumulating?
- Are you recognizing that unless you use what you've got, it may be wasted?
- What dreams are being realized?
- Is the fulfillment of some desire what you imagined it would be?
- What desires or dreams might you put on the shelf?
- What could you be overdoing?
- Are you sharing or tithing your wealth?
- What accounts for your complacency?
- Are you aware that a spiritual foundation supports your material world?
- Are you conscious that material acquisitions are transitory, whereas spiritual acquisitions are eternal?
- Might you profit from counting your blessings?
- Are you enjoying or lacking emotional security?
- Are you feeling contented, or are you in a state of want?
- What love is in the bank?
- Are you enjoying some well-earned pleasure and satisfaction?
- What emotional support and sustenance is available or unavailable?
- Are you contemplating the magic behind your achievements?

Nine of Swords

Universal archetype: A woman is seated in bed with her head in her hands, perhaps in prayer. Nine swords, symbolizing mental formulation and analysis, hang overhead. Psychic surgery, or surgery on one's erroneous thought patterns, is being performed so that healing may occur. The image suggests how painful it can be to let go of what you want and accept what is.

- Are you agonizing over a decision?

- What are you feeling miserable about?

- Are you a habitual worrier?

- What are you mourning, or what do you foresee mourning?

- Is anger beneath your depression?

- How might you safely release your anger?

- Who could shed some light on your situation?

- After doing all in your power, are you surrendering to a higher power?

- Are you frustrated because others misunderstand you?

- What's lowering or raising your self-esteem?

- Are you having difficulty sleeping?

- Are you waking up anxious?

- Might you benefit from a medical checkup?

- What are you coming to terms with?

- What are your tears releasing or cleansing?

- Are you praying for guidance?

- Are you admitting your powerlessness?

- What pain are you enduring alone?

- Who is your harshest critic?

- Are you thinking too much and acting too little?

- Are you feeling self-destructive?

- Does mental illness run in your family?

- Might being proactive relieve your oppressive situation?

Nine of Pentacles

Universal archetype: An elegantly dressed woman with a hooded bird on her gloved hand stands in the middle of a flourishing garden in prospering and protected surroundings. Material security has been established. Time and energy spent amassing material possessions could be coming to a close for now. The bird symbolizes that an opportunity to fly off and explore other ways of living and seeing the world — perhaps the beginning of a spiritual journey — is at hand.

- Are you enjoying or wanting to enjoy a sense of physical well-being?

- What recognition are you receiving?

- Are you experiencing material fulfillment but lacking spiritual fulfillment?

- Is a physical situation suffocating you?

- Being comfortable alone, is a relationship next?

- Would you like to fly away from worldly concerns?

- Do you have too much leisure time?

- What are you doing regarding your concerns about the ecology?

- What ease is turning into dis-ease?

- Do you like being on a pedestal?

- Is prosperity burdensome?

- What are you flaunting?

- Are you recuperating from illness?

- What might you inherit?

- Are you financially independent or financially dependent?

- What are you achieving through right livelihood, hard work, and clarity of purpose?

- What project are you procrastinating about completing?

- What are you sacrificing for success?

- Do you need help managing your finances?

- Are you wanting to play more and work less?

- Is it time to refresh and reward yourself by traveling?

Ten of Wands

Universal archetype: A man weighed down by ten wands, symbols of will, intention, and attention, edges towards his destination. It's taken an act of supreme will and clarity of purpose to keep his intention and attention on the goal, now in sight. The time to conclude his mission is imminent. Because all his energy is directed into the moment, what may follow is not suggested in the picture.

- What's weighing you down? Are you overextended?

- What inspiration and energy are you gathering together?

- What have you set your mind on doing, no matter what?

- How did you get where you are?

- Who dropped their responsibilities and left you to pick them up

- Do you want to unburden yourself?

- Is your goal in sight?

- Are you at your destination?

- What burden is lifting?

- How can you best fulfill what you've taken on?

- How can you shift your load?

- Are you hesitating to go on?

- What are you dedicating yourself to?

- When are you taking a break?

- Why don't you ask for help?

- What are you trying to prove by overworking yourself?

- Are you performing a spiritual exercise?

- Are you thinking about dropping everything and letting others figure out what to do?

- Is what you're doing training you for something important?

- Is your burden becoming lighter or heavier?

Ten of Cups

Universal archetype: Ten cups form a rainbow. Its wonder is being celebrated by a family below. A rainbow symbolizes promise, and this scene suggests that the people's hopes and dreams, symbolized by the cups, show the promise of coming true. Children and adults celebrate together, suggesting peaceful coexistence and the possible healing of long-term familial relationships.

- Are you sharing love and intimacy with others?

- Do you dream of having a home and family?

- Are you and others working diligently to maintain your contentment?

- Are you living your sweetest dream?

- Why do you think you don't deserve happiness?

- Is dysfunction lurking beneath the idyllic picture your family presents?

- Do you desire a family but feel uncertain that you can handle the emotional issues it raises?

- Are you healing your childhood traumas through marriage and children?

- Are you brimming with gratitude?

- Might you be unable to appreciate your happiness?

- Are you too unstable for a committed relationship?

- Do you think marriage and family will solve your craving for emotional security?

- Might illness, loss, or discontentment be disrupting your home life?

- What are you sacrificing for the good of your family or group?

- Do you have an easy or stressful relationship with your parents or children?

- Are you blessed with a good support system?

Ten of Swords

Universal archetype: A prostrated man is pierced by ten swords. The sun rises in the background. The scene implies that when thing get so difficult that they can't seem to get any worse, they will start easing up. The man is in the process of facing the fact that no matter how hard he struggles to hold on to worn-out mental constructs, things are constantly changing — being cut away and eliminated. Surrender to this universal principle brings release, relief, and renewal of his body, mind, and spirit. Acceptance brings fresh energy and the dawn of a new day.

- What has unexpectedly struck you down?

- What are you being forced to realize?

- What might uplift you?

- What reality are you in the process of accepting?

- How and why are you being pinned down?

- How might relinquishing control liberate you?

- What is overwhelming you?

- What situation are you being forced to accept?

- Are pain and defeat functioning to transform you spiritually?

- What's crushing your pride or ego?

- Could you be contemplating a radical change of attitude?

- What cycle is ending for another to begin?

- Are you requiring surgery?

- What are you learning from your downfall or suffering?

- What might be causing your mental anguish and depression?

- Are you experiencing impotency?

- What thoughts are undermining your health and sanity?

- What humiliation are you planning to avenge? Is stagnant energy being released?

- Are you recuperating from an accident or life-threatening illness or surgery?

- You've lost the battle, but how might you win the war?

Ten of Pentacles

Universal archetype: A man and woman stand beneath an archway leading to a family compound. They are accompanied by a child, looking curiously at two dogs attending to an old man who is seated in the foreground. Ten pentacles forming the Qabalistic Tree of Life are overlaid onto the scene, suggesting fruition and completion — another turn of the spiraling wheel of life. A multi-generational family is experiencing the security of home and one another. The old one seated in the foreground, who resembles the emperor, suggests that things are being overseen by a power greater than what can be depicted — the changeless reality, which expresses itself through continuous change.

- What traditions or values are you upholding, questioning, or breaking?

- What new tradition are you introducing?

- Are you materially blessed?

- Is the balance of power within your family or group shifting?

- Are you acknowledging the divine spirit hidden within daily life?

- What family matter are you dealing with?

- What event is motivating you to be civil towards an untrustworthy family member?

- Why are you being disinherited?

- Are you declaring bankruptcy?

- What order is being established or disrupted?

- Are you using money to control another's behavior?

- Who is helping you get your start in the world?

- Are you accepting or rejecting an arranged marriage?

- Do you break free of others' expectations?

- Are you in a nontraditional living situation?

- Are you courting danger by not paying your taxes?

- Is maturity prompting you to accept and value your family?

- Are you caring for an aging parent or sick family member?

- Might you prune your finances so that they can flourish?

Chapter 9

A Magic Kingdom: The 16 Court or Royalty Cards

Welcome to the Magic Kingdom! It's time to meet the royal family. Unlike meeting other royalty, you don't have to bow or curtsy — you don't even have to take a bath or change your clothes. All you need to do is remember that just like you and me, each member of the royal family has a distinct personality.

In this chapter, you complete your journey through the tarot's 56 minor arcana cards by getting to know the 16 court or royalty cards. Before I show you the cards themselves, I list some of the interesting card names that some tarot decks use instead of the traditional *page, knight, queen,* and *king.* I also detail several ways of relating to the court cards.

Finally, I provide sketches of each of the 16 court cards. So get into a royal frame of mind and let's get going!

Naming the Court Cards

Similar to the houses of Windsor, Savoy, and Burgundy, the tarot has different royal households: the houses of wands, cups, swords, and pentacles. Every house has its page, knight, queen, and king. Each house presides over its particular suit or domain, as I explain in Chapter 7. These suits are as follows:

▶ **wands** = spiritual inspiration
▶ **cups** = imagination and feelings

✔ **swords** = thinking and mental formulation

✔ **pentacles** = physical actions and manifestation

Each page, knight, queen, and king does a particular type of work within that suit, which I explain later in the chapter.

Traditionalists stick with calling these cards page, knight, queen, and king. But like the cards in the major arcana, and like the four minor arcana suits, the court cards are given different names in different tarot decks. Following is a listing of just some of the names used:

✔ **page:** maiden, princess, daughter, child, youth

✔ **knight:** warrior, prince, son, man, seeker, horseman

✔ **queen:** matriarch, priestess, woman, guide

✔ **king:** chief, knight, shaman, sage, guardian

Bringing the Court Cards to Life

Historically, a page was a knight's squire or assistant. Until recently, both the page and knight were thought of and depicted in tarot decks as males. With the changes in contemporary culture, some newer tarot decks personify the pages and knights as females. Because these cards are linked with the middle pillar, or neutral pillar, of the Qabalistic Tree of Life (see Chapter 15), I believe that the sexes of these cards are interchangeable.

The court cards represent you, your occupation, someone you know, or someone who will be coming into your personal or professional life. As you read through the interpretations of the court cards later in this chapter, consider matching them to your various roles or to people in your life. Here's how I try to match the court cards to my life:

✔ When working with clients, I'm like the Queen of Wands, ferreting out the spiritual issues that underlie what a client is presenting. When teaching, I tend to be more like the Knight of Cups, passionate about teaching, yet always a student at heart. Going about my day-to-day life, I think of myself as the Knight of Pentacles, becoming better and better at experiencing my daily chores and responsibilities as part of my spiritual practice.

- The Knight of Wands reminds me of my older son, Kurt, the personification of a spiritual warrior.

- The Knight of Cups reminds me of my younger son, Jonah, a highly imaginative and especially warm and loving person.

- The Queen of Pentacles reminds me of my friend Penny, an excellent doctor and patroness of the arts.

- The King of Cups signifies my sweetie Bernard, who's a master of expressing his feelings and listening to the feelings of others.

Royal occupations

To help you identify which cards resonate with you and your loved ones, here's a list of some occupations and interests the court cards can personify:

- **wands:** inventors, administrators, teachers, mentors, innovators, diplomats, politicians, competitors, salespeople, leaders, wheelers and dealers, seekers of spiritual knowledge, business consultants, managers.

- **cups:** mental health professionals, social workers, hypnotherapists, artists, musicians, spiritual healers, psychics, astrologers, drug and alcohol counselors, lovers of the arts and music.

- **swords:** scientists, researchers, engineers, writers, mediators, lawyers, military personnel, computer consultants, methods analysts, travel agents, pilots, Secret Service, detectives, surgeons, problem solvers, thinkers.

- **pentacles:** doctors, dentists, craftspeople, bakers, students, builders, construction workers, herbalists, farmers, gardeners, money and property managers, hair and beauty operators, gamblers, athletes, dancers, massage practitioners.

Stages of life

In addition to occupations and interests, I believe that the court cards relate to our stages of life — childhood, adolescence, and elderhood/sagehood. These stages refer to both chronological age and levels of maturity.

Childhood

Pages are prepubescent persons of either sex. They are novices or apprentices learning about the tools of each suit: wands (spiritual inspiration), cups (imagination and feelings), swords (thinking and mental formulation), and pentacles (physical actions and manifestation). Pages learn with the help of others. A page card can signify someone who is young in years or someone who behaves immaturely. The card can also represent someone who's involved in the process of healing his or her inner child.

Adolescence

Knights are adolescents or young adults of either sex who are getting out into the world and using the tools of the suit. Knights represent apprentices or interns transforming into skilled practitioners by trial and error. The knight cards represent people of any age who are learning through doing.

Elderhood/Sagehood

Queens and kings are people of any age or sex. (I explain the issue of males with female cards and females with male cards in the next section.) Usually thought of as mature adults or elders, queens and kings can also signify younger people who behave with wisdom and maturity (sagehood) or a level of responsibility beyond their years. Queens and kings are mistresses/masters of their tools and domains. They can represent leaders in any field — administrators, teachers, mentors, and/or guides.

A balancing act

If a woman gets male cards, it suggests that she is developing, needs to develop, or already has developed male character traits. This occurrence is what Jungian psychologists call the *animus,* or inner male. The predominance of male cards can also indicate a man living inside a female body.

If a man gets female cards, it suggests that he is developing, needs to develop, or already has developed female character traits. This occurrence is what Jungian psychologists term the *anima,* or inner female. Such cards may also indicate a man's inner or spiritual guides. Finally, the predominance of female cards can also indicate a woman living inside a male body.

The development of qualities of the opposite sex helps you and I become more complete people. These qualities also help you form healthy interdependent relationships, so you don't become overly independent or dependent.

Filling in the Gaps

The court cards can show you the roles in life that you want others to perform due to rightful need. For example, for Taylor, a 13-year-old I know, the King of Swords symbolizes his need for his father, who was killed in Operation Desert Storm when Taylor was a toddler.

The court cards also signify you "living through" others. The cards represent people doing what you'd like to do or need to do, what you fear, what you are unable to do, and so on. For instance, say that you tend to hold onto your feelings. As a result, you choose relationships with people who are unafraid of expressing what they feel. This behavior might appear as the Knight of Swords. Here are a few other examples:

- Brian, a dental school dropout, marries a dentist. This behavior could show up as the Page of Pentacles.

- Sally loved ballet and desired to be a ballerina. Although athletic and musically inclined, her parents discouraged her from pursuing her dream. Lacking the self-confidence and motivation to proceed, Sally's interest waned. Sally was further distracted by her conflicting desire to spend time with friends (rather than practice her dance). Now the mother of a 7-year-old, Sally pushes her daughter to pursue a career in dance. This behavior might present itself as the Queen of Pentacles.

- Larry had just run his first professional race when he was hit by a car. Unfortunately, the accident left him permanently crippled. Larry now coaches young runners at the local Boys and Girls Club. This behavior could be indicated by the King of Wands.

Introducing the Court

Before you explore each of the court cards, I encourage you to visit Chapter 6 if you haven't yet done so. If you have read Chapter 6 already, please keep in mind the information I share in the section called "Amber's approach to interpreting." It goes a long way toward explaining what you find in the following interpretations of each minor arcana card.

Also, for a reminder of what each suit represents in the minor arcana (which includes the court cards), take a quick tour through Chapter 8.

As you read the following interpretations, keep in mind that certain arche-types apply to the royal or court cards:

✔ From the archetypical perspective, all the **pages** signify curiosity, new energy, interest, enthusiasm, innocence, and optimism in regard to dis-covering the powers of their particular tool.

✔ From the archetypical perspective, all the **knights** signify enthusiasm and action aimed at perfecting the use of their particular tool and the power that accompanies it. The knights are service-oriented — dedi-cated to integrating universal and natural laws and principles linked with their tool into what they think, say, and do.

✔ From the archetypical perspective, **queens** and **kings** represent mastery. Having mastered the powers that the tool of their suit represents, they are dedicated to selfless service, and they rule by divine right. The queens and kings are vehicles through which divinity consciously expresses itself.

Interpreting or reading the cards is a matter of your response to the image presented. As I explain in previous chapters, how you and I respond to or "read" the situations, picture symbols, or archetypes of daily life is based on factors such as your own experiences in similar situations and your present state of mind and health.

PAGE of WANDS.

Page of Wands

Universal archetype: The page stands near pyramids, symbol of spiritual aspiration. He contemplates his wand, suggesting his willingness to bring ideas and inspirations from on high into the world. As a new student of the wand, he represents the will to pay attention and become aware of his intentions or motivations. The Page of Wands is receptive to the lessons his tool brings. He is learning about aligning what he believes is his will with the one divine will.

- What's inspiring you?
- What are you intending to do?
- Are you curious, or resistant to learning?
- How are you preparing to deal with the future?
- Is it possible that you're biting off more than you can chew?
- Is your sexual energy awakening or reawakening?
- How are you being naive or staying pure?
- Is your behavior childlike or childish?
- What journey are you beginning?
- Is your mind opening to new possibilities?
- Where are you a novice or a student?
- Might your high energy and spontaneity make others nervous?
- Is your lack of experience showing?
- Are you seeking or receiving potent insights?
- Are you taking a spiritual teacher or expanding your spiritual horizons?
- What's inciting your enthusiasm?
- Who's saying that you show great promise?
- Is some message difficult to decipher?
- Are you making contact with your spirit guide?
- What are you being honest about despite the consequences?
- What are you paying special attention to?
- What are you realizing about your Self?

PAGE of CUPS.

Page of Cups

Universal archetype: The page contemplates a fish, symbol of fertility, rising from a cup to look at him. This interaction represents how feelings lead to the proliferation of creative imagery. As a new student of the cup, he signifies discovering and exploring his feelings, psychic sensitivity, spiritual and mystical experiences, and the power of his imagination. The Page of Cups is receptive to the lessons his tool brings. He is learning about aligning his wants, desires, and fantasies with the reality of what he's given, as well as offering selfless service to others.

- What's activating your imagination?
- Who is offering you help, or who are you offering help?
- Is someone dependent upon you? Are you emotionally dependent?
- Do you feel like a kid?
- Are you facing your painful childhood?
- Is a child entering your life?
- What's drawing you out of your fantasy world?
- Are you seeking emotional growth?
- How might you train your psychic abilities?
- Do you want to be a monk or a nun?
- Is desire seducing you?
- Are your emotions running wild?
- Are your feelings grounded in reality?
- Do you crave love and/or sex, but not the responsibilities that go with it?
- Are you celibate?
- Are you escaping emotional pain, sensitivity, or anxiety via drugs?
- Do you follow the psychic advice you give others?
- Do you work with children?
- What emotional tie is being revived?
- Would you like to be carefree?
- Are you discovering your artistic side?
- Are you behaving like a spoiled child?
- Are you toying with others' feelings?

PAGE of SWORDS.

Page of Swords

Universal archetype: The page walks briskly while holding a sword, symbol of mental planning, analysis, and discernment, upright in both hands. The terrain is rugged and clouds gather quickly overhead. As a new student of the sword, he indicates receptivity to mental stimulation — formulating plans, using discretion, discovering the importance of setting limits and boundaries — and the logic of eliminating what is extraneous in order to bring his ideas into being. The Page of Swords is receptive to the lessons his tool brings. He is learning about mental clarity, making the best choices he can, and being willing to take responsibility for and learn from what results.

- Are you mentally adaptable, or are you too adaptable?

- Are you being pulled in two directions?

- What needs eliminating?

- Are you experiencing mental confusion or paranoia?

- What communication are you cutting off?

- Where might you be more decisive?

- Do you think someone's out to get you?

- Are you learning about protecting yourself?

- Do you follow through on your ideas?

- What might you examine more closely before acting?

- Are you acting rashly?

- Could you be making an irrational decision?

- What might you need assistance cutting through?

- Are you becoming more detail-oriented?

- Are you being spiteful?

- Who are you detaching yourself from?

- What are you looking out for?

- Are you hesitant to get help?

- Are you starting something you can't stop?

- What conflict are you on the fringes of?

- What are you preparing to fight for?

- How might you train your sharp mind or quick wit?

- What immature person or decision are you learning from?

Page of Pentacles

Universal archetype: The page stands in nature, staring intently at a pentacle — symbol of the material world and everything in it — which seems to float over his upraised hands. As a new student of the pentacle, he indicates becoming aware of his environment, body, and physical health, and what he needs to do to maintain himself and survive on a daily basis. The Page of Pentacles is receptive to the lessons his tool brings. He is learning that the physical world is spirit thought into form, his body is a living temple, and all physical bodies are divine in essence and origin.

- Are you burdened by others' debts?

- Are you burdened by survival issues?

- Might you place the physical needs and safety of your child first?

- Are you receiving a scholarship or financial assistance for schooling?

- Might you be smart but lack common sense?

- Are you an athlete or dancer who'd benefit from coaching or taking classes?

- Are you entranced by life's magic?

- Are you studying ecology?

- Are you aware that your body is a living temple?

- Are you accepting an entry-level position?

- Are you in or out of synch with the world?

- Are you blessed with manual dexterity and technological skills?

- Are you pulling yourself up in the world?

- Are you grateful, or do you take for granted the help you're receiving?

- Do you possess or lack financial ingenuity?

- Is your child ill?

- Are you immersed in survival issues?

- Are you learning to listen to your body?

- Do you want to travel the world?

- How could you be more in touch with your body?

- Would you like job training or mentoring?

Knight of Wands

Universal archetype: The knight carries a wand and gallops past pyramids, symbol of spiritual aspiration, on a high-spirited horse. The Knight of Wands enthusiastically takes the power to pay attention, learned as a page or apprentice, and integrates it into his life. This knight is intent and focused on actively applying the principle of aligning his will with the one divine will to as many situations as he can remain mindful of.

- Are you beginning or completing an important transition?

- Is a lack of ties making a change of job, career, or residence easy for you?

- Are you taking necessary or unnecessary risks?

- What oppressive person or situation are you fleeing from?

- What ideas or insights are you needing to pursue?

- What teachings or philosophy are you enthusiastic about?

- Are you heading out on an adventure?

- What's getting you fired up?

- What spiritual inspiration is guiding you forward?

- Are you fighting your battle?

- Are you undergoing a spiritual initiation?

- Why do you have difficulty making commitments?

- Do you want to focus your energies?

- How are you dealing with opposition?

- What are you suddenly inspired to try?

- What are you seeking to prove or overcome?

- Might following intuitional guidance help when you get immobilized by too much information or input?

- Are you feeling sexually adventurous?

- Why can't you calm down or get energized?

- Are you filled with energy, or lacking it?

- Why are you feeling impatient?

KNIGHT of CUPS.

Knight of Cups

Universal archetype: This graceful (not warlike) knight rides quietly along, extending a cup, symbol of creative imaging and desire, in his right hand. His winged helmet suggests his imagination taking flight. The Knight of Cups is taking what he's learned from being a page — the power of his feelings and imagination — and is integrating it into his daily life. This knight actively envisions himself aligning his wants, desires, and fantasies with the reality of what he is given as a means of further developing himself and providing selfless service to others.

- Are you following your dreams?
- What opportunity are you offering or being offered?
- Is a relationship changing direction?
- Are you open to giving or receiving love?
- What services are you volunteering?
- Are your dreams bearing messages?
- How are you dealing with your super-sensitivity?
- What feelings or dreams are you sharing?
- Are you discovering the power of creative imagery?
- Do your fantasies keep changing?
- Might you have a passive-aggressive personality?
- Are you experiencing a period of emotional tests and trials?
- Are you exploring your feelings?
- Are you waiting for someone to come to your rescue?
- Are you losing or keeping your innocence?
- Are you taking your dream trip?
- Are you exploring other worlds via mind-expanding substances?
- Are your actions often motivated by compassion?
- Might you be caring too much for others and not enough for yourself?
- What illusion are you attempting to pull off?
- Are you seeking a period of Self-reflection?

KNIGHT of SWORDS .

Knight of Swords

Universal archetype: With his sword drawn, this knight races at full speed as if charging into battle. The Knight of Swords takes the skill he learned as a page — the power of mental formulation, analysis, and discernment — and is actively integrating it into his everyday life. This exceptionally alert knight uses his mental clarity to cut through issues — separating the wheat from the chaff — thereby making the best and most healing decisions he's capable of. He then willingly accepts responsibility for, and learns from, what results.

- Are you being courageous in the face of adversity?

- What violence is occurring?

- What conflict is your Self compelling you to enter?

- What point are you bent on making?

- Who are you speaking out for or against?

- Are you waging a righteous battle?

- Are you fighting for a lost cause?

- Where is your headstrong attitude getting you?

- What truth or facts are you armed with?

- Who might be approached more cautiously?

- Could tact be useful?

- Are you taking a new course of action?

- Are you mindful of the consequences of your thoughtless or thoughtful words?

- Where are you hurrying off to?

- Is a learning opportunity stimulating you?

- Is a period of mental stagnation behind you?

- Who's threatening your rights?

- What are you resisting or surrendering to?

- What could you be too eager to get involved in?

- What are you attached to acting on?

- Are you feeling very virile?

- Are you mentally energized, or are you experiencing burnout?

KNIGHT of PENTACLES.

Knight of Pentacles

Universal archetype: Riding a heavy-boned working horse, the knight holds a pentacle in his outstretched hands. He is integrating what he learned from pagehood — the power of physical things to serve as spiritual tools. The Knight of Pentacles is dedicated to handling day-to-day situations in spiritual ways — work, finances, environment, and his physical health are all tools for his spiritual development. He's committed to living a spiritual life in the physical world.

- What are you committed to completing?

- Are you becoming increasingly reliable or detail-oriented?

- What new responsibilities are you welcoming?

- Do you enjoy being productive?

- What matter is requiring your immediate attention?

- Do you feel like a workhorse — overworked and underappreciated?

- Are you enjoying your sexuality?

- Do you regard everything you do as spiritual practice, dedicating yourself fully to whatever is at hand?

- Are you seeking or avoiding worldly recognition?

- How are you developing your work?

- Do you take pride in being well-organized and prepared, or do you prefer flying by the seat of your pants?

- Are you persistent, and do you take the initiative?

- Do you work hard, or are you a slacker?

- Are you trying different types of work to find one that you like?

- Do you love the outdoors?

- Are you resourceful — can you make something out of nothing?

- Are you physically active or are you letting your body go?

- Are you looking for work?

- What routine do you want to break out of?

Queen of Wands

Universal archetype: The queen of wands sits holding symbols of her dominion, a wand in her right hand and a sunflower in her left, signifying her connection with divinity. Her throne is decorated with lions, indicating willfulness, self-pride, dignity, and dominance. A black cat, a domesticated animal, sits at her feet, suggesting that she has cultivated supernatural powers. The assertive, extroverted, and self-confident Queen of Wands intends to rule with love and understanding, and attends to her duties with this thought at the forefront of her mind.

- Whom or what are you inspiring or being inspired by?

- Are you brimming with ideas and energy?

- Do you prefer spontaneity to planning?

- Are you feeling vital and powerful?

- What female authority are you encountering?

- Do others consider you someone of insight and intuition?

- Do you use spiritual insights for practical purposes?

- Why are you overextending yourself?

- Who is challenging your authority?

- Why are you being so willful or egotistical?

- Who are you protecting?

- What or who are you feeling passionate or unimpassioned about?

- Are your leadership skills being called upon?

- Are you an independent thinker?

- How might you use the power of positive thinking?

- What ambitions are you realizing, or what ambitions are being thwarted?

- Are you proud of your Self?

- Do you need to be more extroverted?

- What are you gaining or losing by climbing the corporate ladder?

- What understanding are you receiving?

- Are you sharing or imposing your ideals?

Queen of Cups

Universal archetype: The queen of cups sits at the seashore *scrying,* or using her cup to see into the future. Decorated with water nymphs, her throne symbolizes her dominion over the element of water. The intuitive, psychic, imaginative, creative, emotional, and prophetic Queen of Cups is a dreamer and a visionary. She understands that what she conjures up reflects her state of consciousness. Out of respect for her position, the queen interprets what comes to her in terms of spiritual laws and principles.

- What are you dreaming about?

- How are you living your dreams?

- Are you withdrawing inside yourself to handle unresolved feelings?

- Who are you punishing by withdrawing?

- Is this an emotional time for you?

- Are you ruling your feelings, or do feelings rule you?

- What are you receptive to or rejecting?

- Is it easier to sympathize or empathize?

- Who showers or drowns you in love?

- How is your unconscious surfacing?

- What's enchanting you?

- Are you living in another world?

- Are you dealing with an emotional imbalance or depression?

- Could you be self-medicating with drugs or alcohol?

- Might you be too impressionable?

- What are you brooding over?

- What do you keep imagining?

- Who are you unconsciously seducing?

- Is your sensitivity heightened or dulled?

- Are you expressing or censoring your feelings?

- Who are you feeling romantic about?

- What are you understanding through psychic or mystical experiences?

- Who might you be loving too much?

- Are you loving yourself unconditionally?

QUEEN of SWORDS.

Queen of Swords

Universal archetype: The Queen of Swords faces sideways, with her right hand holding her sword upright and her left hand extended in greeting. Her serious expression and upright posture suggest she's familiar with the duties of rulership. She's blessed with the powers of fairness, independence, multidimensional thinking, and self-determination. Her throne is decorated with winged cherubs and butterflies. Her crown is also made of butterflies, which symbolize that she understands the transformative power of analytical thinking that's motivated by love.

- Might you be a woman in a man's world?
- How are you asserting yourself?
- Might you set better boundaries?
- Are you intolerant?
- What truth are you upholding?
- Do you enjoy your own company?
- Where might you add a dash of love, kindness, compassion, or humor?
- Are you relating to a highly motivated and independent woman?
- What do you think you need to separate or detach yourself from?
- Are pain and sorrow making you less emotional and more rational?
- Are you using or hiding your intelligence?
- What are you being called on or asked to analyze?
- Would you rather be alone than be with unintelligent people?
- Are you too cool?
- Could you be an intellectual snob?
- What laws are you enforcing?
- Do you love learning and critical thinking?
- Are you being too judgmental of your Self or others?
- Why might others interpret your unemotionality as coldness?
- What plans are you carrying out?
- What is your mind set on doing?

QUEEN of PENTACLES

Queen of Pentacles

Universal archetype: The queen sits in a beautiful garden, meditating on a pentacle in her lap — looking into it as one might look into a crystal ball (à la the Queen of Cups and her cup). Goat heads are carved into the arm rests of her throne, symbolizing her willingness to look after her herd and her ability to make her way up and over any obstacle in order to do so. The nurturing, hardworking, common-sensical, steadfast, and sensuous Queen of Pentacles understands the spiritual reality present in the physical reality.

- Are you materially secure?
- Is your common-sense attitude your strength?
- Are you contributing to the planet's well-being?
- Are you nurturing or overnurturing others?
- Are you a responsible mom or a dead-beat mom?
- Is your closeness with nature also closeness with divinity?
- Are you pregnant or mothering?
- Are you impassioned by the healing arts?
- Are you reentering the work force?
- Are you financially independent and philanthropic?
- Do you lack motivation?
- Could you be more interested in what others have rather than in who they are?
- Are you masterful at managing money?
- Are you in a homemaking cycle?
- Are you content with your home life?
- Are you bored or excited with your routine?
- Are you a sensualist?
- Do you think of the physical world as divinity in form?
- Are you a natural athlete, dancer, or yogi?
- Might you be more in touch with your body?
- Are you a woman in a man's body?
- Are you coping with health problems?

King of Wands

Universal archetype: Facing sideways, the king grasps a wand in his right hand. His throne is embroidered with lions denoting his lineage of courage, dignity, self-pride, and dominance. A salamander, once believed to inhabit and withstand fire, stands at the base of his throne. When the heat of life gets turned up, the King of Wands wisely directs attention inward for cooling inspiration.

- What or who is inspiring you?

- What are you focusing on?

- What are you impassioned or angry about?

- What are you getting off the ground?

- Is your intention being misinterpreted?

- Are you required to direct others?

- What motivates you to reach for the stars?

- Do you feel energized or stalled out?

- What male authority are you confronting?

- Do you love challenges?

- What wisdom are you using or sharing?

- Do you think you're always right?

- Are you responsible for others?

- How do you use your executive abilities?

- Are you standing your ground or being egotistical?

- Why are you being domineering or argumentative?

- Are you increasingly Self-directed?

- Do you follow your spiritual insights?

- Are others pulled toward or away from you?

- Might you be more open to input?

- Why are you being rigid or unyielding?

- What are you optimistic about?

- Might you cultivate patience?

- Are you serving as a role model?

- Could assertiveness be received better than aggressiveness?

KING of CUPS.

King of Cups

Universal archetype: Holding a short scepter in his left hand and a cup in his right, the king floats comfortably on the ocean. On one side, a dolphin is leaping; on the other, a ship is at full sail. These symbols suggest the king can ride life's tides. Mastery of the power of self-reflection makes him the captain of his ship, himself, and his kingdom. Whether the seas are rough or calm, the wise and highly imaginative King of Cups is full of creative possibilities.

- What dreams are you listening to?

- Do you love love?

- Are you expressing your feelings or fantasies through creativity?

- Do you work in the helping professions or psychic arts?

- Are you mastering your sensitivity?

- Who are you lovingly caring for?

- Could you use some loving care?

- What feelings or fantasies are you expressing or hiding?

- What's upsetting you?

- What psychic wisdom are you receiving?

- Are you realizing that the most compassionate thing you can do for another is to be a good listener?

- Are you a master dreamer?

- Who are you no longer enabling?

- Who are you alienating by always being the giver?

- How are you nourishing your soul?

- Are you mastering an addictive personality?

- Do you want others to know your feelings without speaking?

- Are you kind and generous to a fault?

- Might you manipulate others through their feelings?

- When are you going to write your poem, paint your picture, or make your sculpture or music?

KING of SWORDS.

King of Swords

Universal archetype: Similar to the Justice card in the major arcana, the king of swords holds an unsheathed sword in his right hand, suggesting that he holds the awesome power of life and death. Butterflies, symbolizing the transformative power of analytical thinking motivated by love, adorn his throne. When ruling the domain, the King of Swords sets aside personal bias and prejudice to base his advice and judgments on sound discernment and universal wisdom.

- Are you always being the peacemaker?
- Why do you need to keep the peace?
- What are you decisively planning out or strategizing?
- What are you analyzing or criticizing?
- Where is discretion being called for?
- Do you enjoy brainstorming with others?
- What are you eliminating from your life?
- Are your intellect and feelings balanced?
- Is your judgment distorted?
- What plans are being implemented?
- What if you stopped trying to keep things harmonious?
- Are your mediation skills being called for?
- Is your integrity being questioned?
- What laws must you carry out and live by?
- What information are you sharing?
- Are you thinking too fast?
- How might emotional detachment help you?
- What are you guarding against?
- What truths are you upholding?
- Are you being headstrong? What legal situation requires your time?
- Are you willing to fight for your or another's interests?
- What have you lied about? Are you being arrogant?
- What are you tolerating, or what won't you tolerate?

KING of PENTACLES.

King of Pentacles

Universal archetype: Sitting peacefully in the midst of a garden in full bloom, the King of Pentacles wears a robe embroidered with grapes, suggesting material well-being. Bulls' heads, symbols of leadership and fertility, adorn his throne. The king holds his scepter in his right hand and a pentacle in his left. His eyes are closed, intimating that he wisely knows that his power comes from the invisible world of spirit, as well as from what he's amassed.

- Do you enjoy life and your senses to the max?

- Are you meeting your agreements?

- Do you honor or deny the spirit within the material world?

- Are you a responsible or a deadbeat dad?

- Might you be too materialistic?

- Might you be more charitable?

- Do you control the physical well-being of others?

- Do you manage the money or properties of others?

- Do you need to be more practical?

- Are you a health professional, massage therapist, or healer?

- Are you satisfied or dissatisfied with your level of worldly success?

- Are you well-respected in your work or community?

- How are you protecting the environment?

- Do you feel materially fulfilled yet spiritually unfulfilled?

- Do you respect your coworkers? Are you detail-oriented?

- Are your sexist attitudes changing?

- Do you love being in nature?

- Are you a master athlete or craftsperson?

- Do you possess or lack stamina, endurance, or a strong constitution?

- Are you a man in a woman's body?

Part III

The Tarot and You: The ABCs of Tarot Reading (And Then Some)

The 5th Wave   By Rich Tennant

THE SOLITAIRE SPREAD

" ...8 of swords on the 9 of cups,
4 of wands on the 5 of pentacles..."

In this part . . .

*P*art III offers you numerous ways of experiencing the tarot. In Chapter 10, you discover how to find your soul and personality cards, as well as cards that correspond to any day, week, month, or year. In Chapter 11, I explain the basics of caring for your cards, selecting and using card rituals, and shuffling. Also in this part, I discuss when to consult the cards, the best questions to ask the cards, predictive tarot, and tarot consultations. I show you how you can use color, musical tones, affirmations, dreams, and writing to deepen your experience of the tarot cards. Plus, I offer you a wide array of tarot spreads to try out for yourself (and others, perhaps). Finally, I explain what it takes to become a tarot professional.

Aleister Crowley Thoth Tarot Deck

The Hierophant

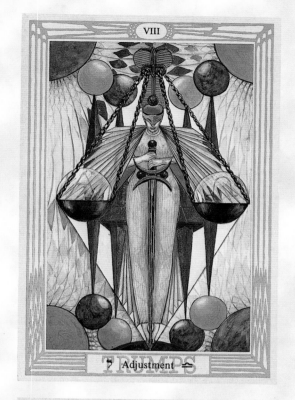

Adjustment

The Hermit

Fortune

Tarot of Marseilles

THE FOOL

VI

THE LOVERS

X

THE WHEEL OF FORTUNE

XII

THE HANGED MAN

XVI

THE TOWER

XIX

THE SUN

The Visconti-Sforza Tarocchi Deck

The Magician

Strength

The Devil

The Moon

Tarot of the Ages

KING OF BATONS

SEVEN OF BATONS

QUEEN OF CUPS

NINE OF CUPS

QUEEN OF SWORDS

KING OF COINS

Native American Tarot

THE FOOL

HOSTEEN COYOTE

STRENGTH

MEDICINE WHEEL

DEATH

THE WORLD

Cosmic Tarot

The Magician

The High Priestess

The Hierophant

The Lovers

Nine of Wands

Ace of Cups

The Witches Tarot

V THE HIGH PRIEST

XVIII THE MOON

IX THE SEEKER

THE ACE OF SWORDS

The Halloween Tarot

IV   The **Emperor**

IX   The **Hermit**

XI   **Justice**

XIV   **Temperance**

XVI   The **Tower**

XIX   The **Sun**

Chapter 10

Experiencing the Tarot

T his chapter provides you with the opportunity to see how the tarot cards can work for you.

In this chapter, I explain how you can find the cards that symbolize your soul, or essence, as well as the cards that symbolize the way you express this essence via your personality.

I show you how to figure out your card for this year and *every* year, past and future, as well as your card for today. Do I hear you asking, "Are these things I can also do for other people?" Yes, you can *definitely* use these methods to find cards for your friends, boss, co-workers, that person you'd like to date — even the President of the United States!

I demonstrate the how-tos of finding cards for any day, week, or month. Along with this, I outline cards for special occasions such as weddings and historical events. Finally, you get to discover and explore your personal court card.

In the spirit of keeping things simple, all the exercises in this chapter, with the exception of finding your personal court card, work only with the 22 major arcana cards. All the information in this chapter is yours for the taking, *without* needing to know how to do an actual tarot reading! (I cover tarot spreads in Chapter 13.)

You need absolutely no experience to get started — only this book, a sheet of paper, and something to write with.

Finding Your Soul and Personality Cards

About six or seven years into my tarot training, I was shown how to find my soul and personality cards. At the time, teachers believed that students needed extensive preliminary training before being shown how to find these cards. But that was long ago. I believe that if you're reading these words, you're ready to give this fun and insightful exercise a try.

Your *soul card* shows who you essentially are: your higher soul, spirit, Self — the part of you that's immortal and is believed to separate from your physical body at death. According to many belief systems, the soul assumes the particular personality it needs for expressing and developing itself in each physical incarnation or lifetime.

Your *personality card* shows your ego, or external individuality: your personal "I" or "Me." It shows the group of character traits that make up you — your distinctive behavior, temperament, and mental and emotional traits, in contrast to mine and others'. These traits create your personality, with its strengths and weaknesses.

Your personality card suggests how your soul is being expressed and perfected. Although there's usually some conflict (or a lack of understanding) between what your personality or ego desires and what your soul needs, your personality is *ultimately* the way you express more and more of your higher soul, spirit, Self, or essence.

Because your personality is an extension of your soul, your soul card comes before your personality card. You can find your cards by using Table 10-1 and the easy step-by-step directions in the following sections.

Numbering The Fool

Because the tarot's creators regarded The Fool to be the beginning and end of all things, it was given the circuitous number 0 and put at the beginning of the tarot deck. If you lay out the major arcana in a circle, The Fool is also the end of the major arcana.

Problem: Numerologists wanted to include The Fool in their tarot-oriented exercises, but 0 has no value, and The Magician was already numbered 1. Solution: There are 22 cards in the major arcana, so numerologists cleverly gave The Fool the value of 22. (If you think this is confusing, consider that every Hebrew letter has a different numerical value than the number on the card! In this system, The Fool has the values of 1 and 1,000.)

Table 10-1		Numbering the Major Arcana Cards	
Card Number	**Card Name**	**Card Number**	**Card Name**
1	The Magician	12	The Hanged Man
2	The High Priestess	13	Death
3	The Empress	14	Temperance
4	The Emperor	15	The Devil
5	The Hierophant	16	The Tower
6	The Lovers	17	The Star
7	The Chariot	18	The Moon
⑧	Strength	19	The Sun
9	The Hermit	20	Judgement
10	Wheel of Fortune	21	The World
11	Justice	22	The Fool

The Fool is actually card number 0, because it is the first card in many tarot decks. However, The Fool is often assigned the number 22, for reasons explained in the sidebar "Numbering The Fool."

Determining your soul card = 8

Follow three easy steps to find your soul card:

1. **Add up the month, day, and year of your birth.**

   For example, Cate was born August 2, 1946. August is the 8th month of the year. Cate would add as follows:

8 (month)	10
2 (day)	30
1946 (year)	1966
1956	2006 2+0+0+6 = 8

2. **If your total is greater than 22 (the total number of major arcana cards), reduce it by adding the numbers together. If the reduced number is still larger than 22, add its numbers together.**

   For example, Cate would add together 1 + 9 + 5 + 6, for a total of 21. Because her number is less than 22, she can move on to Step 3.

However, say that Brandon was born on July 2, 1970. Following Step 1, he adds together 7 + 2 + 1970, for a total of 1979. If he adds together 1 + 9 + 7 + 9, his total is 26. He must go the extra step by adding together 2 + 6, for a total of 8.

3. **Using Table 10-1, find the major arcana card that corresponds with the number you arrive at in Step 2.**

   Cate's soul card is The World, because it is card number 21 in the major arcana. Cate finds the following question from the list in Chapter 7 to be the most meaningful: "How is the fulfillment of your day-to-day responsibilities honoring your spiritual obligations?" This card suggests that Cate experiences joy, inner peace, and freedom through self-discipline. (This intuition is derived from the card's link with the planet Saturn; see Chapter 16 on astrology and the tarot.) It looks like Cate is adept at running her life, and perhaps the lives of others, very efficiently. (This intuition is derived from The World card's being the Administrative Intelligence; see Chapter 15 on the Qabalistic Tree of Life.) Because she innately enjoys regimentation, she might lack sensuality and spontaneity — traits that, as we see in the next section, she could be developing through her personality card.

   Brandon's Soul Card is card number eight in the major arcana, Strength.

To determine what your soul card represents, turn back to Chapter 7 and consider its interpretation.

Identifying your personality card = 8

Follow two easy steps to find your personality card:

1. **If the number of your soul card is a double-digit number, add the digits together.** Cate would add together 2 + 1 for a total of 3.

2. **Use the number you arrive at in Step 1 to find your personality card.**
- **If the number of your soul card was a single-digit number, your soul card and personality card are the same.**

   Cate's personality card is The Empress, the number three card in the major arcana. Cate responds to the question, "Are you feeling sensual?" Aha, just as I suspected. The Empress suggests that Cate is learning about her sensuality and sense of aesthetics as part of her soul's development. (This intuition is derived from the card's link with the sense of touch and the planet Venus's link with aesthetics.)

   Brandon's soul and personality cards are both Strength.

Intellect and intuition: Interpreting the tarot

Interpreting the tarot is a whole brain activity, meaning it involves a combination of intellect and intuition. After receiving an intellectual understanding of what each card means (through books, study, and/or a teacher and classes), you use your intuition to select the meaning appropriate for that card.

For me, looking at a card is like clicking on a file in my computer — dozens of thoughts come to the screen of my mind. While scanning information, such as the card's astrological, numerological, and alchemical correspondences, and its intelligence, symbols, and colors, my intuition cues into what questions to ask and information to share.

If some of the interpretations in this chapter seem different from those appearing in Chapters 7, 8, and 9, it's because they are examples of my intuitive comments on people's cards. I do my best to let you know how I arrive at these comments whenever they appear.

✫ Having the same soul and personality card

If your soul and personality cards are the same, you tend to experience an innate agreement between your soul purpose and your personality — what your ego and personal desires are pulling you toward. Simply put, you may not feel conflicted about what you do in the world and who you are in your heart of hearts. This configuration also symbolizes a state that you are growing into.

Consider two examples of how this works. First, Brandon's soul and personality cards are the same: Strength. Strength suggests that Brandon is an innately creative and nurturing man. He expresses this creativity and tendency to nurture through his daily work of teaching art to handicapped children.

Mia's soul and personality cards are also the same: The Hierophant. Mia is naturally a spiritually oriented person. Because she had years of dogmatic religious training, Mia won't presently participate in anything that has to do with religion. In time, Mia's innate connection with divinity is likely to draw her into practicing, or even teaching, some type of nondogmatic spirituality.

A special case: Totaling 19

If your birthday numbers total up to the number 19, you get one more card than everyone else. I call this the *mediating card* because it helps mediate conflicts, power struggles, or tension between your soul and personality.

For example, Andy's birthday numbers total 19, which means that Andy's soul card is The Sun. Adding 1 + 9 shows that Andy's personality card (number 10) is the Wheel of Fortune.

In this unique case, the digits of Andy's personality card can also be added: 1 + 0 = 1, so Andy's mediating card is number 1, The Magician.

With The Sun as his soul card, Andy is essentially a warm, charismatic, and radiant person. His personality card, the Wheel of Fortune, makes his warmth and radiance dependent on life's ups and downs: When life goes according to Andy's plans, he shines; when it doesn't, his light is eclipsed.

The Magician is his mediator card. Among other things, the card reminds him of the principle of Ageless Wisdom that says, "The only constant is change." As Andy gets better at accepting this truth, he's able to let his light shine no matter what's going on in the outside world. The mediator card helps reduce the tension between Andy's soul purpose and personal expression of this purpose.

Finding Your Card for the Year

If you have found your soul and personality cards, then you already know the basics for finding your card for this year and for all years.

Your card for the year shows you the key issues or lessons that you face. At the same time, the card shows you ways to handle these issues. One of my students wisely said of this, "Within your problems, lie your solutions."

Before proceeding, it's important to realize that you're figuring out *your* card for the year. Because it's *your* card, it must go along with *your* birthday. This means that if the calendar shows that it's April, 2002, but your birthday isn't until June, you're still in a 2001 cycle.

For example, Yuri was born on December 30th. It's now March 25th, 2002. True, the year changed on January 1, but Yuri's birthday is still more than nine months away. What year will Yuri add to the day and month of his birth to find out the card for his present year? You're correct, it's 2001!

1. **Add together the day and month of your birth, as well as the year for which you'd like to find your card.**

   For example, September 30th is Ruth's birthday, and on her birthday in 2001, she wants to know her card for the year ahead. She adds 9 + 30 + 2001 for a total of 2040.

2. **Next, add together the digits of the number you calculated in Step 1. If the number you arrive at is larger than 22, add the digits of that number together.**

For example, Ruth adds 2 + 0 + 4 + 0 for a total of 6. Ruth's card for the year is card six in the major arcana, The Lovers. It looks like she could be entering/reentering the area of relationships. Maybe she's been less than discerning in past relationships, dating married men and/or getting involved with her friend's boyfriends? Perhaps she's been out of a relationship for awhile and has gotten to know herself and her needs better? Perhaps Ruth is realizing that she really wants to be in relationship with a woman, not a man? Ruth's life could be getting revitalized by a new love. In any event, she has the chance to have a more fulfilling love life. There are hundreds of possibilities. (Turn back to the major arcana descriptions in Chapter 7 for further interpretations.)

Bert wanted to see his card for 1995, the year he and his wife divorced. He took the year of his divorce and added it to the day and month of his birth and here's what he got:

6 (month)

28 (day)

1995 (year)

2029

Adding 2 + 0 + 2 + 9 gives 13. Card number 13 in the major arcana is the Death card. Pretty interesting!

The Card for Today

There are two ways to figure out which card corresponds to today. One way is to figure it out *generally;* the other way is to figure it out for you *personally.* The card for the day can act as a point of reference or *touchstone* for the day ahead. (I discuss touchstones in Chapter 13.)

Finding today's general card

If you want to know the card for today, or any day, here are the steps to follow:

1. **Add the day, month, and year together.** Take November 16, 2001, for example.

11 (month)

16 (day)

2001 (year)

2028

2. **Add together the digits of the number you calculated in Step 1.** 2 + 0 + 2 + 8 = 12. The *general* card for November 16, 2001 is card number 12 in the major arcana, The Hanged Man.

Much like the movement of the moon in the practice of astrology suggests the general mood of the day, the general card for a day does likewise. For example, the general mood of The Hanged Man suggests reversals — the day, or your view of the day, turning 180 degrees opposite of how it's been planned. The hanged man hangs freely, yet is tied, suggesting that an expansive attitude toward obligations, responsibilities, and restrictions (such as seeing these as divine service) has the potential to free you. (This intuition is derived from "reading" the card's symbols.) The card is also associated with people who listen to their inner promptings or intuition, rather than the mood of the crowd. Finally, the hanged man has an introspective quality, suggesting that the day may be quieter and more reflective than an ordinary day. (This intuition is derived from the card's Hebrew letter *mem,* meaning "water," intimating Self-reflection.) Turn to Chapter 7 for other possibilities.

Pinpointing today's personal card

If you've done the exercises earlier in the chapter, this should be old hat!

1. **Add together the month, day, and year of your birth *plus* the current day, month, and year.** For example,

8 (month)	5 (month)
2 (day)	23 (day)
1956 (year)	2002 (year)
1966	2020

2. **Add the two totals from Step 1 together and reduce the resulting number. If that number is higher than 22, add its digits together to reduce it again.** From our example in Step 1, 1966 + 2030 = 3996. 3 + 9 + 9 + 6 = 27. 2 + 7 = 9.

If your birthday was August 2, 1956, your personal card for May 23, 2002 would be card number 9 in the major arcana, The Hermit. Your personal card suggests the issues or experiences facing and/or involving you during the day ahead.

For example, the hermit shines his light, which might suggest being called to assist a friend. The card might show you seeking more spiritual direction than usual over the course of the day. It also illustrates the possibility of feeling unsociable, going into retreat, or isolating yourself. Chapter 7 offers you numerous other options.

The exercises in this section show you how to figure out cards for today and *any* day, past or future.

Cards that Correspond to Weeks and Months

Following the same types of formulas that are used to find cards associated with certain days, you can also find cards that correspond to entire weeks or even months. You may find these formulas useful when planning significant events.

Week by week

Figuring out the card for a particular week in this year (or any year) is a snap. All you need is a calendar. For example, Larry, a hard-working corporate executive, wants to know the card for his solo retreat vacation at an alpine lake in the fourth week of August, 2002. He counts the weeks of the year until he gets to this week — week number 34 — and then adds it to the number of the year.

$$\begin{array}{r} 34 \text{ (week)} \\ \underline{2002 \text{ (year)}} \\ 2036 \end{array}$$

Adding together $2 + 0 + 3 + 6 = 11$, the Justice card. After perusing the list of questions under Justice, Larry zeros in on, "What imbalances are you correcting?" Curious about the card's astrological link, he turns to Chapter 16. Finding that Justice is connected with Venus, the planet of beauty and harmony, Larry decides that the card is appropriate for getting rebalanced in nature.

Month by month

To figure out the card for a particular month in the year, add together the number of the month and the number of the year. For example, to find out what card corresponded to January, 2001, add the number of the month (1) to 2001, for a total of 2002. $2 + 0 + 0 + 2 = 4$, and card number four in the major arcana is The Emperor.

Cards for Special Occasions

The information provided in this chapter comes in handy if you want to choose a date for a wedding, a shower, or another special event based on the card that corresponds with it. In this section, I offer examples of how some people put this information to practical use.

One of the most wonderful aspects of my work is officiating at weddings and other ceremonies. When Gloria and her fiancé Greg made an appointment to plan their wedding ceremony, the couple carefully explained to me that they wanted their marriage on a harmonious day. (I interpreted this to mean a day that did *not* correspond to The Devil or The Tower cards!) The couple had selected some tentative dates for the ceremony, and I suggested showing them the corresponding tarot card for each.

After a heated debate, trying to decide between The Lovers and Justice cards, Gloria and Greg opted to marry on the day of the Justice card. Gloria, a legal secretary, first thought the card warned of divorce. But because the Justice card is associated with the astrological sign of Libra, which is ruled or presided over by the planet Venus, the couple finally decided on this date. (I discuss astrology in Chapter 16.) Venus is the goddess of love. She's also associated with balance, harmony, aesthetics, partnerships, agreements, and legal contracts. (Another factor that helped Gloria and Greg choose is that they were both born under the astrological sign of Taurus, ruled by the planet Venus.)

Daniella, a longtime tarot student, wanted to host a baby shower for her best friend, Stacy, on a day when The Empress, the card most associated with birth and motherhood, would be the day's card. Unfortunately, she came up with a problem: No days during the nine months of Stacy's pregnancy would add up to The Empress's number, 3. After some brainstorming, Daniella decided to hold the shower on the third day of the third month instead.

Paul, another tarot student, held a bachelor party for his best friend, Julian, on the day when The Emperor, the card most connected with manhood, was the card of the day.

Carla and her partner wanted their commitment ceremony to take place on a day when The Lover's card was the day's card. Because The Lovers came up only on a Tuesday during the month of May, it just wouldn't work out. Ultimately, they exchanged vows privately on that Tuesday, but scheduled their formal ceremony and party on a day when friends and family could attend.

Studying History with the Tarot

It's interesting to contemplate the cards that are associated with various historical events. In the following list, I show you how the tarot connects with a few well known events:

✔ **Pearl Harbor:** On December 7, 1941, Pearl Harbor was attacked and the United States formally entered World War II. Adding the day, month, and year, 12 + 7 + 1941 = 1960. Adding 1 + 9 + 6 + 0 = 16, The Tower card, which is associated with the planet Mars. The Tower is the tarot card most linked with upheaval, destruction, and war.

✔ **The 2000 presidential election:** November 7, 2000, is the date of the controversial 2000 United States Presidential Election, which was ultimately decided by the United States Supreme Court. 11 + 7 + 2000 = 2018. 2 + 0 + 1 + 8 = 11. Card number 11 in the major arcana is the Justice card, associated with cosmic justice, laws, and lawsuits. (Contrary to what people think, eventually laws and lawsuits do work in accord with what is cosmically just.)

✔ **The end of the Cuban Missile Crisis:** On October 26, 1962, the Cuban Missile Crisis was resolved. 10 + 26 + 1962 = 1998. 1 + 9 + 9 + 8 = 27. Because there are only 22 cards in the major arcana, we add together 2 + 7 to get 9, The Hermit card, one of the cards associated with seeking higher guidance — something the whole world sought during this crisis.

✔ **The Kennedy assassination:** On November 22, 1963, President John F. Kennedy was assassinated. 11 + 22 + 1963 = 1996. 1 + 9 + 9 + 6 = 25. 2 + 5 = 7, The Chariot card, the card most associated with a car or moving vehicle. President Kennedy was shot while driving in an open-topped car in Dallas, Texas.

✔ **Martin Luther King, Jr.'s assassination:** On April 4, 1968, Martin Luther King, Jr. was assassinated. 4 + 4 + 1968 = 1976. 1 + 9 + 7 + 6 = 23. 2 + 3 = 5, which is The Hierophant, the card most associated with the intuition or inner-knowing. Dr. King is said to have spoken about his death the night before his assassination.

Locating Your Personal Court Card

As I explain in Chapter 9, the court cards can offer insight into your life and personality. In this section, I show you a potent way to develop some awareness of your current personal development or a pressing life situation using the court cards.

Before I show you the steps, Table 10-2 lists the court cards and shows their numbering.

Table 10-2	Numbering the Court Cards		
Card Number	**Card Name**	**Card Number**	**Card Name**
1	The Page of Wands	9	The Queen of Wands
2	The Page of Cups	10	The Queen of Cups
3	The Page of Swords	(11)	The Queen of Swords
4	The Page of Pentacles	12	The Queen of Pentacles
5	The Knight of Wands	13	The King of Wands
6	The Knight of Cups	14	The King of Cups
7	The Knight of Swords	15	The King of Swords
8	The Knight of Pentacles	16	The King of Pentacles

1. **Add the month, day, and year of your birth.** For example, Jewel was born on April 12, 1965. 4 + 12 + 1965 = 1981.

2. **Add together the digits of the total you arrive at in Step 1. If your total is higher than 16 (the total number of court cards), reduce it by adding its digits together.** For example, 1 + 9 + 8 + 1 = 19. 1 + 9 = 10.

3. **Add the number you arrive at in Step 2 to the number of the current year (reducing if that number adds up to more than 16).** 10 + 2001 = 2011. 2 + 0 + 1 + 1 = 4.

4. **Find the court card associated with the number arrived at in Step 3.** Looking at Table 10-2, the fourth court card is the Page of Pentacles, which is Jewel's court card for the year 2001.

After you follow these steps, look at Chapter 9 for help interpreting what your personal court card means. You can also pull this card out of your favorite tarot deck and give it a closer look.

Connecting a Court Card with Your Personal Development for the Year

If you'd like to dig a bit deeper into what your court card says about your personality, try the following exercise. You'll need some paper and something to write with so that you can record your responses to the questions.

1. **My court card is . . .**

2. **The figure on my card reminds me of . . .** The answer should be someone you know, someone you'd like to know, or someone you'd prefer not to know.

3. **The aspects of my personality, qualities that I'm developing, and/or the roles that I'm playing this year are . . .** Following are suggestions to consider when answering this question:

   • **Wands (spiritual):** Being open to ideas, insights, and inspirations directly from my higher soul, spirit, Self, as well as from other sources of wisdom in the world around me.

   • **Cups (creative/feeling):** Developing my imaginative/creative side, tuning into dreams and fantasies, and/or becoming more aware of feelings and desires — both mine and those of others.

   • **Swords (mental):** Developing my ability to think clearly, eliminate what is extraneous, and improve my capacity for formulating plans of action.

   • **Pentacles (physical):** Developing my ability to bring my ideas, imaginings, and goals into form; digging in and finishing my work cycles; carrying out plans to completion and/or taking better care of my body and surroundings.

   After considering these suggestions and the information about your card's suit in Chapter 9, add your comments and insights.

   For example, my court card for 2001 is 14, the King of Swords. After considering how the swords function, I'd respond to question number 3 by indicating that this year is presenting me with the challenge of integrating the principle of Ageless Wisdom that suggests that I recognize the manifestation of the undeviating Justice (also known as cosmic justice) in all circumstances of my life.

4. **What's the astrological sign linked with my card?** You can find this information in Chapter 16. **What does this tell me?**

5. **What stage of life is my card in: childhood, adolescence, adulthood, or elder/sagehood?** (See Chapter 9.) **What does this suggest to me?**

6. **What are my card's personality traits?** Answer this by looking at the card and describing what you see.

7. **How does what I just wrote relate to my personality and the qualities I'm developing during this year?**

8. **How am I already developing these qualities? What steps can I take to carry this out further?**

Chapter 11

Handling, Mixing, and Interpreting the Cards

. . . .

In This Chapter

▶ Protecting your tarot cards

▶ Considering the value of ritual

▶ Asking the tarot cards questions

▶ Predicting the future

. . . .

This chapter begins by explaining tarot etiquette, including the basics of caring for your cards: wrapping, storing, and protecting. I describe simple rituals that might accompany your tarot use, from washing your hands and lighting incense and candles, to repeating Sanskrit and Latin prayers or mantras. I also touch on the treatment of orphaned and aged tarot decks.

Next, I show you how to mix and turn over the cards with a minimum of confusion. I also explain the best times and places for doing tarot readings.

I discuss how to formulate questions and offer suggestions for understanding the answers you receive. I also touch on the ever intriguing topic of predictive tarot. Finally, I give you a look at the main differences (subtle and otherwise) between tarot reading and tarot consulting.

Special Handling Required

If I want a tool to continue functioning, I know that I must treat it with respect and care. My tarot cards are an important tool, so I treat them very carefully.

Storing, wrapping, and protecting

Traditionally, tarot decks are kept wrapped in cloth — preferably a natural fiber such as silk, cotton, hemp, or wool. Decks are also stored in cloth or leather pouches and ornate wooden boxes. This practice has two origins:

- ✔ Sacred objects of all types are given special treatment. For example, the Jewish holy scrolls, or *torah*, are dressed in special silken and hand-embroidered garments. Between uses, the scrolls are placed inside a wooden cabinet or container called a holy ark. (One of the definitions of the word *arcana* is "container.")

- ✔ During the time of the Inquisition, when owners of tarot cards and other nontraditional spiritual tools were persecuted, tortured, and murdered for *heresy* (beliefs that varied from the established beliefs of the Roman Catholic church), the cards were hidden. Tarot cards were wrapped in cloth and buried; the cloth kept them clean and holy. The cards were also hidden away among the kitchen spices in wooden spice boxes, making their detection less likely. (The word *arcana* also means "box.")

From these practices came the modern traditions of keeping tarot cards in special cloth, pouches, and decorated wooden boxes.

I keep my cards wrapped in a large square of especially beautiful silk velvet cloth. Within the velvet cloth is a pouch, or card container, of the same material. I loved hand-sewing the wrapping cloth and pouch for my cards. The pouch is fastened by an antique button that was given to me around the time I received my first tarot deck. The very act of unwrapping my cards reminds me that I am about to do something special.

As a tarot teacher, I have numerous tarot decks. Each has its own special container and all are kept in a place of honor, a lovely hand-painted wooden cabinet given to me by one of my students.

When I lay out the cards, I place them on the cloth in which they were wrapped. No matter where I might spread out the cards, I think of this cloth as creating a sacred space for the work I'm doing.

Setting your intention

When you first obtain a tarot deck, you can do several things to make the deck personally yours. First, you can find a special piece of cloth to wrap your cards in, and you can make or purchase a pouch.

You can also consecrate or dedicate your deck. The word *consecrate* means "to set apart as sacred." Consecrating your tarot deck means simply acknowledging that you're using the cards for something special — you're setting your intention. I like to state my intent to use the cards only for the greatest good of all concerned. I use these words to set my intention: "Dear Higher Self, please help me to use these cards for the greatest good of myself and others."

You might like to take the process of consecrating your cards a few steps further. For instance, I always wash my hands before and after working with the cards. Providing that you (or whomever you're reading for) aren't allergic to incense, you can *smudge,* or sanctify and cleanse, your cards by waving them through the smoke from a stick of your favorite incense. You might also like to light a candle (scent-free if necessary), signifying your desire to bring in the divine light. Incense and candles are one of the simplest ways of creating a sacred space or energy field around you and the cards. Keep in mind that candles of different colors signify different things. In Chapter 12, I provide the meanings of ten colors. You may want to burn a candle that's in harmony with your tarot work.

If you're reading the cards for someone else, be sure to ask if that person has allergies before lighting up a candle or incense. I recall one young man's eyes watering so badly from a combination of incense and my cat that we had to finish working in the garden.

You can also consider saying a prayer or mantra over the cards that holds a special significance for you. Here are a few examples of prayers or mantras provided by students of mine from varying backgrounds:

> One hand to receive, one hand to give. I dedicate this work to the service of divine love and the One.

> Dear God (any name can be substituted — Jesus, Divine Mother, Buddha, Krishna, and so on), make me a vehicle for your life, love, and energy. Without you, I am nothing.

> Make me a center of expression for the primal will-to-good, which eternally creates and sustains the universe.

> *Allah Hu* (a Sufi and Moslem name for God, repeated seven times).

> *Deus In Adjustorium Manum Intende* (Latin, meaning "Oh God come to my aid").

> *Sh'ma Yisroyel Adnoi Elohaynu, Adonai Echod* (Hebrew, meaning "All of creation is Most High God in form, and therefore holy").

> Hail Mary Full of Grace (part of the Roman Catholic rosary).

> *Hum Mani Padme Hum* (a Tibetan Buddhist prayer that means "Hail to the jewel or Buddha in the heart of the lotus").

So' Ham (Sanskrit for "I am That, That I am" or "I am one with the source of all").

Om Namah Shivaya (Sanskrit for "Everything is God").

Dambusa (Yahi Indian, meaning "beautiful, gentleness, sweetness").

My friend Bob, a Buddhist practitioner, turned me on to the following two prayers:

Buddhist prayer

May all sentient beings (compassionate, feeling, or sympathetic beings) have happiness and the causes of happiness.

May all sentient beings be free from suffering and the causes of suffering.

May all sentient beings never be separated from the happiness that knows no suffering.

May all sentient beings abide in equanimity, free from attachment and anger that hold some close and others distant.

Buddhist dedication prayer

Through this virtuous action may I and others quickly attain the state of Buddhahood and lead every living being, without exception, into that pure world.

To consecrate their decks, other students report doing things as diverse as:

- Holding their new deck of tarot cards up to the heavens and asking for a blessing and guidance.
- Dribbling a few drops of water from the Ganges River over the deck.
- Creating a Native American Medicine Wheel and walking the deck through the four directions.
- Sprinkling *verbuti*, or sacred ash manifested by the great Indian Master Sri Sathya Sai Baba, over the cards.

Whatever you do to dedicate your cards, even if it's nothing, is certain to be right for you.

Requesting divine protection

Some people believe that others can put a curse on them through a deck of tarot cards. As a result, these people don't like others to use or even touch their cards. If you find yourself thinking that this is probable, you can certainly prohibit people from touching your cards, which could limit your use of them. Or, like me, you might request *divine protection* before using your cards, and then request *divine cleansing* of any harmful energies after using your cards. Even the simplest request for protection and cleansing works perfectly! Some people even burn incense and candles before, during, and after working with the cards to ensure purification or "a clean psychic environment."

When I first started working with the tarot, I unwittingly violated another person's privacy. I did some unsolicited tarot work aimed at gaining insight as to why my good friend Barbara's 9-year-old child was stealing. When I told my friend what I'd learned, she became enraged because I had stuck my nose in her business. Although I apologized and tried explaining that I was coming from a place of love and concern, she remained closed and angry.

Before these events, I'd lent Barbara a deck of my tarot cards to study. When I asked her to return my cards, she hotly told me that she'd never give them back and that she was using them to put a curse on me and my family. I am not a superstitious person, but I proceeded to write her a letter of apology and put up a wall of psychic protection around my home and family. This experience taught me that invading another's privacy is a type of psychic voyeurism. Even when such an act is done with the best of intentions, it's an absolute no-no.

If you put a curse on someone, you're also putting a curse on yourself. Actions like this bring the principle of *karma* ("what goes around comes around") into play.

Adopting orphans and retiring older cards

Over the years, I've been given or have purchased orphan tarot decks. *Orphans* are decks that their owners felt incompatible with and have gifted to someone or sold at yard sales, flea markets, or used book stores. Although it's supposed to be bad luck to use another person's cards, I make the decks mine by rededicating them.

When teaching a workshop, I'm sometimes asked, "If I have a tarot deck that gets too old and damaged to use, what should I do with it?" Because the cards are treated with chemicals that preserve their paper and colors, they don't decompose in the earth easily. Over the years, I've cremated two decks in my fireplace. I thank the deck for the service it's given, then throw it card by card into the fire. I take its ashes and bury them in the earth. I'm hoping to sprinkle the ashes of my next deck into the ocean!

But I Can't Shuffle!

In order to use tarot cards, you need to be able to mix them. Mixing has two purposes. The first is to get you focused on working with the cards. The second is to put both your energies and the energies of a person you might be working with into the cards.

There are several ways to mix the cards. You can shuffle them like regular playing cards, being sure not to *stack the deck,* or make all the cards come up in the same direction. If the cards are too big, your hands are too small, or you've never learned to shuffle (one of my students was forbidden to play card games as a child), you have another option: the Cauldron.

It's not necessary, but you may repeat the famous chant from the three witches in Shakespeare's *Macbeth* ("Double, double, toil and trouble; fire burn and cauldron bubble") while stirring the Cauldron.

Stirring the Cauldron is as easy as one, two, three!

1. **Spread the entire deck face down on a firm surface.**

2. **Stir the cards around using both hands.** (You might like to consecrate the cards with a prayer as you do this.)

3. **Gather the well-mixed cards face down into one pack.**

Now you're ready to lay the cards out in a tarot spread, which I discuss in Chapter 13.

I've found that the best way to lay out the cards is to turn them over like the pages in a book, from right to left, rather than flip them over as you would regular playing cards. If you're working with someone, sitting next to them while spreading the cards can eliminate any confusion about whether the cards are upright or reversed.

Shuffling is a lone activity, and tarot reading often is not — there's the reader/consultant and the person being read for. Because the Cauldron can allow both the reader and the person being read for to mix the cards simultaneously, it's a good method to consider when mixing the cards.

Why, When, and Where?

Do I hear you asking, "*Why* might I lay out the tarot cards? *When* is a good time to lay out the cards? And *where* should I lay out the cards?"

It's a good idea to be clear about why you want to use the tarot cards, whether you're doing an entire spread or drawing a single card from the deck. For example, I draw a card from the deck every morning. Before doing this, I ask that the card give me guidance and direction during the day ahead.

As I explain in Chapter 1, you and I are trained how to see ourselves and life situations. I use the tarot cards because they give me another, often different perspective on myself and life situations. The cards open my mind and heart to following my higher soul, spirit, Self in my thoughts, words, and actions. This includes releasing worn-out *constructs* — ways of seeing myself, others, and life situations.

If I am willing to step out of my own way, the cards can also help me see more than what I want to see, or have been trained to see. They put me in touch with what's true and real. It's possible that the cards can do likewise for you.

I've found that it's best to lay out the cards when I have time to give them a really good look-see. Of course, there are times when I don't understand (or I resist understanding) a card's meaning. At such times, I leave the card in question where I can keep seeing it. Doing this allows the image to work on my subconscious, the part of me that knows everything. It usually doesn't take long — perhaps a day or two — before I get insight into the card's meaning.

Because silence helps me focus on what I'm doing, I prefer to lay out the cards in quiet and peaceful surroundings. This doesn't mean that you can't take the cards to the beach. It simply means that I find that a less distracting environment is the best place to read the cards. Truthfully, where you read the cards has to do with what you're comfortable with — I've seen people do excellent tarot stationed on a busy city sidewalk.

Asking Questions and Getting Answers

When using the tarot cards, it's preferable to have a question in mind, even if it's a general one. Be aware that the more specific your question is, the easier it is for the cards to provide answers.

At best, the answers to your questions come in the form of suggestions and the identification of new options. Working with tarot cards is like getting input from a wise friend. It's aimed at expanding your point of view. The best input comes in the form of suggestions and general guidelines rather than advice and directives. This means to carefully consider the suggestions and options that come from each card, then decide what rings true for you. In other words, let your conscience or sense of inner-knowing be your guide!

The tarot is a tool that facilitates self-empowerment and the development of higher consciousness. Blindly following the tarot's suggestions is the antithesis of what the tarot is about. This type of behavior is a actually *dis*empowerment.

Jill wanted to get back together with her ex-husband. After hearing about a tarot reader who specialized in repairing relationships, Jill quickly scheduled an appointment. At the beginning of her session, she told the reader she wanted to know, "Will I get my husband back?" The reader used the cards to instruct her how to rekindle the relationship. Jill unthinkingly carried out the reader's instructions to the letter, but her husband still got engaged to his new girlfriend. Jill became furious, blaming the reader for what happened.

By giving up her role in the decision-making process, Jill gave up her power. She also denied herself the growth and learning that exercising her free will and taking responsibility for her actions offer.

The best questions start with the words *how, why, what,* and *might*. Because the tarot only deals with possibilities, it's best not to start questions with the words *should I, will I,* and *when*.

Here are a few examples of good questions to pose to the tarot:

- ✔ "How might I proceed with my relationship with my father for the greatest good of all concerned?"
- ✔ "Why am I experiencing difficulty finding a new job?"
- ✔ "What might I learn from leaving teaching to become a school administrator?"
- ✔ "Might it be in my child's best interest to move her to a school for gifted children?"

There are several purposes that you shouldn't ask the tarot to serve:

- ✔ Don't use the tarot as your financial consultant. I learned this while working with a man who wanted me to make stock market predictions.
- ✔ Don't use the tarot to solve legal issues. I learned this while working with a district attorney who wanted to know if the man she was prosecuting was guilty of killing his brother.
- ✔ Don't use the tarot to diagnose a medical problem. I learned this while working with a man who wanted to know if his headaches were being caused by a brain tumor.
- ✔ Don't use the tarot when a psychiatrist is needed. I learned this while working with a schizophrenic woman.

When Will I Meet the Love of My Life? Win the Lottery? Become Enlightened?

If you are like most people, you may want to use the tarot to find out when an event is going to happen. Except for a very few, exceptionally gifted individuals, most tarot readers cannot determine the timing of an event without using some guesswork. (I know a psychic tarot reader who's being sued for malpractice.)

Predicting probabilities

Most people who make predictions base them on the laws of nature, the tendency of events to occur in cycles, and cause and effect. Yes, history does have a way of repeating itself. Mental, emotional, and physical states tend to recur in definite patterns and rhythms. And, of course, when you or I act, there's bound to be a response to that action at some point in time. Yet pinpointing events is a whole other thing! Although human behavior runs a somewhat predictable course, you and I grow and change, and nature has a way of intervening in the most unexpected ways and at the most unexpected times. Such factors need to be added to the issue of timing.

Certain tarot books and teachers do correlate time with the numbers on the tarot cards. For instance, they may say that the Five of Cups as a final card means that the thing you're asking about will occur within five days, weeks, months, and so on. Or they may say that because tomorrow is the 5th, you should bet on horse number five in the fifth race. This type of thinking is misleading and sometimes dangerous.

If an event doesn't come to pass, you could get angry and end up discounting what the cards can do: reduce stress; assist in problem solving; increase Self-confidence; offer hope, support, and encouragement; and affirm your choices, responsibilities, and options.

If the event does come to pass, you might start using the cards to run your life. Using the tarot cards in such ways is a setup for disaster and contributes to the tarot's somewhat dubious reputation.

The tarot cards themselves don't cause problems, but the people who use them sometimes do!

Trusting in divine time

With lots of practice, you might be able to make an educated guess regarding the timing of an event. For example, I recently did some work that kept repeating the astrological signs of Cancer and Leo in both the major and minor arcanas. (I discuss astrology and the tarot in Chapter 16.) Based on this information, a bit of intuition, and the remaining cards, I told my client that the summer of 2001 could *possibly* bring the fruition of her project. Yet I was extremely careful to mention that unknowns such as the future political and economic conditions (as well as the potential for natural disasters) carry quite a bit of weight and need additional investigation and attention.

While it's helpful and ethical to inspire hope, it is harmful and unethical to create false expectations. Therefore, in my opinion, the best answer to the question of when something's going to happen is, "in divine time."

Comparing Tarot Reading with Tarot Consultation

When I was teaching an introductory tarot workshop many years ago, one student boldly stood up and said, "A tarot reading is a form of entertainment." Her words made me stop and think. Over time, her comment changed my entire way of explaining the work I do with the tarot. I believe a similar change has been slowly permeating the tarot community as a whole. A significant number of professionals in the tarot community are presenting themselves less and less as entertainers, and more and more as consultants to be taken seriously.

I spent years repeatedly insisting that tarot groups, such as the American Tarot Association, refer to me as a Tarot Consultant rather than a Tarot Reader. Finally, people began catching on. Last year, the American Tarot Association "borrowed" my title and started offering their students degrees as Tarot Consultants!

So what's the difference between a consultant and a reader?

In a tarot reading, the *reader* reads the cards for a client or friend. A tarot reading focuses on what the reader sees and says. Because the reader is active (she does all of the work), and the client is passive (he sits and listens), a tarot reading can be seen, like entertainment, to focus on and empower the reader. Also like entertainment, the reading must fit into a measured period of time — such as 60 minutes.

The tarot consultation is an interactive process. During a tarot consultation, the *consultant* and client exchange their views of the cards. Even if you know nothing about the cards, you or a friend can look at a picture and describe what you see, how it makes you feel, and what it brings to mind. A tarot consultation is a session at which information, or in this case views of the cards, is exchanged.

When you consult with another person — whether a friend, doctor, or lawyer — it's a deliberative process. A tarot consultation is a slow and Self-reflective process in which you discover and carefully examine your choices so that you can take responsibility for your actions and their results.

Chapter 12

Going Deeper: Meditating with the Tarot

This chapter explains how to deepen your understanding of the tarot through meditation and contemplation. *Meditation* is simply giving your full attention to something for a particular period of time. I tell students that meditation is like zeroing in on someone or something that's very important to you; it requires being fully present. Not only can meditation relax you, it can also provide you with insights into the meanings of the tarot cards and, subsequently, your life.

There are several ways to meditate with the tarot. First, I show you unique ways of tuning into the tarot cards through simple exercises involving color and sound. I encourage you to color your own set of tarot cards and/or try out the musical tones that accompany them. Next, I offer you an herbal menu of the tarot devised by master herbalists.

The section called "Composing Affirmations" explains that to affirm something is to acknowledge it as fact. This section zooms in on the attitudes and behaviors that you wish to develop using the tarot cards as your inspiration.

Also in this chapter, I take you through a tried-and-true method of making inroads into the tarot cards through your dreams and through writing. And finally, I illustrate ways to integrate the tarot's principles into your daily life.

It's one thing to have spiritual or mystical knowledge and information, but it's another to use it to improve your day-to-day life. I believe that the true aim of all knowledge is the practical application of that knowledge.

When first experimenting with any of the techniques I discuss in this chapter, your insights may come slowly. Yet, with practice and patience, you can find yourself growing more attuned to the workings of the tarot, and your understanding can grow deeper. Don't be surprised if you actually start viewing life as a set of pictures, the interpretation of which depends upon *your* perspective!

So dig out your crayons, markers, colored pencils, paper, and pens — or borrow some from your children. Resurrect that musical instrument from the garage, basement, or attic, and pull out the teapot. Oops, don't forget the dream crystal you've got tucked under your mattress. Now you're ready to get going!

Exploring Color and Sound

Wisdom teachings from both Western and Eastern traditions state that all living beings and things vibrate at different rates of speed, creating color and sound. This section shows you fun and simple ways to explore these mediums.

Meditating with color

If I suggested that you sit and meditate on a tarot card for 20 minutes, you'd probably tell me, "I can't sit and stare at a card for 20 minutes." But, if I suggest that you color in a black-and-white image of the card, as you would a picture in a coloring book, you might just take me up on it.

Coloring the tarot cards is a potent meditation exercise, especially when you start by taking several long, deep, relaxing breaths while looking at the card and you don't let your meditation period get interrupted. Coloring helps fix the image of the card in your mind. Fixing the card in your mind may help you gain insight into its many meanings. Essentially, coloring is an enjoyable, yet truly powerful way of becoming more intimate with each tarot card.

There are several ways to go about coloring the tarot cards. You can color in the pictures of the Rider-Waite Tarot cards in Chapters 7, 8, and 9 of this book. Or, if you feel especially motivated, you can make enlarged copies of the cards from this book on a heavier paper. You may also enjoy working with coloring-book-style decks, such as the **Builders of the Adytum Tarot**, **The Hermetic Tarot,** and **Church of Light**. A beautiful black-and-white deck that is wonderful to color is the **Daughters of the Moon Tarot;** unfortunately, it's presently out of print, so it may be difficult to find.

Choosing your hues

You can color the cards however you please. Color has a subtle way of stimulating your subconscious mind. Writings on the psychology of color show that colors trigger certain states of feeling, thinking, and ultimately, being.

It's no mistake that The Empress, associated with nature, creativity, and fertility, has so much green in her card. The High Priestess, associated with coolness, self-containment, and spirituality, is dominated by the color blue. The lion in the Strength card, a symbol of unbridled passion, is a vibrant red.

Because the tarot cards are aspects of you, consider coloring the cards with *your* hair, eye, and skin tones. More than one student has put small photos of their own face on the card! People who create tarot decks sometimes do the same thing. For example, The Hierophant in Paul Case's deck (Builders of the Adytum Tarot) is Case himself. The faces of all of the cards in **The Gendron Tarot** have Melanie Gendron's features.

Here's a list of the primary, secondary, and neutral colors and their basic meanings:

- **Red:** Highly energizing and exciting, red is associated with fire and heat, life and life blood, courage, passion, embarrassment, inflammation, and anger.

- **Blue:** Linked with trustworthiness and principled behavior, blue produces mental and emotional tranquility through its soothing and cooling properties. Blue also signifies spiritual and religious tendencies.

- **Yellow:** Yellow denotes clear mindedness and intellectual maturity. It stimulates the thinking processes, raises the spirit, and eliminates fear (despite the fact that the term *yellow* is linked with cowardice!).

- **Green:** Green exerts balancing, soothing, and healing influences, and it neutralizes other colors, especially red, making it calming and revitalizing. It's also nature's color, connoting fertility and abundance (If you live in the United States, the money in your pocket is green!), as well as what's unripe and inexperienced.

- **Orange:** Mildly stimulating, orange is energizing, but not as much as red. It relieves worry and anxiety, stimulates mental alertness, improves circulation, and promotes physical vitality.

- **Violet:** Violet restores mental alertness, stimulates creative energy, and enhances sensitivity. In certain instances, it can set off depression. Violet is associated with wealth, royalty, social status, spirituality, and self-confidence.

- **White:** Linked with the positive polarity that's found in all of life, white signifies purity, holiness, and unconditional love. White not only reflects all colors, but it is the color from which all others originate.

- **Black:** Linked with the negative polarity that's found in all of life, black signifies darkness, death, and the absence of light (although without light, you wouldn't perceive darkness). Black absorbs all other colors back into it, signifying how every creature and thing is born from and returns to the dark womb of life.

- **Gray:** The union of white and black, gray is associated with neutrality, maturity, wisdom, and superior intelligence (as in "using your gray matter").

- **Brown:** A combination of all other colors, brown signifies earthiness, groundedness, dependability, and solidity.

Sometimes, when a client or I can't quite understand the meaning of a card, I will pull out the same card from another deck, or even several others. Seeing the card in different colors and different styles of artwork can evoke a response, when none was previously possible.

Coloring the major arcana

Table 12-1 provides a listing of the colors associated with each of the 22 major arcana cards (see Chapter 7). When a card's color is a combination of two colors, its function is a combination of those two colors. For instance, The Hierophant's color is red-orange, a combination of the highly energizing red and anxiety-relieving orange.

When reading Table 12-1, please do not think that you *must* color the cards in this way. (I colored my first deck of tarot cards with whatever colors "felt right," and completely out of order!) I'm introducing you to the traditional associations between color and the major arcana because the colors are known to send subtle suggestions to your subconscious mind that help to reinforce the principles of each card.

Table 12-1	Colors Associated with the Major Arcana Cards		
Card	*Color*	*Card*	*Color*
The Fool	light yellow	Justice	green
The Magician	yellow	The Hanged Man	blue
The High Priestess	blue	Death	green-blue
The Empress	green	Temperance	blue
The Emperor	red	The Devil	indigo blue
The Hierophant	red-orange	The Tower	red
The Lovers	orange	The Star	violet
The Chariot	orange-yellow	The Moon	red-violet
Strength	yellow	The Sun	orange
The Hermit	yellow-green	Judgement	red
Wheel of Fortune	violet	The World	indigo blue

Dressing for success

When I'm focused on integrating the teachings of a particular card into my life, I wear and/or surround myself with the card's color. Doing this is a subtle reminder to use the card's teachings.

For instance, in situations where creativity is called for, I pull out The Empress and wear my mother's jade bracelet. Or, if after asking for guidance and direction I draw The Star card, I move my pot of African violets closer to my desk. When you wear or surround yourself with a card's color, you subtly align yourself with that card's principles and energies.

Trying symbols on for size

While you color your tarot cards, notice what you're *thinking* about the cards' symbols. (For example, the angel in The Lovers card makes me think of healing.) Notice also how you're *feeling* as you color the card. (The Tower card makes me feel nervous.) Also consider the general *mood* of the card. (The Sun card seems cheerful, while The Star is peaceful.)

While coloring a card, notice what symbols stand out. Ask yourself, "What does this symbol mean to *me?*" I strongly encourage you to make your own associations with the symbols. Later, you may want to check out a tarot book or dictionary of symbols to learn more.

Books on the tarot or symbolism reflect one writer's point of view. Each symbol can have hundreds of meanings. So, while it may be helpful to learn what someone else thinks about a symbol's meaning, don't be discouraged if your own interpretation differs.

Try a card's symbol on for size. For example, when I'm feeling caged-up, I borrow a friend's puppy and go for a walk. Doing this reminds me of The Fool's carefree attitude and increases my understanding of both the symbol and the card.

Tuning in

My teacher, Paul Foster Case, was a master musician who taught that you can tune into each of the 22 major arcana cards by sounding its particular musical note. When you sound the card's specific musical note, you are attuning yourself to that card's particular vibration. If you find this intriguing, I suggest using a chromatic pitch pipe (12 semitones), but any instrument with the ability to play this scale will do. Here's the process:

1. **Place the card you're meditating on in front of you.**

2. **Take several long, deep breaths and relax.**

3. **Play the note linked with the card for pitch.**

4. **Hum or sound along with the pitch anywhere from three to seven times while looking at or tuning into the card.** To do this, it's imperative that you put aside what your mother or third grade teacher told you about moving your lips but not singing, because you were throwing everyone else off!

5. **Let your eyes wander around the image for a minute or two, or until your attention begins to wander.**

6. **Notice any associations that you make with the picture on the card: thoughts, feelings, or other insights.**

Musical meditation has helped thousands of people tune into each card more deeply.

When working with the cards, I often sound my own (and/or my client's) soul card (see Chapter 10). This increases our attunement and adds another dimension to the consultation.

Table 12-2 lists the notes associated with each of the 22 major arcana cards.

Table 12-2 Musical Notes Associated with the Major Arcana Cards

Card	Note	Card	Note
The Fool	E	Justice	F#
The Magician	E	The Hanged Man	G#
The High Priestess	G#	Death	G
The Empress	F#	Temperance	G#
The Emperor	Middle C	The Devil	A
The Hierophant	C#	The Tower	Middle C
The Lovers	D	The Star	A
The Chariot	D#	The Moon	B
Strength	E	The Sun	D
The Hermit	F	Judgement	Middle C
Wheel of Fortune	A#	The World	A

Sweet sounds of tarot

When Steven Halpern, King of New Age Music, was composing his now world-renowned Spectrum Suite (the first of his "Anti-Frantic Alternative" series of recordings), he and I spent a delightful afternoon discussing the tarot's musical correspondences.

After he took several tarot classes, a well-known jazz pianist told me he was creating a work called "Tarot Jazz," using the notes from each of the tarot cards as his inspiration. I look forward to hearing his finished work!

Tasting the Tarot

I had the privilege of studying herbology with Brysis Buchanan, a master herbalist and wonderful person. Brysis not only knew about herbs, she also knew a great deal about the tarot — she matched the tarot's major arcana cards with North American herbs. One day, Brysis approached me announcing (as only she could), "If Sybil Leek can put together a cookbook for witches, I can put together an herbal tarot for herbalists. Let's you and me do a tarot reading about it."

The work we did energized her project, but Brysis passed on before she ever got it to a publishing company. Another master herbalist, Michael Tierra, with the help of artist Candis Cantin, took up where Brysis left off — and then some. Michael's knowledge of Chinese herbs and medicine added greatly to his world renowned **Herbal Tarot**.

While imbibing a particular card, you may want to cook with or have a cup of tea made from a small bit of the herbs listed below. Meditate on the qualities of the herb while looking at the card it represents, as you sip or eat. In Table 12-3, I've listed herbs only for the major arcana, but the Herbal Tarot lists herbs for the entire tarot deck. If this subject interests you further, you may want to pick up this excellent tarot deck.

Some of these herbs can be toxic! Be very careful that you know about *all* of an herb's properties before eating or drinking it.

Table 12-3	Herbs Associated with the Major Arcana Cards		
Card	**Herb**	**Card**	**Herb**
The Fool	ginseng	Justice	plantain
The Magician	astragalus	The Hanged Man	kelp
The High Priestess	cramp bark	Death	elder
The Empress	dong quai	Temperance	echinacea
The Emperor	ginger	The Devil	lobelia
The Hierophant	sage	The Tower	garlic
The Lovers	parsley	The Star	skullcap
The Chariot	dandelion	The Moon	lemon balm
Strength	cayenne	The Sun	bay laurel
The Hermit	licorice	Judgement	golden seal
Wheel of Fortune	slippery elm	The World	comfrey

Composing Affirmations

To affirm something is to acknowledge it as reality. The purpose of affirmations is to confirm and emphasize the existence of various physical, mental, emotional, and spiritual states and attitudes that you want to be aware of or develop. For instance, the statement, "I welcome change," states my belief in this idea and *affirms* my desire to make it a day-to-day reality.

After working with a tarot card, you can compose a statement affirming a quality of the card that resonates with your state of mind or life situation. For example, the following affirmation goes with The Emperor card: "I, Amber, am getting better and better at organizing my life." Repeating an affirmation while looking at the tarot card that embodies its principles embeds both the card and affirmation in your consciousness.

To avoid setting yourself up for disappointment, don't use affirmations that have definite time frames, such as "I will meet the man of my dreams by September 1," or, "In six weeks, my thighs will be as firm as they were when I was 20." Finally, it's best that you remain open to the fact that in the big picture, your highest good is *always* served.

Here are some guidelines for creating and working with your affirmations:

- Focus on a few affirmations at a time.

- Surround yourself with reminders of your affirmations. Repeat them in the morning and at night. Record and listen to your affirmations whenever possible. Write your affirmations on Post-it notes or index cards and place them where you can easily see them. (I have them in places I frequent, such as my desk, refrigerator, and meditation altar.)

- Have a friend tell your affirmations to you. ("Amber, you welcome change.") Imagine someone you care for saying them to you, or imagine your friends talking about you. ("Did you know that Amber welcomes change?")

- Put as much passion into your affirmations as possible. If you say words without feeling the meaning behind them, it's like saying that you're hungry, but lacking an appetite.

- Make your affirmations as real as possible. When I don't believe my affirmation, I check out why I don't. For example, the likelihood of my thighs being as firm as they were when I was 20 is laughable.

    Joey, a very high-strung and impatient man, desires to be calmer and more patient. Instead of affirming, "I'm a calm and patient man," Joey states, "I am growing calmer and more patient with each passing day." Making your affirmations real increases your chances of success.

- Phrase your statements positively. Using negatives causes confusion. For example, the negative statement, "I no longer reject the dark side of my personality," is confusing. Instead, try "The dark side of my personality is an aspect of my undeveloped divinity."

- Make your affirmations more than just a bunch of words by backing them up with *actions* that support them.

A tarot affirmation is a realistic statement confirming your ability to develop an aspect of the card that will improve your state of mind and/or life situation.

Becoming a Beautiful Dreamer

Another potent form of tarot meditation is *dreaming* on the cards. One avid dreamer (and tarot student) called tarot cards "frozen dreams." I suggest dreaming on the cards if you're stumped by a card's significance or are particularly attracted to a card and want to go deeper into its meaning. (You can try this just for fun, too!) The following steps can help you contact the spirit of each tarot card in your dreams:

- If you plan to dream on a card, keep it visible during the day before your dream journey. It also helps to color in the card and sound its musical tone (which I discuss earlier in this chapter) at bedtime.

- Don't overeat, drink alcohol, or take sleeping preparations or tranquilizers.

- Ritualize the process. Ask for guidance and light incense or a candle that is the same color as the card you're dreaming on. (But be sure to blow out the candle before falling asleep!)

- Station a pen, paper, and flashlight next to your bed so you can jot down key thoughts and images if you wake up in the middle of the night. Make notes first thing in the morning.

- Consider sleeping alone. This might make you feel more comfortable if your dreams wake you up or if the person next to you interrupts your dreaming by snoring or other habits.

- Don't use an alarm clock. Try dreaming on a card on a night when you can sleep until you wake up naturally. An alarm clock may shock you and make you forget your dream.

- Look at the card that you are dreaming on for a few minutes before bedtime. Ask the spirit of the card to link you with the teachings and information that are important for you to receive from the card this time. Write out your request and affirm that you'll remember your dreams, something like this:

    Dear Spirit of Temperance,

    I am open to receiving the information and teachings about (the name of the card) that are important to my growth and well-being at this time, no matter what these might be. I'll remember my dreams when I wake up. Thank you.

    With appreciation and love,

    Your Name

- Keep the image or sense of the card in mind as you fall asleep. (I keep going over and visualizing the symbols of the cards in my mind's eye while drifting off.) Do your best to have the card be the last thing you think about.

- Experiment with sleeping with a dream crystal in your hand. It may keep you just a bit awake while dreaming and also remind you to remember your dreams.

- Pin a note on your pillow saying, "What did I just dream?" It might stir your dream memory.

- If you can't recall your dream, stay in bed. Spend a few minutes lying in your different sleeping positions. Doing this has tuned me into my bodily dream memory time and again.

- Be patient and persistent! If the process doesn't work the first night, keep at it.

Meditating through Writing

One of the meditation exercises I do with students focuses on the tarot cards through writing. After relaxing and zeroing in on a card, I ask a series of questions. Students write down their spontaneous and uncensored answers to these questions.

For example, I may ask students to ask The Hermit:

- Who are you?
- Whom are you shining your light for?
- You are alone on a mountain top. Are you lonely? If so, why? If not, why not?
- Why is your body shaped like the number nine?

The tarot cards have the potential of activating your whole brain; they involve the use of both the left and right sides of your brain. The *questioning* part of this exercise calls on your intellect or linear thinking — your left brain. The *answering* part calls on your feelings and instincts — your right brain. Combined, the questions and answers activate your intuition — your whole brain.

Taking this a step further, sometimes I have a student write questions with her right hand (if she's right-handed), then write out the answers with her left hand. If you are left-handed, you would do the opposite. (It's usually easier to print than write with your nondominant hand.) This exercise has resulted in some pretty remarkable insights!

The Best Form of Meditation

I've found that applying the principles of the cards to my life is the best form of meditation. Instead of just thinking about the meaning of a card, I try to *use* its principles to improve the quality of my life and relationships.

For instance, say I draw the Two of Swords from the deck at the beginning of the day as my touchstone. (I explain the touchstone in Chapter 13.) Looking at the list of questions associated with the Two of Swords (see Chapter 8), the question "What feelings are worth putting behind you?" jumps out at me. Immediately, I think of an old friend who's become distant. I recently learned that he's now caring for his dying father. My grandmother's words, "two wrongs don't make a right," come into my mind. I put my feelings behind me and give him a call.

Sometimes connections aren't as obvious as this one. Yet if you keep the card in mind as you go through your day, you might notice the card popping up. Rereading the card's list of questions at the end of the day is also useful.

If you're interested in pursuing this further, you may want to thumb through my book, *Living the Tarot* (Wordsworth Editions, Ltd.), which is devoted to this practice. This work not only gives examples of myself and students putting the principles of the cards we study to work in our lives, it also offers detailed descriptions of the symbols of the 22 major arcana cards.

Following is a story told to me by Lindsay, one of my tarot students who was living the Wheel of Fortune card:

> Much to the relief of my family, I finally got my certificate in public school administration last spring. It took me nearly four years to finish a two-year program. Although it was a strain on my child and husband, I'm glad I stuck with it. At first, I loved being home, but lately I've been feeling resentful and trapped. I worked oh so hard for my certificate and now it's lying in a drawer!

> But what you said in class about the Wheel of Fortune's link with life cycles really started me thinking that now is probably my time to be a homemaker. I'm fortunate (yes, fortune goes with the Wheel of Fortune card) to have the money to do this. I asked myself, "Why did you have a child? To put her in child care so you can work with other people's children?" I know mothers and fathers who'd trade places with me in the blink of an eye. Soon my daughter will be grown enough for me to start my new career.

> The Wheel of Fortune is about opportunities. Thanks to the card's teachings, I'm letting go of my angst and preconceived ideas about where I *should* be in life, so I can be where I am. I'm taking advantage of my once in a lifetime opportunity to be right here, right now.

Chapter 13

Tarot Spreads Aren't for Sandwiches!

In This Chapter

▶ Understanding what a tarot spread can (and cannot) do

▶ Formulating a question to take to the tarot

▶ Laying out and interpreting six tarot spreads

▶ Preparing for a professional reading

*I*n this chapter, I show you how to do tarot spreads. I explain the importance of setting your intention before laying out a spread, and I detail what a tarot spread can offer. While many tarot professionals advise against reading for yourself, I discuss the value of doing tarot for *you*. I believe that the purpose of working with the tarot is to get better and better at reading tarot cards or taking an honest look at yourself in this magic mirror. This way of doing tarot embodies the inscription on the ancient temple of Apollo, "Know thy Self." For me, reading the tarot cards is about knowing your higher soul, spirit, Self first, *then* facilitating this process in others!

To help you get started, I guide you through all aspects of doing six different tarot spreads. After explaining how to lay out the cards with each spread, I give you examples of the spreads in action. I start with the Touchstone, a simple yet potent one-card spread. Next comes Amber's All-Purpose Tarot Spread. Like its name indicates, this spread can be used for almost *any* question.

While I don't advise using the tarot cards for answering yes or no questions, the Between Extremes Spread shows you an unusual way of approaching decision making.

The Psychological Spread can help you see a question from three psychological points of view: your subconscious, conscious, and superconscious minds. You can tune into the 12 houses, or departments, of the zodiac by way of the Astrological Spread. This spread offers you insight into the kinds of learning and growing you're doing in any or all of these departments of your life. For example, today you can look into your health (the Sixth House), while tomorrow you might look into expanding your horizons through world travel (the Ninth House).

The Relationship Spread was designed for two people (although I taught it to a therapist who now uses it with entire families). It provides you and your partner with pictures of yourselves as individuals *and* partners regarding an issue in your relationship.

As energy moves through your *chakras,* or subtle energy centers, it produces different states of being. The Chakra Spread can help you zero in on how your chakras are responding to a set of circumstances.

As if learning all these great spreads isn't enough, I also give you a few easy and interesting ways to learn more about the cards and yourself at the same time. This chapter closes with tips on getting professional tarot readings: everything from finding the best tarot reader to paying the bill.

How Tarot Spreads Work

When people ask me how the tarot spread works, I say, "It works because *you* want it to work!" Approaching the cards with the *intention* of increasing your self-understanding via a life issue or challenge — no matter what the truth about this situation turns out to be — is key.

If someone wants you to read their cards but wears an "I doubt it" or "show me" attitude, I suggest not wasting your time or theirs.

Starting small

When doing tarot spreads, keep it simple. Bigger does not mean better! Spreads with less cards can show as much as spreads with more cards. Start off working with a one-card spread. As you feel increasingly comfortable, increase the number of cards and the size of the spreads.

Instead of working with the whole tarot deck, consider working with one part of the deck at a time: either the major arcana, number, or court cards. Doing this will help you really get to know that part of the deck.

One of the reasons people give up working with the tarot is because there are 78 cards to learn, and they feel overwhelmed. Working with the cards is not about *memorizing* each card's meaning. Because one picture can be interpreted in so many ways, this is an overwhelming task (even for someone with a photographic memory). Working with the tarot is like making new friends:

Each card is an individual worth taking your time to get to know. Doing this means you can discover meanings that have never even been thought of!

Preparing your intention

When using the tarot cards, it's best to have a question in mind, even if it's a general one. The more specific your question is, the easier it is for the cards to offer suggestions and options to you, or to confirm what you might already know.

I suggest that you frame a question before you begin laying out a spread. This usually involves writing out a question that you're looking for a perspective on. If you're reading the tarot for another person, this step involves discussing the purpose of the reading with that person and having him or her write out the question.

Focusing your question

If you try to cover too much territory with one question, your reading will be an unreadable mishmash.

For example, Paul asks, "Our family's moving to a new state and home. Will it be a safe place for raising children; how will my new boss be; are we going to get along with our new neighbors; is the school system a good one; and will my wife and children make new friends easily?" Paul's question is really five or more questions rolled into one. I would advise him to focus on one question per tarot spread to avoid creating confusion.

Other unreadable questions include "When will I meet the man of my dreams?" "Where will I meet my special someone?" and "Who am I going to marry?" It's inappropriate to ask the tarot "when," "who," and "should" questions. A more readable question would be "Where *might* I go to meet my special someone?"

Avoiding yes or no questions

No matter which spread you use, avoid questions asking for yes or no answers. When laying out a spread, the cards you turn over can help you identify what *has* happened and what *is* happening — the past and present. What's *going* to happen in the future is still undecided, but a card that is laid out in a future position in a spread can indicate what might happen based on your past and present tendencies. (If you change your actions, you just *might* be changing your future.)

Tarot cards are sometimes called *maps of consciousness*. In addition to showing you many routes for reaching the same place — higher consciousness — they can help you change your direction or course of action.

Furthermore, life is full of shades of gray; within every positive is a negative, and within every negative is a positive. What looks positive could work out negatively. What looks negative might work out positively. Here I go again (I'm hoping that you're getting to know this by heart): Whether a situation is positive or negative is mostly a matter of your perspective.

Seeing into the magic mirrors

The tarot cards are like magic mirrors that can help you see yourself and life issues from a different perspective. Achieving this perspective comes down to your willingness to put aside your ego so that your higher soul, spirit, Self might be better seen and heard. It's about temporarily giving up

- ✔ your preconceived ideas about what you want or feel entitled to.
- ✔ how you think things should be.
- ✔ your belief that you know what *the* truth is.

A tarot card spread has the potential of facilitating a bit of objectivity that can

- ✔ reveal new options.
- ✔ expand how you see your options and possibilities.
- ✔ offer you support, hope, and encouragement.
- ✔ reduce stress and anxiety.
- ✔ empower you to become more conscious of your thoughts, words, and actions (bring mental clarity).
- ✔ bring out or restore your sense of humor.
- ✔ reaffirm what you already know.
- ✔ introduce you to universal truths such as "All things in divine time," which help adjust your viewpoint.
- ✔ confirm your intuitive sense of the best course of action to take for the greatest good of all concerned. Often this is something you might be avoiding because of the discomfort, inconvenience, difficulty, and/or hard work it entails.
- ✔ remind you that only *you* are responsible for your decisions and actions.

Tarot is not designed to "program" you or anyone else by making definite predictions. Only your DNA is set in stone (and if you've been reading the newspapers and watching the news, you're aware that even your DNA's becoming more and more subject to change).

Tarot hotlines

Recently, out of curiosity, I called a well-known tarot hotline. I took on the persona of a woman in her thirties wanting a general reading. Without saying one word about the cards she'd turned over, the reader immediately launched into the area that she intuited I'd be most interested in, relationships. She said that a lover, "an older light-haired man," was coming into my life. Although the reader was completely off about my love life (I've been in a relationship for over 25 years), I believe she was trying to give me hope.

I then called another hotline. For this call, I took on the persona of a woman in her forties with cancer wanting a look at my future health. The reader, who was using the Rider-Waite Tarot,

kept repeating that I had angels all around me. When I asked him the name of the card or cards he was talking about, he said, "You know, the card with all the angels on it."

I could sense his discomfort and lack of experience — I heard him flipping through pages of written material between his sentences. He was very sweet and kept telling me not to worry; he suggested that I burn incense to keep calm. At the end of my "free three minutes," he told me that the future looked hopeful and that I wasn't going to die.

Although these hotlines used the disclaimer "for entertainment purposes only," both told me I could ask *any* question I wanted to.

Interpreting a spread's meaning

A tarot reading reflects the level of consciousness of the person who's reading the cards.

No matter which spread you use, I suggest using the following guidelines:

- ✔ Start interpreting by allowing your first thoughts and feelings about the cards to surface.

- ✔ Next, look at the interpretations for each tarot card in Chapters 7, 8, and 9 and see if any of the concepts or questions jump out as being particularly relevant to you.

- ✔ If you're spreading the cards for someone else, follow this same pattern by encouraging their first thoughts and feelings to surface, then begin asking the questions you find in Chapters 7, 8, and 9.

- ✔ Write or tape record your interpretations so you can refer back to them.

If you don't like the interpretations that are coming your way, consider what you might do to make things different. Often this means changing your attitude toward someone or something, because stopping time is impossible. For example, some events are unavoidable — such as the death of someone who's terminally ill.

If you're unclear about the meaning of one or more cards, slow down. Leave the card in question out where you can see it — this encourages the card's images to work on your subconscious mind. You might also ask a friend to give you his or her thoughts about the card. You'd be surprised at how another person's ideas can spark your own.

When reading a spread for another person, encourage him or her to comment. Sometimes the best insights will come from that person.

If, after all this, you find that your reading doesn't feel complete, I'd suggest asking the tarot for further guidance and direction and then selecting one more card whose meaning may provide clarity. Naturally, I call this the *clarity card.*

Spreading the cards: From A to Z

Following are the steps that I take when preparing for and reading a tarot spread:

- ✔ **Create a comfortable environment, preferably one in which you won't be interrupted.** Perhaps you want to light some incense or a candle.

- ✔ **Clear the air and get present.** Focus on what you're doing. Have a few moments of quiet and/or request spiritual guidance.

- ✔ **Frame your question.** (See the "Preparing your intention" section earlier in the chapter.)

- ✔ **Decide which spread to use.** No spread is better than another. All spreads aim at the same thing: offering you a new perspective. Choosing a spread is a matter of deciding what view you'd like to have of your question: a psychological view, a view related to relationships, an astrological view, and so on.

- ✔ **Shuffle, or mix, and cut the cards.** After shuffling/mixing the deck, I cut the pack into four piles. Either I or the person I'm working with puts them back together in any order.

  The four piles represent the four-fold process of creation, the Word or name of the Most High (see Chapter 8). Dove, a student from a Native American background, designates each pile as one of the four directions and their qualities: North (Wisdom), South (Innocence), East (Illumination), and West (Introspection). (The four directions can also be used as an interesting format for a tarot spread.)

  Just because I cut the deck into four parts doesn't mean you must do the same. I suggest doing what feels comfortable to you.

- ✔ **Lay out the cards according to which spread you want to use.** When you lay out the cards, instead of flipping them over, turn them as you'd turn pages in a book — from right to left.

- ✔ **Interpret the cards.** (See the section "Interpreting a spread's meaning" earlier in the chapter.)

- ✔ **Create an affirmation based on your reading.** The point of creating affirmations is to keep a particular idea or attitude at the forefront of your mind (see Chapter 12).

- ✔ **Close your reading.** Pick up the cards. I always thank my higher soul, spirit, Self and wash my hands after a reading.

Taking Precautions When You Read for Others

If you choose to read cards for other people, keep the following cautionary tips in mind:

- ✔ **Confidentiality is key.** You talk about the reading *only* with the person you're working with. Gossiping is sure to backfire!

- ✔ **The tarot is not a doctor, attorney, psychiatrist, or money manager.** If the person you're reading for wants guidance about health, legal, psychiatric, or financial issues, encourage him or her to get a second opinion from a specialist.

  I worked with an accountant who eventually went to federal prison for aiding tax fraud. One of the first things I asked when he called for an appointment was if he had legal counsel. He and I used the tarot for focusing on the spiritual implications of his situation.

- ✔ **If someone is in danger, get help.** If you believe that someone is in danger of harming him or herself or another, report the situation to that person's family and/or the proper authority as soon as possible!

  I once reported a client who told me she was planning to kill her teacher. I told the teacher and the police, and doing so spared lives — including the client's own.

  I also once informed a man that his partner was considering suicide. His partner was extremely angry at me, but I may have saved her life.

- ✔ **Avoid getting in over your head.** Tell the person you're reading for that you're just learning and that you recommend getting help elsewhere for certain problems such as health, legal, psychiatric, and financial issues. It isn't easy to know when outside help will be necessary before you start working with someone, but you can make such a recommendation in the context of the reading itself.

Often, you can avoid getting in over your heard by doing two things before laying out the cards: asking why someone wants to work with the tarot, and informing that person of the types of situations you are comfortable working with.

✔ **It's better to stop a reading than to force it.** If you feel that you can't finish a reading, don't force yourself to continue. Doing so has harmed many people and contributed to the tarot's image problems. Contrary to what you might think, knowing that you can't handle a situation and suggesting that someone seek a different kind of assistance is a sign of wisdom.

✔ **Working with friends and family can be dicey.** If you can keep what you already know about the person out of it by reading the *cards* and not the *person,* go ahead. If you can't do this, consider not working with them.

You must tell the truth as you see it, no matter what this means. I stopped doing tarot with friends after suggesting that one severely depressed friend consider seeing a psychiatrist for anti-depressant medication. He stopped talking to me after that reading.

You can't control how another reacts to a reading.

✔ **Never threaten anyone with dire consequences if they don't follow your directives.** Let the cards speak for themselves! For example, instead of saying, "This card means you're definitely heading for burnout, so you'd better quit your job," try "This card suggests you might be heading into burnout — what do *you* think about that?" I often use a disclaimer such as "I'm telling you what I see in the cards, but you may see something else. It's essential that you do what you believe is right for you."

Let love and compassion motivate each and every word you say!

The Touchstone Spread

As you begin working with spreads, less can be best. The Touchstone is a simple yet powerful one-card spread. Using the Touchstone spread is a super way of getting intimately acquainted with one card at a time.

Consider working with just one segment of the deck at a time — the major arcana, number, or court cards — as a means of focusing your attention and learning.

Touchstone means "a point of reference." Selecting a single card at the beginning of the day or before an important event offers you a reference point for the events ahead. Doing this also offers you a way to reflect on what has happened at day's end. Touchstones help you see *prospectively* (some of your prospects for the day ahead) and *retrospectively* (what you might have missed during an event or a day).

Pulling a Touchstone card

Close your eyes and take several deep, relaxing breaths. Inwardly request spiritual guidance and direction for the day ahead. Mix or shuffle the cards in whatever way works for you (Chapter 11 offers you suggestions). Draw a card from *anywhere* in the downward facing deck.

Now look at the card as if you were looking at a great work of art or into the face of your lover. Imagine that you are the figure(s) in the picture. How does it feel to be that person in that situation? If you like, list your first thoughts and feelings. Just let the ideas flow — don't censor what comes to mind.

When I draw a major arcana card as my touchstone, I sound the musical note associated with that card; this process is explained in Chapter 12. Doing this helps me tune into the card.

Locate the card that you pull in Chapter 7, 8, or 9 of this book and add to your list any interpretations that jump out at you. Consider how these thoughts, feelings, and questions might guide you over the course of the day. If you'd like, jot down your ideas.

Reflect back on this card after the upcoming day or event. Consider whether what you thought at the beginning of the day did or didn't match with what actually happened. Ask the card if it has any other messages for you. Add any additional insights to your list.

Sample spread

The morning of the 1989 Loma Prieta earthquake, I drew The Tower card from my deck (see Chapter 7). My first thoughts were of my plans to walk with a friend who was recovering from a nervous breakdown after losing her husband to a younger woman. Because The Tower card's Hebrew letter *peh* means "mouth," the card reminded me of being very aware of what I said to her.

Considering that the tower is the most physically destructive (yet constructive) omen in the tarot deck, I also thought about potential disasters. Yes, my car did need new windshield wipers before the torrential winter rains. Yes, the roof of our home needed to be cleared of debris to avoid it flooding and leaking. It might also be a good idea for my school to hold a "Tarot Benefit" for the local Red Cross Disaster Relief Fund. As my processing ended, I reminded myself that I'd have more insights by nightfall.

Of course, mere seconds after the earthquake struck at five o'clock that evening, I was able to look back at the potential for natural disasters (actual earth-shattering events) also present in The Tower card.

Amber's All-Purpose Tarot Spread

Betty Crocker has her all-purpose flour, and this is my all-purpose tarot spread. You can use this spread for almost any question and spend almost any amount of time interpreting it.

Laying out the cards

The cards in this spread are laid out as shown in Figure 13-1. Each card is given a position number (card 1, card 2, and so on), and each represents something unique, such as *past experiences* and *opportunity for growth*.

Follow these steps for laying out Amber's All-Purpose Tarot Spread:

1. **Frame your question.**

2. **Look through the cards in the deck and pick one card that represents you.** Traditionally, this card is called the *significator*. Most readers pick this card according to their own or their client's birthday (see Chapter 16) or physical appearance. (For example, a woman with long light-colored hair might pick a card that shows a woman with long blond hair.) Because you are so much more than your sun sign or physical appearance, I suggest that you go through the deck and pull out the cards that resonate with you, or that you feel connected with, and put them aside in a pile. Next, go through this pile and select one card. This is your significator. Place it in position 1 in the spread, which represents you and the present time.

   When picking your significator, go with the card that seems like a good fit. Spending time worrying over your decision won't make a huge difference. (Also, there's a good chance that some of the cards you reluctantly discard will show up in the spread!)

3. **Take several deep relaxing breaths and request inner guidance and direction.**

4. **Mix or shuffle the cards in whatever way works for you.** (See Chapter 11 for mixing and shuffling tips.) While mixing, mentally repeat your question.

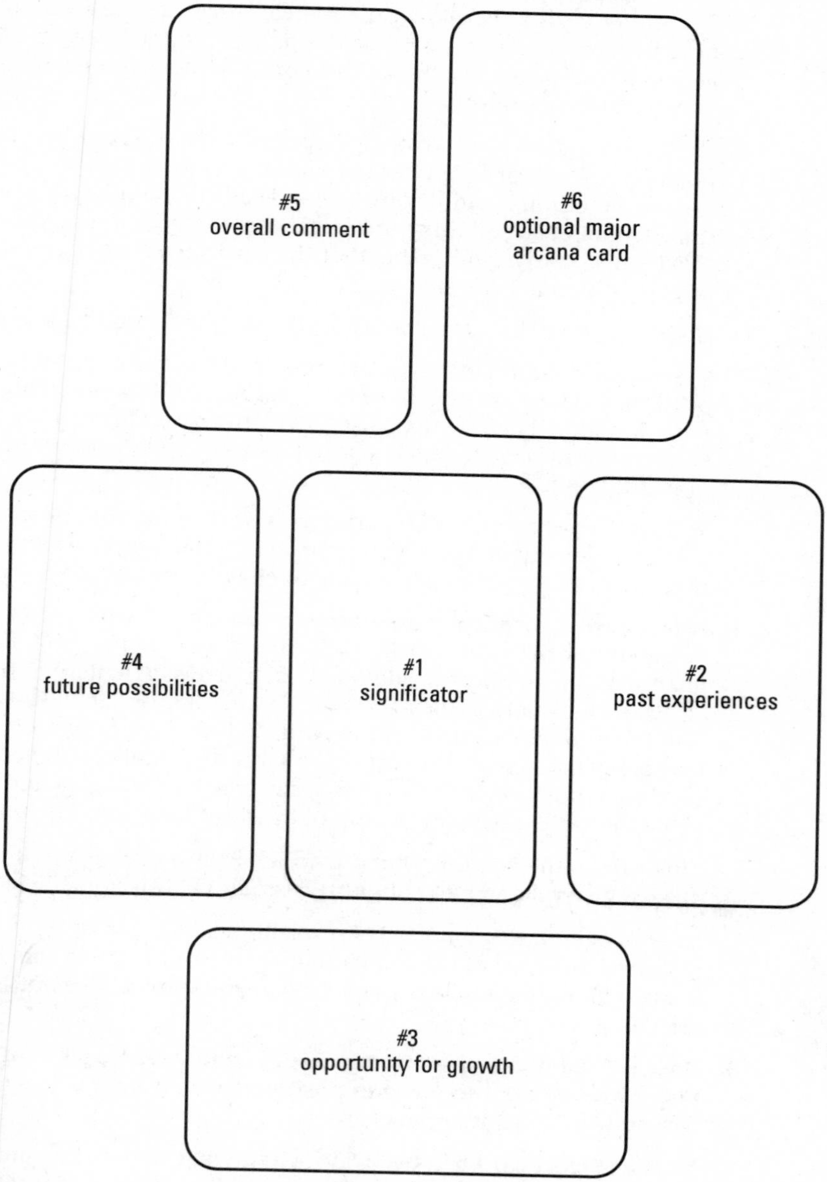

#5
overall comment

#6
optional major
arcana card

#4
future possibilities

#1
significator

#2
past experiences

#3
opportunity for growth

Figure 13-1:
Amber's All-
Purpose
Tarot
Spread.

5. **Turn over card 2.** Turn over the top card from the deck and place it in position 2. Remember, instead of flipping the cards over, turn the cards as you'd turn pages in a book. This card signifies your *past experiences* in regard to your question.

6. **Turn over card 3.** Turn over the top card from the deck and place it in position 3. This card signifies the *opportunity for growth* — spiritual, mental, emotional, and/or physical — that's being offered by your situation. I sometimes call this the *karmic knot* that you're untying. I place this card sideways, indicating that the card shows what you're growing or going through.

No matter how this card comes up, it's read in an *upright* position.

7. **Turn over card 4.** Turn over the top card from the deck and place it in position 4. This card signifies *future possibilities* that are being offered by your situation. I can't emphasize the word *possibilities* enough. The card shows your future tendencies based on what you've done and are presently doing.

You are a co-creator, meaning that you work along with divinity and nature. If you change how you're presently thinking and what you're presently doing, you *might* be able to change the future.

8. **Select card 5 by adding the numbers associated with cards 1 through 4.** Except for the court cards, each card has a number on it. If you are unsure of the numbers, or if you choose to assign a number to the court cards, turn back to Tables 10-1 and 10-2 in Chapter 10 for these listings. Add the numbers from all of the cards in the spread together, then count that many cards from the top of the tarot deck and place the card you stop on in position 5. For example, say cards 1 through 4 add up to 18; place the 18th card from the top of the tarot deck into position 5.

This card is the *overall comment,* which is interpreted as, "If you could make a general comment about this situation, this is it."

Instead of counting out cards for position 5, you can opt to use the major arcana card of the *same* number for your total. In this instance, 18 is the major arcana's The Moon card. If you want to use both cards, see step 9.

9. **If card 5 is not a major arcana card, you have the option of choosing a major arcana card to place in position 6.** Many people like to end their spread with a major arcana card.

You can select card 6 in two ways. First, you can use the number you arrived at in step 8 (for example, 18) and find the major arcana card associated with that number (for example, The Moon).

The major arcana contains 22 cards. (Although it is numbered 0, numerologists regard card 22 to be The Fool.) If you get a number over 22 in step 8, add its digits together to get a usable number for step 9. For instance, if you get the number 48 in step 8, add together 4 + 8 to get 12.

A second way to select card 6 is to use either your soul, personality, year, or day card, which Chapter 10 can help you find.

Because card 6 is optional, some people will start a layout without it. If you do this but find that the spread just doesn't feel complete, don't hesitate to add card 6 or pull a *clarity card* (a card that isn't part of the spread but can help clarify the question at hand).

10. **Look at the image on each card.** Consider how it might feel to be the person on that card, in that situation. If you'd like, write out or tape record your impressions — the thoughts and feelings you have about the image. (Doing this when getting to know the cards can really benefit your long-term understanding.)

Pay attention! In addition to noting your overall sense of the card, note the card's colors and symbols (such as plants or animals), the look on a person's face, and the way that person holds his or her body. These elements might key you into other important ideas.

If you're doing the spread for another person, involve him or her in this process. After all, it's that person's reading!

11. **Locate each card in Chapter 7, 8, or 9 of this book and add any interpretations that jump out at you.**

12. **After reading each card individually and according to its position in the spread, look at all of the cards together.** I call this "putting the story together." Each card is like a sentence in a story; together you get the whole story. What does this story suggest about your question?

13. **Create an affirmation about the attitude you're intending to take from this reading into your life situation.** See Chapter 12 for a discussion of affirmations. Repeat or write out this supportive self-talk reminding you of your intention.

Sample spread

Derrick asks, "Spirit of the tarot, what's the best way for me to go about getting a job promotion for the greatest good of myself and my family?" Derrick lays out the cards shown in Figure 13-2.

#5: Eight of Cups

#6: The Star

#4: The Magician

#1: Eight of Pentacles

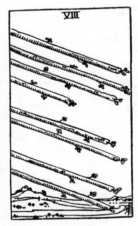

#2: Eight of Wands

Figure 13-2:
An example
of Amber's
All-Purpose
Tarot
Spread.

#3: Knight of Swords

Derrick interprets each card according to his first thoughts and feelings, the card's position in the spread, and the ideas prompted by the interpretations in Chapters 7, 8, and 9:

✔ **Card 1 (significator): Eight of Pentacles.** "I picked this card because, like the man in the card, I'm doing the same job over and over again. I've got it down and I'm bored doing it."

✔ **Card 2 (past experiences): Eight of Wands.** "I've put a lot of energy into trying to get a promotion so I can do something new and make more money for my time. I'm willing to work a different shift. I've been teaching a new employee about my job. I keep asking for more responsibilities. I've even sent my resume to another company."

✔ **Card 3 (opportunity for growth): Knight of Swords.** "He looks like he's in a big hurry. I'm a quick learner. My manager promised me a promotion by winter and now it's spring. I keep reminding him, and he keeps telling me I'm doing great work, but that I need to be patient. Patience is not one of my strengths. The whole technology industry is experiencing a slowdown. I have friends who've been laid off. I guess I should be happy I've got a job. But I'm bored out of my gourd."

✔ **Card 4 (future possibilities): The Magician.** "Okay, The Magician. Making magic. The magician sets his mind on something and manifests it. I've set my mind on a promotion. It's off somewhere in my future. Yes, things come in their time, not mine. Maybe I should find some outside activity that brings some magic into my life."

✔ **Card 5 (overall comment): Eight of Cups.** The numbers on cards 1 through 4 add up to 17. (Derrick chooses not to assign the Knight of Swords a number, and The Magician is card number one in the major arcana.) Derrick counts out 17 cards from the top of the deck and turns over the Eight of Cups.

"Looks like I should take my vacation now. As my daughter would say, 'Dad, chill.' I think I need to chill out, or else I'm going to burn out."

✔ **Card 6 (optional major arcana card): The Star.** The Star card is the 17th card in the major arcana.

"Stars mean hope, so I guess there's hope for me. The woman is on her knee. I need to surrender to reality."

✔ **Putting it all together:** "The reason I'm not getting promoted has to do with the state of the industry, not with the state of my skills. I can be so ego-centered. I'm not going to stop looking for another job — but only after a good vacation. I'm going to do it in a different frame of mind — one that's more detached and realistic."

✔ **Creating an affirmation:** Derrick states, "I will get promoted or find a better job at exactly the right time."

When the same number or court card appears more than once, it's a signal to pay attention. Derrick has three eights in his spread: the Eight of Pentacles, Eight of Wands, and Eight of Cups. The Star, the 17th card in the major arcana, reduces to an eight (1 + 7 = 8) as well! I'd suggest that Derrick pull out Strength, the eighth card from major arcana, for further insight. If Derrick had three or four Knights, I'd suggest that he carefully study the qualities they have in common.

Between Extremes Spread

Although I don't advise using the tarot cards for answering yes or no questions, this spread allows the tarot to offer some balanced insight into your decision making. For example, maybe you want to ask, "Would it be in my best interest to enroll in school for an advanced degree, or continue working?" You put down one card for enrolling in school, a second card for continue working, and a third for another possibility. This spread offers a look at what your choices now look like, plus another possibility.

Laying out the cards

This spread is different than most because it's *your* job to name the positions for the cards; the choices you consider determine what each card signifies. The layout of this spread is shown in Figure 13-3.

#2	#3	#1
choice two	new possibility	choice one

Figure 13-3:
The Between Extremes Spread.

Follow these steps for laying out the Between Extremes Spread:

1. **Frame your question.**

2. **Take several deep breaths and ask for guidance and direction.**

3. **Mix or shuffle the cards in whatever way works for you.** (See Chapter 11 for tips.) While mixing, mentally repeat your question.

4. **Turn over card 1, which signifies what your first choice looks like.** In the example we're working with, the first choice is enrolling in school.

5. **Turn over card 2, which signifies what your second choice looks like.** In our example, continuing to work is the second choice.

6. **Turn over card 3, symbolizing what your new possibility looks like.**

When I say "turn over the cards," I mean pick the card from the top of the deck after it's mixed. It also works to divide the deck into as many piles as there are positions in a spread, turning over the top card from each pile for each position. This method is demonstrated in the sample spread that follows. By the way, I have a student who makes piles for the positions, but then picks a card from *anywhere* in each pile to fill them.

There are many different ways of laying out and turning over the cards. Over time, you will surely find those that suit you!

7. **Interpret the meanings of the three cards.** See the section "Interpreting a spread's meaning" earlier in the chapter.

8. **After reading each card individually and according to its position in the spread, put your story together.** Each card is like a sentence in a story; together you get the whole story. What does your story suggest about your question?

9. **Consider creating an affirmation about the attitude you're intending to take from the reading into your life situation.** Repeat or write out this supportive self-talk reminding you of your intention.

Sample spread

The following is an example of this unique tarot spread in action.

Samantha asks, "Dear Higher Self, is it in the best interest of all concerned that I start a family or continue developing my career in the coming year?"

Before mixing the cards, Sam assigns a meaning for each position.

✔ Card 1: What continuing my career presently looks like.

✔ Card 2: What starting a family presently looks like.

✔ Card 3: A new possibility, the middle ground between cards 1 and 2.

After mixing, Sam divides the deck into three piles. She draws a card off the top of the first pile and places it in position number one. She does likewise for the two remaining positions.

Sam interprets each card according to her first thoughts and feelings, the card's position in the spread, and the ideas prompted by the interpretations in Chapters 7, 8, and 9:

- ✔ **Card 1 (continuing her career): Justice.** "Since my boss got unjustly fired and I was reassigned, I've been feeling like everything's off balance. So, I've been thinking about other options. I love the company, but don't like my new job. So, I'm thinking about starting a family. I even went to the doctor to be sure I'm healthy."

- ✔ **Card 2 (starting a family): Two of Swords.** "Here, I am undecided. I don't know if I'll ever really be ready to start a family. But I'm thinking it would be a way out of my job. Yes, I know that's not the best reason for having children."

- ✔ **Card 3 (new possibility/balance between cards 1 and 2): The Fool.** "Great, The Fool! I'm dying for an adventure alright. But do I really want to go off the cliff into God only knows what? (I guess I do that every morning when I get out of bed.) The card is telling me that whatever I choose will be a journey that will end up okay in the end. I guess it's gonna depend on my attitude towards what I do and what comes from it.

- ✔ **Creating an affirmation:** Samantha creates the following affirmation to remind her of her intention: "I'm resolving my negative feelings about work, and by doing so I'm getting my life into a better balance."

Next, Samantha puts together her story:

"Yeah, I'm feeling pretty upset about my job — I've got tons of anger at the company that needs dealing with. Being angry isn't a good reason for fleeing work and starting a family, especially when I'd really like to do some traveling first. My husband and I have been planning on going to Africa and Asia next summer. I can just imagine dragging around a backpack in my third trimester — right! I think I'd best stay put and work through my work drama for now. Hey, maybe I'll feel more ready for a family after my work situation's resolved and we take our trip."

Psychological Spread

A tarot student who was finishing grad school in psychology showed me this spread. It's meant to help you look at an issue or problematic situation from three different psychological viewpoints:

    ✔ **Your subconscious or child self.** How you instinctively feel, view, and respond to life. Your natural and/or automatic responses in regard to your question.

    ✔ **Your conscious or adult self.** How your personality or ego views and responds to life. Your conscious thought-out responses to your question.

    ✔ **Your superconscious or wise self.** How your higher soul, spirit, Self views and responds to life. Your intuitive responses.

This spread offers you a broader perspective of, and possibly insight into, your situation.

Laying out the cards

The positions of the cards in this spread are shown in Figure 13-4.

Follow these steps for laying out the Psychological Spread:

1. **Frame your question.**

2. **Take several deep breaths and ask for guidance and direction.**

3. **Mix or shuffle the cards in whatever way works for you.** (See Chapter 11 for tips.) While mixing, mentally repeat your question.

4. **Lay out cards 1 through 4 in the positions shown in Figure 13-4.** Again, you may do this either by turning over the first card from the top of the deck, by dividing the deck into three piles (one for each card that you will be pulling and selecting from the top of each pile for each position), or by any other way that suits you.

5. **Interpret the meanings of the four cards.** See the section "Interpreting a spread's meaning" earlier in the chapter.

6. **After reading each card individually and according to its position in the spread, put your story together.** Each card is like a sentence in a story; together you get the whole story. What does your story suggest about your question?

7. **Consider creating an affirmation about the attitude you're intending to take from the reading into your life situation.** Repeat or write out this supportive self-talk reminding you of your intention.

Sample spread

This section gives you an example of the Psychological Spread at work.

Elliot asks, "How might I handle my discomfort about meeting my girlfriend Sue's family for the greatest good of everyone concerned?"

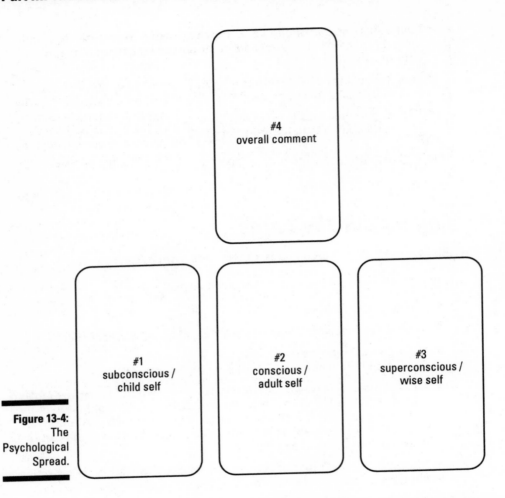

#4
overall comment

#1
subconscious /
child self

#2
conscious /
adult self

#3
superconscious /
wise self

Figure 13-4:
The
Psychological
Spread.

Elliot interprets each card according to his first thoughts and feelings, the card's position in the spread, and the ideas prompted by the interpretations in Chapters 7, 8, and 9:

- ✔ **Card 1 (subconscious): Three of Swords.** "I grew up in family of college professors, but preferred working with my hands to school. My family has put down my work as a carpenter and cabinetmaker. I feel hurt and sad, and wish my parents could understand me. I'm extra nervous because the last time I met a girlfriend's family I tried being someone I wasn't and it led to us breaking up."

- ✔ **Card 2 (conscious): Ten of Wands.** "I see myself putting down the heavy burden of being so concerned about what others think of me. I am who I am. Sue loves me and thinks enough of me just as I am to bring me home. I really want my discomfort to end."

✔ **Card 3 (superconscious): The Hermit in reverse.** Elliot feels stumped, so he turns back to Chapter 7 of this book for some ideas. The following jump out at him: "Are you concerned about fitting into the world? What lesson are you assimilating? Is there some way you can shine your light without being attached to whether or not others can see it?"

Elliot realizes, "I've been concerned about fitting into the world of my parents and now Sue's parents. I'm assimilating the lesson that I am a good and worthwhile person, although I don't have any college degrees. I'm going to let my light shine and trust that her parents can see it. I'm alright for Sue, and I'm on the right track for me."

✔ **Card 4 (overall comment): The Lovers.** As explained under Step 5 in the all-purpose spread, instead of counting out cards from the top of the deck, you have the option of putting a major arcana card in this position. Elliot opts to go for the major arcana card. Adding up the numbers on all of the cards in his spread, Elliot gets the number 24. Because there are only 22 cards in the major arcana, he reduces this number by adding 2 + 4 = 6 and gets The Lovers as his overall comment card.

Elliot thinks, "Yes, this love relationship with Sue's giving me a chance to heal my feelings of sadness and inferiority."

✔ **Putting it all together:** "It looks as if I have the opportunity to be in a better relationship with not only Sue, but with myself. If that isn't great, I don't know what is."

✔ **Creating an affirmation:** Elliot composes the following affirmation: "I deserve to be loved for who I am."

Astrological Spread

Before trying this spread, you may want to read Chapter 16 about astrology and the tarot.

The zodiac is divided into 12 *houses*. Each house is connected with a different department, or area of your life. The Astrological Spread is a simple way of gaining insight about the kind of learning you're doing in these areas.

Picking cards

To do this spread, first read through the list of 12 zodiac houses:

✔ **House One:** Your birth and new experiences. Your general health and physical vitality. Illnesses you might be prone to.

✔ **House Two:** Your money. How you earn, handle, and acquire money, property, and material comforts. What you value most in life.

- **House Three:** Your communication. How you think, communicate, express yourself, and maintain relationships — through writing, visiting, traveling, e-mailing, and phoning. Contact with your immediate family, especially brothers and sisters.

- **House Four:** Your home life. How you've been nurtured and what you need to feel secure. Your home life, parents, and environments in early childhood and at life's end.

- **House Five:** Your love life. Romance. Creative self-expression through work, hobbies, children, or mentoring others.

- **House Six:** Your service to others. Community service, jobs, paid and unpaid responsibilities, and people who work for or with you. Interests in health and healing of yourself, others, and the environment.

- **House Seven:** Your one-on-one relationships. Your general attitude toward relationships, from marriage to business partners. How you work and live in harmony with the people in these relationships.

- **House Eight:** Your attitudes toward sex, power, and death/transformation. Money or inheritances that you do or don't receive.

- **House Nine:** Your attitudes toward expanding your horizons and developing your mind through international travel, religion, philosophy, science, and education.

- **House Ten:** Your ambitions and career, and the challenges that accompany these. How you relate to authority figures. What others think of you.

- **House Eleven:** Your friends and acquaintances. People who support you realizing your ambitions. Your relationships with groups of people. Humanitarian activities.

- **House Twelve:** Your spiritual development. The private or secret side of your life. Fears and sacrifices.

Select one or more houses that match the department(s) you'd like to look into.

Next, frame a question for each house that you're interested in. Mix and cut the cards (see Chapter 11). For each house that you're asking about, draw one card from the face-down deck. Interpret each card as it relates to the meaning of the house in question.

Sample spread

Because Gabrielle's having an especially difficult time communicating with her sister and mother, she wants to look at House Three — communication.

Gabrielle asks, "Dear Mother Goddess, What's the best way for me to improve communications with my sister and mother for our greatest good?"

After asking for guidance and direction and mixing the cards, Gabrielle turns over the Three of Cups. She is flabbergasted! The picture on the card shows *exactly* what she wants but isn't getting! She focuses in on the card for a bit and then comes to a realization:

> "I've been living in the United States for years and my family lives in France. Because I've been avoiding my domineering and controlling father, I haven't communicated very much — you know, birthdays and Christmas and phone calls once in a blue moon, but not much more than that. Now that papa's died, new possibilities are opening."

After a while, Gabrielle starts understanding that rekindling closeness isn't going to happen overnight. She also realizes that being pushy or childish and needy won't work, but being more available and involved in family life will. Gabrielle tearfully admits, "I'm just like dear old papa, I want to control the situation and everyone in it." Gabrielle resolves to attend her sister's fortieth birthday party in France next month. The outlook is promising.

For a variation on this spread, do it on your birthday and lay out cards for all 12 houses. Interpret them as the type of learning that might be coming your way in the different departments of your life in the coming year.

Relationship Spread

This spread is designed to be done with, or for, two people. It offers you and your partner views of yourselves as individuals and partners, with regard to a question involving your relationship.

Although the Relationship Spread was designed for two people, it can be used for groups. To do this, you'd add another column of cards for each person involved. Of course, each person must participate.

Laying out the cards

The layout of this spread is shown in Figure 13-5.

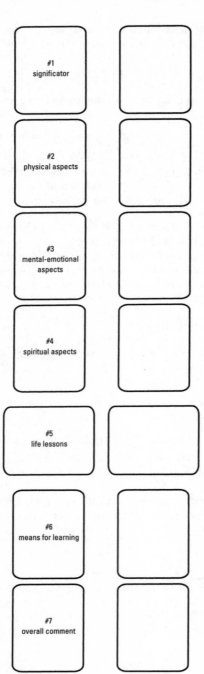

Follow these steps to lay out the cards for the Relationship Spread:

1. **Frame your question.**

2. **Take several deep breaths and ask for guidance and direction.**

3. **Mix or shuffle the cards in whatever way works for you.** (See Chapter 11 for tips.) While mixing, mentally repeat your question.

4. **Each person turns over cards 1 through 7 and lays them out in columns.** The two columns of cards are laid out next to each other.

   Card 1 is the significator. You and your partner each select a card that represents you, as explained in the section on "Amber's All-Purpose Tarot Spread." The significator cards can also be your soul cards (see Chapter 10), or you and your partner can agree upon a single card to represent you both.

   Card 2 signifies the physical aspects of you and your partner in regard to your question.

   Card 3 signifies the mental–emotional aspects of you and your partner in regard to your question.

   Card 4 signifies the spiritual aspects of you and your partner in regard to your question.

   Card 5 signifies the life lessons being learned through your relationship in regard to your question. This card is placed sideways, indicating what you're growing or going through.

   Card 6 signifies the means for you and your partner to learn the lessons suggested by Card 5.

   Card 7 is the overall comment on the spread/relationship. It can be a single card selected by summing up the numbers of all cards in both columns, or each person can select a card by totaling the numbers on their separate cards.

5. **Interpret the meanings of the seven cards in each column.** See the section "Interpreting a spread's meaning" earlier in the chapter.

6. **After reading each card individually, put your story together.** Each card is like a sentence in a story; together you get the whole story. What does your story suggest about your question?

7. **Consider creating an affirmation about the attitude you're intending to take from the reading into your life situation.** Repeat or write out this supportive self-talk reminding you of your intention. Each partner can create an individual affirmation, or both can work together to create a single affirmation.

Sample spread

Jenny and John have been married almost 30 years. Their children are grown and well into their own lives. Now Jenny would like to be living more simply and working part time. John, who enjoys spending money and taking expensive vacations, keeps pressuring her to stay at her very stressful but high paying job for "a few more years." Jenny, who between working and commuting is away from home 14 hours a day, does not see an end in sight.

The couple agrees to work on the following question: "What's the best way for us to come to terms with our desires for different lifestyles for our greatest good and the greatest good of our relationship?" Here are John and Jenny's cards:

- ✔ **Card 1 (the significator): Two of Cups.** After going back and forth about whether to use their soul cards, The Empress and The Hierophant, Jenny and John decide on the Two of Cups, because "it looks like the two people really like each other and are open to making an agreement. That's us."

- ✔ **Card 2 (physical)**

  Jenny turns over the **Eight of Swords:** "I feel like I'm living in a prison. I feel like I'm trapped into running a maze every day. Yes, I see the gate's open, but I'm blindfolded. I'm just going to have to feel my way out."

  John turns over the **King of Pentacles:** "I grew up in poverty, I like living in luxury. I like being the king of my castle."

- ✔ **Card 3 (mental/emotional)**

  Jenny gets the **Six of Cups:** "I feel like I'm a little girl waiting for my Daddy to give me a present, my freedom."

  John gets the **Six of Pentacles:** "My brothers and sisters and I had to take care of my mother because dad's illness wiped out their retirement. I don't want my children or anyone else to stop living their lives to take care of us."

- ✔ **Card 4 (spiritual)**

  Jenny draws the **Four of Swords:** "Something deep inside keeps telling me I'm going to get sick and not be able to enjoy retirement if I keep having to go at this fast and furious pace. I really need a break, and not just a week off."

  John pulls **The Devil:** "Whoa, I'll admit I've been making money and physical pleasure a kind of God. But I've had so many years of taking care of other people, I just want to indulge myself before I'm too old to enjoy."

✔ **Card 5 (life lessons)**

Jenny turns over the **Ace of Wands:** "As uncomfortable as it is, I'm think-ing I need to be more assertive about what makes me happy. I must set a limit on how much longer I'm going to work like this, rather than wait for John to give me permission.

"I know what our financial situation is, and we're fine. If we do about a third less spending and don't go first class all of the time, my working part time will work. Hey, I can go coach and John can travel first class. With his long legs, he really needs the leg room."

John selects the **Seven of Cups:** "That's me alright. I want it all! But I want Jenny too. And if she's so unhappy, I'm willing to make some adjustments."

✔ **Card 6 (the means for learning the life lessons)**

Jenny turns over **The Empress:** "The Empress is my soul card. I need to treat myself with respect. I need to create a more nurturing life for myself, one that isn't as wrapped around working and making money as it now is."

John gets the **Ten of Cups.** "I really want to feel how the people in the card look — content with the simple things in life. We're going to have our second grandchild next winter. I love playing grandpa. I guess I want to have more and more money, because I also want to give more and more to the family I love.

"Maybe it's time to start giving right now, by supporting Jenny to cut back like she wants to. Hey, maybe I'll slow down some too. Perhaps I'll be able to feel more relaxed at home and need fewer vacations."

✔ **Card 7 (overall comment): The Chariot.** Jenny and John agree that The Chariot card puts their story together for them.

Jenny begins, "Marriage is sometimes about making compromises. If horses are pulling in different directions at once, a chariot gets torn apart."

John adds, "We've definitely been pulling in different directions. Now we're going to be working together. I think we're already heading toward a better relationship."

✔ **Creating an affirmation:** Jenny and John create affirmations to keep their purpose at the forefront of their minds.

Jenny says, "I feel good taking control of my life."

John says, "I think I'll use my soul card, Justice, for this. I enjoy living a more balanced lifestyle."

The Chakra Spread

Your chakras are ever-active psychic or subtle energy centers. The word *chakra* is Sanskrit for "wheel." The Ageless Wisdom of the tarot proposes that everything comes from, and returns to, spirit. The chakras are wheels or vortexes of energy that spin clockwise and counterclockwise simultaneously. Originating from your spiritual Self, their energies pass through your mental and emotional bodies to your physical body, then cycle back to your spiritual body.

As you live, your life energy moves through your chakras. This movement results in different states of awareness. (This explains in part why some people believe all physical imbalances and diseases are spiritual in origin.) Some psychics and intuitives use the chakras for "reading" the body's energy systems. In this section, I show you how to do something similar, using the tarot.

The Chakra Spread can help you focus on how you're responding "energetically" to a particular life change or situation. Because it helps you to see yourself more clearly, looking at your chakras through the tarot cards can assist problem solving and introspection.

The chakras

Before I explain the spread itself, here is an overview of the seven chakras. For each, I explain the position of the chakra in the body, the parts of the self that the chakra influences, the kingdom on the Qabalistic Tree of Life that the chakra relates to (see Chapter 15), and what aspects of your mind, body, and spirit the chakra is linked with.

- **Root Chakra** *(Mudlahara)*. Situated at the base of your spine, between your sexual organs and rectum, the root chakra influences your feet and organs of elimination. It is associated with the sphere of Kingdom on the Qabalistic Tree of Life.

  This chakra is linked with your need for grounding or physical security — how you meet your basic physical needs; establishing and regulating your basic behavior patterns associated with survival (working, eating, sleeping); connecting with your physical surroundings and body; how well you accept and work with and within the limits of the world and society; and awareness that your physical body is a tool for doing spiritual work.

- **Procreative Chakra** *(Svadhisthana)*. Situated below your navel, this chakra influences your sex glands and sex organs. It goes with the sphere of Foundation on the Qabalistic Tree of Life.

This chakra is coupled with your sex drive — your biological drive for living and procreating — because after you've got the basics down (whew!), you start having other desires. It is linked with imagining the forms these pleasures may take. It is also linked with using "the drive to survive" for procreation, as well as for bringing your "other children," your dreams and desires (creative inspirations), into the world.

✔ **Solar Plexus Chakra (Manipura).** Situated (appropriately enough) at your solar plexus, the area of the abdomen just below your sternum, your solar plexus chakra influences your digestive organs, hips, and legs. It goes with the spheres of Victory and Splendor on the Qabalistic Tree of Life.

This chakra corresponds with developing your personality/ego and identification in the world: attending to gaining personal power and recognition, and satisfying your plans, dreams, and desires, with little or no thought about if and how your actions might impact others.

✔ **Heart Chakra (Anahata).** Situated at the middle of your chest, this chakra influences your heart and lungs. It goes with the sphere of Beauty on the Qabalistic Tree of Life.

This chakra is connected with unconditional love; selflessness, spiritual devotion, and bliss; awareness of your role in life and the potential power of your actions; and your motivation to live a balanced life.

✔ **Throat Chakra (Visuddha).** Situated at your throat, this chakra influences your organs of speech and hearing, thyroid gland, shoulders, and arms. It goes with the spheres of Mercy, Severity, and Knowledge on the Qabalistic Tree of Life.

This chakra is associated with walking your talk — integrating and creatively expressing your knowledge of higher truth through your values and actions — and receiving communication and communicating to others.

✔ **Brow Chakra/"Third Eye" (Ajna).** Situated at the space between your eyebrows, this chakra influences your pineal gland, left brain (intellect), and right brain (intuition and psychic perceptions). It goes with the spheres of Wisdom and Understanding on the Qabalistic Tree of Life.

This chakra is paired with your insight (wisdom) and foresight (inner knowingness); the past and present coming together; and non-dualistic consciousness, infinite perception, and truth.

✔ **Crown Chakra (Sahasrar).** Situated at the crown of your head, or just a bit above, this chakra influences your connection with the divine (your higher soul, spirit, Self) — your impersonal and infinite reality. It goes with the sphere of The Crown on the Qabalistic Tree of Life.

This chakra is conjoined with effortlessly opening and subordinating your personal will to divine will; letting go and letting God (because it's the only way to go); the higher soul, spirit, Self within; impersonal cosmic energy entering and becoming personal energy for you; and personal energy exiting and becoming impersonal cosmic energy.

Laying out the cards

1. **Frame your question.**

2. **Take several deep breaths and ask for guidance and direction.**

3. **Mix or shuffle the cards in whatever way works for you.** (See Chapter 11 for tips.) While mixing, mentally repeat your question.

4. **Turn over seven cards, one to correspond with each chakra.**

   Card 1 (root chakra) signifies the security issues underlying your situation, the physical energies beneath and behind things.

   Card 2 (procreative chakra) signifies the energy and inspiration to create, the creative energies available to you.

   Card 3 (solar plexus chakra) signifies the personal acknowledgement, gratification, renown, or satisfaction you're seeking from this situation.

   Card 4 (heart chakra) signifies the love, devotion, and/or duty that is motivating you or this situation.

   Card 5 (throat chakra) signifies how this situation is offering you the opportunity to creatively express higher knowledge and wisdom.

   Card 6 (brow chakra) signifies the highest truth (and your intuition) about this situation.

   Card 7 (crown chakra) signifies how this situation is connecting you with your higher soul, spirit, Self.

5. **Interpret the meanings of the seven cards.** See the section "Interpreting a spread's meaning" earlier in the chapter.

6. **After reading each card individually, put your story together.** Each card is like a sentence in a story; together you get the whole story. What does your story suggest about your question?

7. **Consider creating an affirmation about the attitude you're intending to take from the reading into your life situation.** Repeat or write out this supportive self-talk reminding you of your intention.

Sample spread

When Hungry Minds, Inc. offered me the chance to write this book, I wanted to consult the tarot for a look-see at the project. Contemplating the various spreads I might use, I decided on Chakra Spread because I believed it could provide the most complete picture of how my energies were responding to the possibility of undertaking the book.

First, I framed my question: "Dear higher Self, please reveal if it's for the greatest good of all concerned — me, my publisher, and potential readers — to be the vehicle for bringing *Tarot For Dummies* into the world at this time." I then pulled seven cards.

- ✔ **Card 1 (root chakra): The Empress.** Over the years, I've learned that I can't push Mother Nature — things grow in the garden of The Empress in *their* time and season, not mine. I have had a secret desire to write a mainstream book about the tarot for years. The Empress helped me to reflect on this desire. Because the offer was now in my hand, the time might finally be ripe.

  The chakra and card's connections with physical security made me consider that the book would be paying me a living wage while I write it — something that's the exception rather than the rule for most writers. But the four-and-a-half-month timeline would necessitate my cutting one class from my upcoming teaching schedule, which would disappoint my students.

  The link The Empress has with creative imagination gave me a glimpse of myself getting inspired by a fun-filled writing style. She also made me take another look at my old tendency to overextend myself due to the desire to do everything, all of the time!

- ✔ **Card 2 (procreative chakra): The Seven of Cups, reversed.** The card reminded me how, as soon as this project came across my desk, I was flooded with ideas — the entire outline came through while taking a shower early one Sunday morning. I immediately recognized that to gain the focus and energy needed, I'd be streamlining both my work and social schedules.

  The card also got me thinking about how every dream or project has its limitations. Writing this book meant that I'd be putting a couple of other projects on hold, something I might later regret.

- ✔ **Card 3 (solar plexus chakra): The Hierophant, reversed.** The word *hierophant* means "revealer of sacred things within." Yes, I'd be getting the satisfaction of turning people on to the tarot and showing them ways they can tune into the cards. As the writer, I'm the person whom the book would come through — the so-called "authority" on the subject. Yet one of the main purposes of the tarot is to inspire and empower every person to be their own authority, one of the esoteric or hidden meanings of The Hierophant (and quite likely why the card came up reversed). I'd be emphasizing that readers should listen to their conscience — they have the final say on what's the best behavior for themselves.

  The Hierophant is connected with the sense of hearing. This got me thinking that I'd be getting input and directions from editors who are more experienced with writing this particular type of book. Am I receptive to learning new ways of writing? I'd also be getting input and direction from editors who know little or nothing about the tarot. Can I be receptive to their questions?

The Hierophant is synonymous with intuition. Writing *Tarot For Dummies* has the potential to be an exciting opportunity for me to tune into my intuition and inner direction in new ways.

✔ **Card 4 (heart chakra): Three of Pentacles.** The card shows me the artist and her patrons. I see the publisher and my agent showing me their design or contract and my needing to follow it. Yes, Hungry Minds and my agent, Bill, are acting as my patrons — they're expressing their support for the tarot and me by contracting me to bring the tarot to readers through this book. Yes, this is going to be a cooperative venture.

The image shows me how much I love my work and that I'm dedicated to producing the best work I can. The card reminds me of my gratitude for coming into a relationship with the tarot. The image helps me look at the service I've been doing, and want to continue doing, in the name of the tarot's Ageless Wisdom.

Because this is a four-and-a-half-month project, concerns about my perfectionist standards come up. Continuing to look at the card, I notice the triangle at the top of the card. It reminds me of the top three spheres, or Divine Triad, on the Qabalistic Tree of Life. Automatically, the words "let go and let God" come through my mind.

✔ **Card 5 (throat chakra): Knight of Cups.** The knight holding his cup makes me think of offerings. I recognize how writing *Tarot For Dummies* will offer the tarot to a group of readers who might find it unapproachable in another type of book. It helps me see the opportunity I'm being offered and the opportunity I will be offering to others.

The image prompts me to recall that I'm someone who follows her dreams. I've been dreaming of doing a book like this for years.

Finally, the active knight reminds me of the importance of balancing all the hours of sitting and writing with physical exercise. I'm recuperating from a back injury, and continuing my rehab will make completing the book without a setback probable.

✔ **Card 6 (brow chakra): The Devil, reversed.** The Devil makes me think that *Tarot For Dummies* has the potential of dispelling some of the bad press and satanic energy associated with the cards. The Devil is also about small-mindedness. I'm getting the chance to communicate that the tarot is a powerful tool that can help you step away from self-limiting views of yourself and life, and see from a more expansive view.

I absolutely must give up any thought of controlling what readers might think of and do with the book — readers will do what they're ready and able to do, and that's that.

Certain people will "dis" me for writing "such a mundane book." Unfortunately, these folks don't recall that no matter how mundane a teaching seems, the mystic perceives the mystical at its core.

Finally, *Tarot For Dummies* encourages me to poke fun at my own learning process and humanness — essential for learning any new subject.

✔ **Card 7 (crown chakra): Wheel of Fortune.** Whatever may come from writing *Tarot For Dummies* — fortune or misfortune — is up to *my* perception. I am acutely aware of fortunate circumstances becoming unfortunate and unfortunate circumstances turning out great.

The card jars my memory — the Qabalistic Tarot calls the Wheel of Fortune the Rewarding Intelligence. I guess I'm getting rewarded for my years of tarot study and practice, as well as for writing the book's outline. The other reward, surely the greater of the two, is my being paid to keep the tarot's teachings at the forefront of my mind.

There's a time for every season. The seeds for writing *Tarot For Dummies* were planted long ago — back to The Empress card. The wheel has turned. It looks like spring is here and my seeds are sprouting.

✔ **Putting the story together:** After reviewing the cards, I put the story together. My heart tells me, if you can write *Tarot For Dummies* without an attachment to what becomes of it or any aversion to the work that lies ahead, get to work. I decided to sleep on it.

✔ **Creating my affirmation:** Along with the decision to start writing, the morning brings the following affirmation, "I can write *Tarot For Dummies* without being attached to the book's success or harboring any aversion to the work the book entails — I'm willing to do my best and Most High will help me do the rest."

Tarot Games

The following activities give you a chance to get to know the tarot, and yourself, a bit better.

For you

Go through the deck and select four cards that you like the least. Note why you don't like them. Now see if you can find something likable in each card.

Next, go through the deck and select four cards that you like the most. Note why you like them. Now see if you can find something unlikable in each card.

For two

Two or more participants can take turns doing one of the following activities:

- ✔ Go though the deck and select four to six cards that you think depict yourself. Talk about why these cards depict you.

- ✔ Go through the deck and select four to six cards that you think represent the person you're playing with. Give those cards to the other person. The person who gets the cards explains why he or she has received each card. Ask if that person would like to hear your comments about why those cards fit him or her. If so, share your comments, and if not, remain quiet. Next, have the other person select cards that represent you, and go through the same steps in reverse.

For any number of you

The following can help you look at the possibilities different situations offer. You draw a card for each possibility. Remember: A possibility is what *might* — may or may not — happen, not what *will* happen.

For example, you may ask, "How might vacationing in Mexico, Costa Rica, or Hawaii during late summer be?" You then pull a card for each location.

The cards reflect what's going on now and, based on this, what might be going on at another time. My friend Bess used this method for selecting her vacation spot. When the card for Hawaii looked the best, she made reservations for Kauai. Little did she know that two months later Hurricane Inniki would hit Kauai, wrecking both her vacation and the island!

This little tarot exercise offers you an essential lesson. When asking questions of the tarot, it's oh so important to remember how frequently things, such as weather conditions in Kauai and personal attitudes, are subject to change. It's essential that you allow room for this and the unexpected, what I call "divine intervention," to occur.

Getting a Professional Tarot Reading

If you haven't already had a professional tarot reading, it might be interesting to have one. Or, if you have already done so, now that you know more about the tarot, it might be worthwhile to have another.

Finding a reader

One of the best ways to find a reader is by word of mouth. If this doesn't work, try the Yellow Pages, local entertainment guides, spiritually-oriented newspapers, or community newspapers for ads.

Interviewing

I suggest talking with the reader *before* making an appointment. Doing this can help you decide if the reader's right for you. Some readers are willing to do this, others are not. For some, "time is money," and they charge for any time they spend talking with a client or potential client. I wouldn't recommend making an appointment without being able to interview the reader first.

If you select a tarot hotline, you're randomly assigned a reader. You can get around this by having a friend recommend a particular reader. However, what's right for your friend may not be right for you.

If you call a tarot hotline, be prepared to be inundated by a stream of phone calls and advertisements. If you prefer to avoid this, tell the reader that you don't want to be put on any lists. (I didn't do this and am being continually pestered!) Also, although I used only the three free minutes of time advertised by the hotlines, my phone bill reflected $80 in additional time charges. It was not easy getting the phone company to remove these charges, which they later revealed was a fairly common hotline practice.

Ask the reader what they think their areas of expertise are. If the question you want to ask the tarot falls into one of the categories of this person's expertise, you might ask how long they've been practicing and possibly how they learned tarot. You might ask if the work is passive (you get to listen) or interactive (you get to participate). Find out if the reader tapes the session, or if you can tape it. Taping can help you remember important points.

Interviewing also helps the reader discover if you're a good match with their skills. Recently, a man explained that he wanted a tarot session because he needed help curtailing his sexual attraction to children. I told him I don't know how to work with that particular issue, but referred him to people who do.

Show me the money!

Be certain of what you're paying for a reading before making an appointment. Like everything, prices vary. Some readers charge between $1 and $5 per minute; others work for an hourly fee. A few readers don't work by the clock, but charge a flat fee for the appointment. I work on a sliding fee scale.

Paying more doesn't necessarily mean that you're getting more — it can just be more expensive. If you shop around and carefully interview the reader, you should be able to figure this one out.

If you feel that you haven't paid enough for a great session, consider tipping the reader, or writing them a note of thanks. I can't tell you how much an expression like this can mean.

Chapter 14

Help Wanted!

Are you thinking about becoming a tarot professional? Congratulations, it's a fascinating profession! But it's one thing doing tarot as a hobby, and another doing it full time.

This chapter offers you some wholesome food for thought. I explain the key differences between a tarot professional and amateur, and give you a glimpse of what it *might* be like to quit your day job. Next, I share my experience regarding the many hats a tarot professional can wear — from executive secretary and director of advertising to paramedic, car mechanic, and maid.

This chapter closes with a list of possible job opportunities and a look at the business of tarot certification, from scams and shams to bona fide programs.

Thinking About Going Pro?

Working with the tarot as a professional is incredibly rewarding. You meet all kinds of people (including some famous and infamous people), make your own schedule, and can even travel the world as you work.

Thanks to the evolution of consciousness and the development of the computer and Internet (which are byproducts of this evolution), the tarot is moving into the 21st century with more people aware of its existence than ever before. Need proof? Here *you* are reading these words and thinking about becoming a tarot professional!

Quitting Your Day Job

Before you hand in your resignation, let me offer two truths to consider:

- ✔ If you think you're going to get rich doing tarot work, think again.
- ✔ Tarot professionals are real people.

When I first started doing tarot professionally, I thought, "Fabulous, I'm in a *spiritual* profession. In this field, people treat each other differently than in corporate America — no more backstabbing, gossiping, super competition, and sexism." Reality bites! Being a tarot professional is like being any other professional; people treat others according to their level of consciousness, not according to what they do for a living.

Deciding to become a tarot professional can mean different things to different people. In addition to offering tarot consultations and classes at metaphysical bookstores, I continued to work other jobs for many years.

Having my tarot work be something I *needed* to do in order to put food on the table and gas in the car just didn't feel right to me. I knew that if I needed to earn a living from tarot, it would be harder to say no to an inappropriate client or student. Instead of taking this route, I baked bread; taught elementary school, meditation, and stress management classes; and wrote several children's books while building my tarot skills and repertoire.

Becoming a master of all trades

Tarot professionals wear many hats. Here are some of mine:

- ✔ Executive secretary
- ✔ File clerk
- ✔ Referral service, offering the names of competent doctors, dentists, drug and alcohol dependency programs, lawyers, psychiatrists, and so on (when they are appropriate to the situation)
- ✔ Director of advertising
- ✔ Hospitality committee, providing beverages and snacks for clients and students
- ✔ Car mechanic, providing jumper cables, wire hangers, and clean-up rags (Among other things, numerous students and clients have forgotten to turn off their lights and/or locked their keys in their cars!)
- ✔ Electronic specialist, keeping my tape recording equipment in tip-top shape (I record my tarot sessions, and often a sick student will request that I tape a class for them.)

- Techie, using computers and the Internet to create flyers and brochures, write articles and books, keep up e-mail correspondences, maintain a Web site (www.practical-mystic.com), and visit other interesting tarot Web sites, such as www.artoftarot.com

- Paramedic, having a supply of bandages, nail files, aspirin, and tampons available for the needy

- Business and booking agent — lots of fun

- Head of the ethics committee

- Bookkeeper

- Writer and editor — a neat trick when I can do it

- Paralegal (Yes, I've taken a few deadbeats to court.)

- Teacher-facilitator

- Stationer, supplying pens and paper to students who've forgotten theirs

- Maid, cleaning up after classes and consultations

- Night owl and early bird, fitting my schedule to the schedules of students and clients (I taught Saturday classes for four years, which meant getting up at 6 a.m. on Saturday mornings.)

Seeking professional opportunities

This profession requires that you make your own opportunities. As you start, try calling appropriate venues and, perhaps, offering free services initially under the condition that the next time around you will be paid. You may also want to speak with entertainment booking agents.

There's work for tarot professionals in the following venues:

- Offering readings at spiritual or psychic fairs

- Providing "entertainment" at social events, fund-raisers, and parties

- Working on a tarot hotline

- Hiring on with a cruise ship company (something I expect some enterprising tarot person will soon help make a reality)

- Doing online readings and teaching

- Speaking and offering readings at metaphysical/spiritual bookstores and cafes

- Offering your services at a spa, beauty salon, or fine resort

- Working with a psychotherapist — tarot can be a great adjunct to traditional psychotherapy

✔ Teaching workshops and/or classes privately and at various programs, schools, and colleges

✔ Writing articles and books

✔ Speaking on the radio or TV (Stations, especially college radio shows, are always looking for people to speak on interesting topics or to do readings on the air.)

While it's certainly possible to get work by networking, it's very helpful to create a resume and gather letters of reference from past clients. You also may want to be prepared to show your skills. For example, when I interviewed at Lewin's Metaphysical Bookstore in Berkeley, California in 1972, I read for Mrs. Lewin. When interviewing to work at East West Bookshop in Seattle, I presented a letter of recommendation from East West Bookshop in California.

Spreading the word

If you decide to work independently, from an office or your home, advertising lets people know that you exist. Consider doing some or all of the following:

✔ Place a small ad in the Yellow Pages.

✔ Create a Web site with links to other sites (which link back to your site).

✔ Post flyers, notices, and brochures in spas, beauty salons, bookstores, coffee shops, and health foods stores (as well as on community bulletin boards).

✔ Advertise in local or events-oriented newspapers and magazines.

✔ Let friends and acquaintances know about your business, and ask them for referrals.

✔ Join a local business association — remember that you are running a bona fide business. Members of a group in my hometown welcomed me into their organization and monthly networking breakfasts.

✔ Do what's appropriate to get your work and name "out there" — people tend to remember what they see and hear about most frequently.

Remember that your business will develop in divine time, not your time. Do your best, and the universe will do the rest!

Corporate tarot

I've had the opportunity to work at many social events, including some sponsored by well known corporations. One of my most fun experiences was getting into costume — an Indian sari complete with a bindi, or red dot, over my third eye (situated between my eyebrows) — and doing card readings at a company's annual Halloween party. Another particularly fulfilling assignment was reading tarot at a charity ball raising money for breast cancer research.

The only down side of these gatherings is dealing with people who've had too much to drink. I stopped participating in events serving alcohol after a woman was so far gone that she began arguing and yelling about the cards she'd turned over. Although I succeeded in calming her down by having her select one more card, she remained unable to relate to the cards because of her intoxication. (Every once in a great while I give in and do a special event serving alcohol, but only with the caveat that I have the right to refuse working with anyone who's drunk or abusive.)

Getting paid

It took me a few years of doing "practice" tarot readings before I felt qualified enough to be paid for my work. I remember exactly when it happened. I'd received a pair of earrings and a beautiful note from an acquaintance thanking me for "practicing" on her. In the note, she told me how much she'd appreciated all the time and energy I'd shared with her, and she stated that she definitely wanted to pay me next time around. Reading her words, my heart knew I was ready for the next step.

When I reflect back on the kind of work I did then and compare it to what I am capable of doing now, I find that there's quite a difference! Yet I believe that I was ready to be a tarot professional because I was fully present, giving my all to each person I worked with.

It's not getting a fancy bag for your tarot cards or having engraved business cards that make you a genuine tarot professional; it's the *quality* of the work you do.

How does a tarot reader set rates? Setting rates depends upon the geographic area in which you are working and your level of expertise. Although you might be able to charge $45 for a half-hour session in New York City, you might only be able to charge $20 for the same amount of time in a small town in upstate New York. No matter where you are, if your work is well known, you're more likely to be able to charge more than someone who isn't well known. It's helpful to check with other tarot professionals to see what the "going rates" in that area are.

Setting up shop

Tarot professionals sometimes establish partnerships with therapists, drug and alcohol counselors, or other types of professionals. I have done this myself, and several of my colleagues work in conjunction with Jungian psychologists. I also know of massage therapists and beauty operators who do client referrals.

Tarot professionals work in many different places. Some work out of their homes, in malls, in bookstores, and in storefront shops. On a recent trip to New York City, I noticed at least a half dozen tarot readers working out of their own "parlors" in uptown Manhattan.

Depending upon where a reader works, overhead varies. For example, I worked at one bookstore that took 40 percent of my earnings, while another took 20 percent. (I adjusted my fees accordingly.) If your reader works for a hotline or service, they could be working on a salary-plus-commission basis.

Working for tarot hotlines

Working for a hotline has definite pros and cons. I've gathered the information in this section from interviewing people who've worked in this venue.

The pros of working for a hotline include:

- ✔ You can be hired with little or no experience.
- ✔ You have the chance to learn a whole lot, quickly.
- ✔ You can make networking connections.
- ✔ You may be able to assist someone in dire need.

The cons of working for a hotline include:

- ✔ You have to work with a large number of people.
- ✔ In order to make more money, you're encouraged to keep people on the phone for long periods of time.
- ✔ The person who owns the hotline takes a big cut out of the money you make (to cover overhead expenses and make a profit).
- ✔ It's sometimes suggested that you overcharge people in order to make money. When I called to protest being overcharged by a hotline, the woman at the phone company told me that some people are too embarrassed to call the phone company to protest an overcharge to a 900 number.
- ✔ Because you must keep talking, the work is exhausting.

- ✔ The work can be saddening because people want you to "fix them."

- ✔ You are encouraged to create dependent or codependent relationships with others.

- ✔ Rather than empowering people to figure things out for themselves, your job is to figure things out for them.

- ✔ Naturally, if things go wrong, you're responsible, not the caller.

- ✔ Because some people are pressed for money, you can't give them all the assistance they need.

Buyer Beware: The Limits of Tarot Certification

Tarot certification has been a topic of much controversy within the tarot community for the last dozen or so years. Because tarot certification programs are not standardized, I don't put much credence in whether someone is certified or not.

I know of a tarot teacher who will make you a Certified Tarot Reader in a weekend for a mere $600. After being hired as a consultant on a tarot book written by one of these "Certified Readers," I felt like suggesting that he either repeat the course or call the Better Business Bureau!

 While writing this section, I received a letter from a man who'd purchased a tarot course and a degree as a Certified Tarot Advisor for $195. He writes, "I was sent a $5 book on how to read tarot and my certification — no instruction, no tutorial, and no assistance!"

He asked me to spread the word about this Sacramento, California based organization offering bogus certifications and ordinations. A shortened menu of the offerings on their *Fast Service Order Form* reads:

- ✔ Certified Tarot Advisor (our most popular diploma), $195.

- ✔ Doctor of Religion (Awarded for life experience), No Course!, $95.

- ✔ Doctor of Metaphysics, $150.

- ✔ Doctor of Theology (Awarded for life experience), No Course!, $95.

- ✔ Certified Clairvoyant, $175.

- ✔ Registered Tarot Advisor Certificate, $55.

- ✔ "Title" Certificate: Evangelist, Rabbi, Priest, Bishop, Deacon, Chaplain, Pastor, Priestess, Missionary, or Monk, $30.

- ✔ Doctor of Apologetics (Awarded for life experience), No Course!, $95.

> ✔ Press/Minister Dash Plate (For vehicle, states "Official Business"), $15.
>
> ✔ Registered Medium Certificate, $55.

I think the best offer was their Sainthood Certificate for only $20! Maybe you'd like to place an order after all?

It's my belief that if an organization certifies you, it's bound to continue assisting you — not to disappear after six months or if you get into trouble. If you go through a substantial number of courses and pay a substantial amount of money, the school might have a job placement service (something that is offered in many educational settings). For credibility purposes, a group of this type should be obligated to pass along and enforce a code of ethics (which is no easy trick).

I completed 13 years of correspondence courses in a Western Mystery School, the Builders of the Adytum, and received no degree of any kind. What I got was the satisfaction of knowing myself and the tarot better than I did when I started out.

I think it's wise to ask yourself exactly *why* you want certification, if indeed you do. Aside from the piece of paper, which can open certain doors, a good certification program can provide teachings, support, and guidance. However, the bottom line is, if you're proficient at what you do, your practice grows. If you're deficient, you either improve, get a second job, go out of business, or end up in some type of legal hassle that closes your doors.

If you want certification, I suggest attending a bona fide graduate program at a university where tarot is taught along with courses in psychology. John F. Kennedy University in Orinda, California is one such school. Because most university-affiliated tarot programs are not comprehensive (they give you appetizers, not entrees), I'd recommend supplementing your education with outside classes.

Some tarot professionals choose a particular approach to the tarot, such as Jungian psychology and symbolism, or the mystery school tradition. Others take an eclectic approach to the cards, studying many different philosophies with many different teachers. I'm certain that you'll find what's right for you.

Tarot Grandmaster

I am associated with the American Tarot Association (ATA), which offers various levels of certification, but I am not certified. My relationship with the ATA is as an *Honorary* Tarot Grandmaster. I was given this honor because of my contributions to the field of tarot and Qabalah, and because I added credibility to the then newly formed organization, not because I took or passed any of the ATA courses or exams.

The Tarot and Her Family: Seeing Through Other Eyes

The 5th Wave By Rich Tennant

@RICHTENNANT

"Just try it! If you can reference an astrological chart in a tarot reading, why not a racing form?"

In this part . . .

Part IV gives you the opportunity to see how the tarot, astrology, numerology, and alchemy are related to the Qabalah and its powerful symbolic representation, the Qabalistic Tree of Life. The chapters in this part introduce you to concepts that can transform the way you look at the tarot and its brothers and sisters — astrology, numerology, and alchemy. This part also shows you how the tarot emulates the cycles of life and spiritual development from birth to elder or sagehood.

Chapter 15

Connecting the Tarot to the Qabalistic Tree of Life

In This Chapter

▶ Climbing the Qabalistic Tree of Life
▶ Using the Tree of Life during a tarot reading
▶ Decoding the Tree's symbols

*F*rom my experience teaching the tarot and Qabalah, I've found that when students get interested enough in the tarot, they eventually want to go deeper. Learning about the connections between the tarot and the Qabalah via the Qabalistic Tree of life is one surefire way of doing this.

In Chapter 5, I introduce you to the Qabalistic mystery school tradition, which believes that the tarot is a pictorial representation of the teachings of the *Universal Qabalah.*

If you haven't yet read Chapter 5, or if you need a quick refresher, the Universal Qabalah is a nonsexist, nonracist, nonhomophobic belief system that blends Judeo-Christian mysticism with the hermetic arts and sciences of tarot, astrology, numerology, alchemy, and sacred geometry.

The Universal Qabalah also embraces essential principles from Hinduism, Buddhism, Sufism, and Shamanism, to name a few; it's both a nondenominational and multidenominational system of teachings and practices that highlight the basic truths that the spiritual traditions of the East and West share. For example, one of those truths is that all of creation comes from a divine source.

In this chapter, I take your understanding of the Qabalah a step further by introducing you to the *Qabalistic Tree of Life,* a diagram that represents relationships between the physical and spiritual worlds. Although opinions on this topic vary, I believe that the Qabalah and the Qabalistic Tree of Life are the parents of the tarot (as well as astrology, alchemy, numerology, and sacred geometry).

First, I show you exactly what the Qabalistic Tree of Life is, and then I explain why I believe that the tarot evolved from it. I discuss how you can use the Tree of Life to further your understanding of the tarot, and vice versa.

I also discuss the *Qabalistic Intelligences:* powers that you can develop when you master various tarot cards. And finally, I discuss some of the "secret" messages or concepts that the Tree of Life can cue you into.

If, at the end of this chapter, you find yourself interested in learning more about the fascinating relationship between the Qabalistic Tree of Life and the tarot, you might look at the following books:

- *The Mystical Qabalah* by Dion Fortune (Samuel Weiser Publications)
- *Qabalistic Tarot* by Robert Wand (Samuel Weiser Publications)
- *A Practical Guide to Qabalistic Symbolism* by Gareth Knight (Helios Books)
- *Principles of the Qabalah* by Amber Jayanti (HarperCollins Thorsons)

Diagramming Your Spiritual Journey

So what exactly is the Qabalistic Tree of Life? The Tree of Life is a physical representation of the inseparable relationship between the physical and spiritual worlds. On a personal level, it represents your own physical and spiritual selves. It diagrams the various stages that you grow through as you strive for enlightenment, making spiritual evolution something you can actually see!

The Tree of Life represents, in picture form, the fundamental principles of the Universal Qabalah (see Chapter 5). Most importantly, it reminds you that each person can take a unique path toward enlightenment.

These concepts, and those that follow, are also depicted in the Tree of Life's child: the tarot.

Fruits of the Tree

Before I show you the Tree of Life and describe its components, I want to give you some ideas regarding the benefits of becoming familiar with this diagram and its meanings:

- The symbols of the Qabalistic Tree of Life can bring you into an intimate relationship with your higher soul, spirit, Self and the godhead. Through this closeness, you begin to understand the divine plan: who and what you *really* are and your place in the scheme of things.

✔ The Tree of Life points out that there are as many paths to know your higher soul, spirit, Self as there are people. It illustrates that spiritual growth is both an individual and universal experience.

✔ The Tree of Life shows you all the possible cycles of life — life in the round. Perhaps this is why psychologist Carl Jung referred to it as "a mandala of life."

✔ The Tree of Life is a model for creation. Its structure illustrates "invisible divinity" becoming "visible divinity" through the birth of the physical world and everything in it.

✔ The Tree of Life shows you that life is simultaneously a stable and constantly changing reality; it presents both the cosmic and personal experiences of life.

✔ If the previous paradox didn't make you dizzy, try this one! The Tree of Life represents the ten aspects of the one godhead and how these aspects are one and the same.

✔ The Tree of Life is a blueprint for living. It lays out how your consciousness develops while you're living in the physical world.

✔ The Tree of Life's structure shows how your personality comes into a conscious relationship with your higher soul, spirit, Self.

Thirty-two paths

Okay, enough build-up — it's time to see this amazing Tree! Figure 15-1 shows the Qabalistic Tree of Life, a diagram that has appeared cross-culturally since the most ancient times. Along with the Tree of Knowledge, the Tree of Life is mentioned in the stories of the Garden of Eden. Because tribal people believed that the Tree of Life carried the power of eternal life, tribe members were buried wearing them as talismans. Recently, the body of a 2,400-year-old Siberian "Ice Maiden" was discovered wearing a funerary headdress in the form of a Tree of Life. Representations of life-giving, pomegranate, cypress, and palm trees are found in Babylonian, Chaldean, and Assyrian engravings. One of the most alluring attractions at Disney's Animal Kingdom is a Tree of Life that lights up the theme park at night.

The Tree of Life has 32 paths. Although they are represented as circles, the first ten paths are the Crown through the Kingdom, from the top to the bottom of the Tree of Life. The remaining 22 paths are the channels connecting, or running between, the spheres. The Fool, path 11, connects the Crown to Wisdom; The Magician, path 12, spans the Crown and Understanding; and so on.

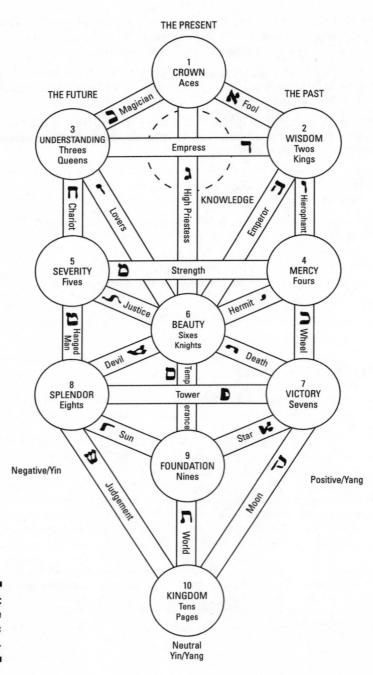

Figure 15-1:
The
Qabalistic
Tree of Life.

Positive and negative

In Qabalah, the terms *positive* and *negative* don't mean "good" and "bad." The entire natural world is made of a combination of active (positive) and receptive (negative) polarities, energies, or forces of nature. Basic biology teaches that the combining of positive and negative forces makes life possible.

The spheres

The Hebrew word *sephiroth* refers to all ten spheres, and *sephirah* refers to each individually. The root of these words, *safar,* comes from the Hebrew word meaning both "to count" and "to emanate." When something emanates, it's generated from a source. The ten spheres on the Tree of Life generate from what Qabalists call the limitless source of life.

Following are descriptions of what each sphere on the Tree of Life represents. In many of the descriptions, I also explain the relationships between spheres.

- **Crown:** The Crown represents the godhead and source of life, the uncreated potential for all of creation, and the universal life force.

- **Wisdom:** The sphere of Wisdom represents the positive polarity within all living things and also represents Father God. Wisdom receives the universal life force from the Crown and sends (or ejaculates) the life force into the sphere of Understanding, the waiting womb of the Mother Goddess.

- **Understanding:** This sphere represents the negative polarity within all living things. It is the Mother Goddess and Mother Nature. Understanding receives the universal life force from Wisdom and shapes it into you and me, other humans, plants, animals, and so on.

- **Knowledge:** This is an *invisible sphere* situated on the middle column in the space between Wisdom and Understanding and above the spheres of Mercy and Severity. (Knowledge is called an invisible sphere because traditional Jewish texts state "there are only ten spheres on the Tree of Life.") An obsolete meaning of the word *knowledge* is "sexual intercourse." On the Tree of Life, things that have been conceived in the spiritual world enter into the physical world through the sphere of Knowledge.

- **Mercy:** This sphere functions to bring loving kindness to the world and alleviate suffering. It represents your social conscience — how you and others make rules, laws, regulations, or social contracts aimed at preserving and protecting life. This is also the sphere where being too permissive may result in you harming yourself or others.

- **Severity:** This sphere represents corrective and limiting behaviors that are motivated by love and compassion — how you and others enforce the rules, laws, regulations, or social contracts aimed at preserving and protecting life. This is also the sphere in which being too restrictive may result in you harming yourself or others.

✔ **Beauty:** Beauty represents who you are at heart and the experience of spiritual bliss and unconditional love. It is the part of you that's in touch with the fact that divinity lives within you and all around you. In Qabalah speak, Beauty is the part of you that "consciously recognizes that you and all of creation are divine in essence and origin." This sphere receives insights and information from both your higher soul, spirit, Self and subconscious mind (the Crown and Foundation) and sends information back to them.

✔ **Victory:** Your passionate, imaginative, and feeling self is represented by this sphere, as is your emotional temperament. Victory contains the visions and imaginings that come from having dreams, goals, and feelings.

✔ **Splendor:** Your thinking and reasoning self is represented by Splendor — how you think and process information, communicate, and learn. Splendor reflects the intellectual faculties that help you sift through your passions, dreams, and feelings and help you plan out the steps needed to bring your dreams and goals to fruition.

✔ **Foundation:** While the sphere of Knowledge acts as a passageway from the spiritual into the physical world on an cosmic level, Foundation has the same function on a mundane level. It's the private laboratory where you can imagine and think about what something's going to be like without actually having to create it. Foundation manufactures the patterns or foundations from which physical forms are constructed. It also stores your personal experiences and memories and those of the entire human race — your personal subconscious and the collective unconscious.

✔ **Kingdom:** In this sphere, spirit comes into form. Kingdom represents the physical world and all that goes with it. It is home to you, me, and everything else in this big wide world.

Each sphere receives and sends energy through the paths running to and from the spheres that surround it. For example, if you look at the sphere of Kingdom, you can see it receives and sends energy in many directions simultaneously!

The channels

The names of the channels or paths that run between the ten spheres correspond to the 22 major arcana tarot cards and their meanings, which I explain in Chapter 7.

In terms of the Tree of Life, the channels signify the *experiences* you might have while moving to and from one level of consciousness, or sphere of the Tree of Life, to another. For example, going from Victory to Mercy would involve mastery of the Wheel of Fortune card — grasping the idea that determining whether an event is fortunate or unfortunate is a matter of your perspective.

The channels also represent what you might confront when achieving a balance between one sphere of the Tree of Life and another. For example, balancing the spheres of Mercy and Severity involves mastery of the Strength card. (One of the secrets to doing this is having gentle yet firm control over your impulses to act.)

In this section, I explain how this connection between the Tree of Life and the tarot emerged.

For generations, the 22 paths between the spheres on the Qabalistic Tree of Life were symbolized only by the 22 letters of the Hebrew alphabet. (This restricted understanding of the Tree of Life to people who read Hebrew.)

There is an ancient practice in which Jewish mystics meditate on the form or shape of each letter of the Hebrew alphabet. Over time, this practice reveals each letter's "inner" or esoteric meaning to the mystic.

I was taught that the images of the tarot's major arcana were arrived at through this meditative practice. In other words, what you're seeing when you look at the 22 major arcana tarot cards is an interpretation of the letters of the Hebrew alphabet.

If you look at Figure 15-1 again, you'll notice that each channel between the spheres is represented both by a Hebrew letter and by the name of the tarot card that emerged from that letter.

Are you wondering how someone meditating on a letter from the Hebrew alphabet might see a tarot image? I recently saw the movie *Cast Away*, starring Tom Hanks. For me, a high point of the movie came when Hanks's character Chuck, who's been lost on an out-of-the-way island for years, is sitting on the beach contemplating a large odd-shaped piece of plastic that's washed up on the shore. After some time, Chuck gets a flash: The three-sided piece of plastic can be made into a sail that he can lash to a raft to escape the island. The meditative process for creating the tarot cards from the Hebrew letters is similar to the process that this character goes through.

Branching out

The purpose of the following information is to clue you into how the physical design of the Tree of Life actually appears in many of the tarot cards in both the major and minor arcanas. While the tree's three pillars can be seen in The High Priestess, The Hierophant, and Justice cards, the entire Tree of Life is laid out in the Ten of Pentacles and suggested in the composition of several others. Picking up on these can deepen your understanding and interpretation of the cards.

The tree's pillars are evident in the following examples: In The Chariot card, the charioteer rides between the black and white sphinx; he maintains control over competing forces by remaining centered and neutral. The design of the Two of Cups intimates that spirit is synergizing the relationship between the man and woman.

Looking again at Figure 15-1, notice that the Tree of Life has three pillars or branches. (The ten spheres are situated among them.) Each pillar symbolizes a segment in time and a type of energy.

The Tree of Life's middle branch, topped by the sphere of the Crown, is called the Pillar of Equilibrium. The middle branch represents present time, the moment, and neutral energy. I sometimes call the middle branch of the tree *synergy*. Synergy is what results when the activities of the two other branches and their pairs of opposing spheres (say Victory and Splendor or Mercy and Severity) mix together.

The Tree of Life's right branch, topped by the sphere of Wisdom, is called the Pillar of Mercy. The Pillar of Mercy represents the past — what's already been born and happened. This branch is also the positive polarity or Yang energy in Oriental tradition.

The Tree of Life's left branch, topped by the sphere of Understanding, is called the Pillar of Severity. The Pillar of Severity represents the future — what's yet to be born and happen. This branch is also the negative polarity or Yin energy in Oriental tradition.

The Minor Arcana and the Tree of Life

As I explain in the section called "The channels" earlier in the chapter, the paths between the spheres on the Tree of Life have the names of the 22 major arcana tarot cards.

Although there are several Qabalistic mystery schools, all agree that the remainder of the tarot deck — the 56 minor arcana cards — are associated with the 10 spheres on the Tree of Life. This means that the principles or core concepts associated with each sphere can be found in the cards bearing the same number. The connections between the minor arcana number and court cards and the 10 spheres on the Tree of Life are shown in Table 15-1.

Table 15-1	Associations between the Minor Arcana and the Tree of Life
Minor Arcana Cards	*Sphere*
aces	Crown
twos	Wisdom
threes	Understanding
fours	Mercy
fives	Severity
sixes	Beauty
sevens	Victory
eights	Splendor
nines	Foundation
tens	Kingdom
pages	Kingdom
knights	Beauty
queens	Understanding
kings	Wisdom

If you are interested in learning more about the connection between the minor arcana cards and spheres of the Tree of Life, turn back to the section in this chapter called "Decoding the spheres." The descriptions of each sphere can surely get you started on this fascinating journey. You might also refer to some of the Qabalah books listed in the introduction to this chapter.

Tapping into the Qabalistic Intelligences

Each tarot card and its corresponding channel or sphere on the Tree of Life has what is called a *Qabalistic Intelligence*. The Qabalistic Intelligences are mental powers that develop when you master the principles of a tarot card or sphere.

The *Sepher Yetzirah,* the mystical Hebrew *Book of Creation,* written somewhere between 600 and 1000 A.D. by an unknown mystic, attributes creation to the emanation of a holy word or vibration (perhaps the big bang?), resulting in the birth of all the letters of the Hebrew alphabet and/or the elements of nature. It's no wonder that some people think of the Hebrew letters as a genetic code of our world! The Book of Creation attributes certain "powers" or Intelligences to the letters of the Hebrew alphabet. The power of each letter, or Intelligence, is activated by your understanding of its inner meaning.

Because the Qabalistic mystery school tradition (see Chapter 5) regards each tarot card to be an elaboration of a letter of the Hebrew alphabet, induced through extended periods of contemplation on that letter, the concept of the Intelligences naturally followed.

For example, The Hierophant card is the Eternal Intelligence. When you master the teachings of The Hierophant, you are completely *certain* that the eternal or divine consciousness is available to assist you, 24 hours a day, every day of the year, throughout your entire lifetime. Furthermore, you call up that Intelligence — which is now embedded in your mind — as needed.

The ten spheres on the Qabalistic Tree of Life also each have an Intelligence that corresponds with the tarot's minor arcana cards. For example, the four sixes and knights (of wands, cups, swords, and pentacles) are connected with the sixth sphere on the Tree of Life, Beauty, and its Mediating Intelligence.

One reason the ancient Qabalists assigned this Intelligence to Beauty is that the sphere is situated in the middle of the Tree of Life. One who mediates is a middleman (or woman) — an impartial party who's placed between dissenting parties in an effort to bring agreement. The Mediating Intelligence acts to harmonize or balance your personal self with your Higher Self, since there are instances when what life presents us with creates dissention between what your ego or personality desires and what your Higher Self, in the form of your day-to-day life experiences, gives you.

Mastery of the sixes and Knights suggests that you are fully aware that the people in the cards are, in their most conscious state, serving as mediators or intermediaries working for the greater good of humanity and the planet, not just for themselves.

Table 15-2 is a listing of the major arcana cards and the letters of the Hebrew alphabet associated with them. Next to the name of each Hebrew letter is its English meaning. Taking the time to consider that The Hierophant is associated with vav, a "hook or link" as well as the conjunction "and," can clue you into some of the deeper meanings of the card. For example, the card represents your divinely given ability to hook up with your higher soul, spirit, Self at will. Contemplating that The Lovers is zain, "the sword," offers similar insights. Some mystics actually meditate on the shape of a letter to tap into its meanings. For example, the letter *aleph* (א), associated with The Fool, looks like a pinwheel, suggesting the whirling energy that fills the cosmos with life. The names of the Qabalistic Intelligences associated with the major arcana cards appear last.

Table 15-2	Hebrew Letters and Qabalistic Intelligences Associated with the Major Arcana	
Major Arcana Card	**Hebrew Letter / English Name(s)**	**Qabalistic Intelligence**
The Fool	*aleph* / ox	Fiery
The Magician	*beth* / house	Transparent
The High Priestess	*gimel* / camel	Uniting
The Empress	*daleth* / door	Luminous
The Emperor	*heh* / window	Constituting
The Hierophant	*vav* / hook, link, "and"	Eternal
The Lovers	*zain* / sword	Disposing
The Chariot	*cheth* / fence	House of Influence
Strength	*teth* / serpent	Secret of All Spiritual Activities
The Hermit	*yod* / open hand	Will
Wheel of Fortune	*kaph* / grasping hand	Rewarding
Justice	*lamed* / oxgoad, to teach	Faithful
The Hanged Man	*mem* / water	Stable
Death	*nun* / fish, to proliferate	Imaginative
Temperance	*samekh* / support, to prop	Testing and Trying
The Devil	*ayin* / eye	Renewing
The Tower	*peh* / mouth	Awakening
The Star	*tzaddi* / fish hook	Natural
The Moon	*qoph* / back of the head	Corporeal
The Sun	*resh* / face	Recollective
Judgement	*shin* / tooth, fang	Perpetual
The World	*tav* / signature, mark, cross	Administrative

Table 15-3 shows how the minor arcana cards are associated with the Qabalistic Intelligences.

Table 15-3	Qabalistic Intelligences Associated with the Minor Arcana
Minor Arcana Cards	*Qabalistic Intelligence*
aces	Admirable
twos / kings	Illuminating
threes / queens	Sanctifying
fours	Receptive
fives	Radical
sixes/ knights	Mediating
sevens	Hidden
eights	Perfect
nines	Pure
tens / pages	Resplendent

Decoding the Qabalistic Tree of Life

A code is a system of symbols, letters, or words used to transmit messages requiring secrecy and/or brevity. The Qabalistic Tree of Life concisely conveys volumes of secret information in shorthand. It is a symbol code for the secret, esoteric, or "inner" wisdom of the tarot, astrology, numerology, alchemy, and sacred geometry. It uses tarot cards, names, astrological glyphs, and numbers to accomplish this end. Here's some of the information this symbol code holds for you:

✔ Exploring the major arcana tarot cards whose names are on the paths between the ten spheres on the Qabalistic Tree of Life can cue you into different views of the tarot.

The major arcana cards on the paths signify both the experiences you can have when moving from one level of consciousness or sphere to another and what you might face when balancing or harmonizing one sphere of the Tree of Life and another.

Understanding the interaction of the tarot and the Tree of Life can enhance and deepen your interpretations of the tarot cards. For instance, reading the "Universal archetypes" listed for The Hanged Man in Chapter 7 will tell you that The Hanged Man suggests temporarily stepping out of ordinary time into eternal time. Yet if you look at The Hanged Man's placement on the path between the spheres of Severity and Splendor, you can get something different. The Hanged Man signifies the mental clarity, inner serenity, and unconditional love required to enact the principle Severity: taking a harsh and/or unpopular course of action that's intended to serve the greater good of all concerned.

✔ Defining the names of each of the ten spheres on the Qabalistic Tree of Life, from the Crown to Kingdom, can cue you into the intimate relationship between spirit and matter. For example, the Spirit and/or your spirit transform into matter by involution — by moving outwards and downwards from the Crown at the Tree's top to the Kingdom at the bottom. Matter and/or you transform into spirit by evolution — moving inwards and upwards from Kingdom at the Tree's bottom to the Crown at its top.

Following the Tree from top to bottom, the ten spheres illustrate "invisible divinity" becoming "visible divinity" through the birth of the physical world and everything in it. The Tree depicts both the universal and personal creative processes.

✔ Because the Tree of Life is a cross-cultural symbol that's existed since antiquity, there are innumerable diagrams of it. Some of these show astrological symbols in the spheres, while others do not.

Tuning into the astrological symbols on each sphere can cue you into a surprising view of astrology. For example, knowing that Jupiter is linked with the sphere of Mercy offers a different view of this planet. It suggests the spiritual importance of being as generous towards yourself as you are with others. The astrological correspondences are shown in Table 15-4.

Table 15-4	Astrological Correspondences to the Tree of Life
Sphere	*Planet*
Crown	Neptune
Wisdom	Uranus
Understanding	Saturn
Knowledge	Pluto
Mercy	Jupiter
Severity	Mars
Beauty	Sun

(continued)

Table 15-4 *(continued)*

Sphere	Planet
Victory	Venus
Splendor	Mercury
Foundation	Moon
Kingdom	Earth, a composite of nature's elements: fire, water, air, and earth

Being aware of the astrological correlations for each tarot card presents you with fascinating perspectives of both tarot and astrology. For example, knowing that The Fool is coupled with the planet Uranus communicates how spirit behaves unexpectedly. (I discuss astrology in Chapter 16.)

✔ Discovering the meanings of the numbers on the ten spheres and the numbers of the tarot cards on the Qabalistic Tree of Life's pathways can cue you into numerology in picture form. For example, finding out that the sixth sphere on the Tree, Beauty, is linked with reciprocation adds this idea to the sixth tarot card, The Lovers. (See Chapter 16 for a discussion of numerology and the tarot.)

✔ Although there are no overt alchemical symbols on the Qabalistic Tree of Life, the whole tree symbolizes the process of spiritual alchemy — the transformation or change of the ordinary person into the enlightened person. (I discuss alchemy in Chapter 17.)

Linking the Tree of Life to Your Chakras

The Tree of Life places your *chakras,* the seven spiritual energy centers connecting your spiritual and physical body, alongside the spheres. This makes the Tree of Life a living being — you and me and everyone else are living Trees of Life!

There are ten spheres on the Qabalistic Tree of Life and only seven chakras. Three chakras share the opposing spheres of Wisdom and Understanding, Mercy and Severity, and Victory and Splendor. Because Knowledge is in a latitude similar to Mercy and Severity, it shares a chakra with these spheres.

Table 15-5 is a listing of how all seven chakras match up with the spheres of the Tree of Life.

Table 15-5	The Chakras and the Tree of Life
Sphere	*Chakra*
Crown	Crown
Wisdom	Third Eye
Understanding	Third Eye
Knowledge	Throat
Mercy	Throat
Severity	Throat
Beauty	Heart
Victory	Solar Plexus
Splendor	Solar Plexus
Foundation	Reproductive
Kingdom	Root

If you're interested in finding out more, here are three books that touch on bringing the Tree of Life and chakra system together:

Wheel of Life by Anodea Judith (Llewellyn Publications)

Anatomy of the Spirit by Caroline Myss, Ph.D. (Crown Publishers)

Principles of the Qabalah by Amber Jayanti (HarperCollins Thorsons)

Chapter 16

Connecting the Tarot to Astrology and Numerology

*O*nce upon a time, I was thinking about becoming a professional astrologer so I could study the influence of the planets or cosmos on human affairs. But because of my consuming love for the tarot, I felt that I didn't have time to fully develop both skills. Then I made a discovery: The tarot is astrology in pictures.

As it turned out, I didn't have to stop working with astrology. I found that I could present it in new ways through the tarot. I love seeing astrology come to life in pictures! Discovering each tarot card's astrological correspondence — its planet, sign, and house — may increase your understanding of the tarot. Conversely, exploring each planet, sign, or house's corresponding tarot card may increase your understanding of astrology.

In this chapter, I explain how the tarot can add meaning to the symbolism of both astrology and numerology. First, I show you the relationships between the 12 signs of the zodiac, the 8 planets, and 2 luminaries, and I explain how the tarot's minor arcana cards are connected with the signs of the zodiac. You may have noticed that some astrological calendars give you the birth-days of people born throughout the year; in this chapter, I give you the tarot cards that correspond with birthdays.

I describe the 12 houses of the zodiac — the places where the planets *reside* or sit in an astrological chart — and link those houses with major arcana cards. The 12 signs of the zodiac also correspond with the four elements, so in this chapter, I show you how to link the elements, the signs of the zodiac, and the tarot.

This chapter also describes how *numerology* — the secret meanings of numbers and their influence on human life — is coupled with the tarot.

Linking Signs, Planets, Luminaries, and the Major Arcana

There are 22 cards in the major arcana. There are 12 signs in the zodiac, 8 planets, and 2 luminaries. 12 + 8 + 2 = 22. Each of the major arcana cards is linked with an astrological sign, planet, or luminary. Pretty convenient, huh?

While no one's looking and before you read the rest of this section, let loose and try writing your own guess list of which astrological sign, planet, and luminary may go with each tarot card. Even if you don't know much about astrology, give it a shot!

First, list the 12 signs of the zodiac: Aries, Taurus, Gemini, Cancer, Leo, Virgo, Libra, Scorpio, Sagittarius, Capricorn, Aquarius, and Pisces. Next to these signs, jot down the 12 tarot cards that may match up.

Now list the eight planets: Mercury, Venus, Mars, Jupiter, Saturn, Uranus, Neptune, and Pluto. Then list the two luminaries: the sun and moon. Next to these, jot down the tarot cards that may match up.

You may be surprised at how good a guesser you are, or at how much you already know about the tarot!

Zodiac signs and the major arcana

The 12 signs of the zodiac describe the dominant personality traits of people born under these signs. Connecting the major arcana cards with the zodiac involves matching the cards' personalities with the signs.

In addition to being associated with a major arcana card, each sign of the zodiac is also associated with an element — fire, air, water, or earth.

Ancient astrology

When the ancient astrologers first started studying the planets and luminaries, they were (to the best of my knowledge) standing on . . . the Earth. Believing, as they did in antiquity, that the Earth (rather than the sun) was the center of the universe also contributed to the fact that the Earth was not included among the heavenly bodies. Finally, astrological charts are cast or figured from where you and I were born and now live. Only when humans colonize the moon, Mars, Venus, and so on, will the planet Earth appear in your chart.

The following sketches of the 12 signs of the zodiac indicate the element and major arcana card that are associated with each sign. As you read through these descriptions, I encourage you to look at the tarot cards that match the signs.

Aries

Element: Fire

Card: The Emperor

I am, energize, do, order, motivate, think, protect, excite, initiate, reason, and activate. I am willful, energetic, impulsive, inflexible, headstrong, assertive, forceful, enterprising, and pioneering.

Taurus

Element: Earth

Card: The Hierophant

I own, have, endure, persevere, conserve, and listen. I'm artistic, self-possessed, contemplative, intuitive, possessive, controlling, sensual, dogmatic, stubborn, determined, and explosive when aroused.

Gemini

Element: Air

Card: The Lovers

I invent, adapt, flirt, change, think, communicate, and mediate. I'm restless, indecisive, quick witted, people-oriented, and curious. I take things apart to put them back together. (Interestingly, in Vedic or Hindu astrology the sign of Gemini is called *Maithuna,* meaning "Lovers.")

Cancer

Element: Water

Card: The Chariot

I remember, feel, receive, imitate, nurture, nag, protect, pinch, avoid, resist change, domesticate, and like repetition. I'm supersensitive, home-oriented, tenacious, shy, imaginative, resentful, spiritually inclined, moody, sentimental, and romantic.

Leo

Element: Fire

Card: Strength

I love, perform, forgive, risk, control, strengthen, and empathize. I'm protective, intense, in charge, generous, fun loving, warm, emotional, lazy, powerful, creative, proud, egotistical, vain, courageous, quick tempered, and helpful.

Virgo

Element: Earth

Card: The Hermit

I utilize, select, harvest, dissect, worry, and sympathize. I'm attentive to details, serviceable, modest, quiet, serious, a perfectionist, industrious, practical, fussy, picky, health conscious, discerning, and humane.

Libra

Element: Air

Card: Justice

I agree, balance, appease, dislike conflict, harmonize, intuit, adjust, idealize, dream, and love beauty. I'm refined, artistic, fastidious, socially oriented, logical, versatile, just, cooperative, moody, perceptive, impartial, and honest.

Scorpio

Element: Water

Card: Death

I calculate, argue, survive, transform, act quickly, and penetrate. I'm desirous, intense, vital, reserved, powerful, sexy, resourceful, energetic, magnetic, psychic, secretive, argumentative, vengeful, vulnerable, cruel, stinging, cool, and complex.

Sagittarius

Element: Fire

Card: Temperance

I test, try, verify, examine, gamble, have a passion for life, and love a good laugh. I'm astute, adventurous, daring, talkative, faithful, candid, determined, jovial, vain, open-minded, philosophical, and pursue my inner promptings. (Interestingly, in Vedic or Hindu astrology, the sign of Sagittarius is ruled by the planet Jupiter, called *Guru,* or teacher, suggesting the value of being tuned in philosophically and spiritually while experiencing life to the max.)

Capricorn

Element: Earth

Card: The Devil

I persevere, achieve, aspire, endure, crystallize, apply, aspire, use, control, limit, and rule. I'm conservative, serious-minded, tactful, determined, disciplined, prudent, loyal, powerful, focused, narrow-minded, dutiful, critical, ambitious, stable, authoritative, and resourceful.

Aquarius

Element: Air

Card: The Star

I detach, know, invent, cooperate, intuit, and lead. I'm detached, humane, and philanthropic (I love humanity, but not people). I'm inventive, self-reliant, individualistic, idealistic, friendly, open-minded, inquiring, and a visionary who envisions unconventional solutions to problems.

Pisces

Element: Water

Card: The Moon

I sacrifice, love unconditionally, believe, hide, deny myself, observe, undermine myself, live in other worlds, heal, and transcend. I'm changeable, despondent, devoted, mystical, understanding, empathetic, guilty, sensitive, kind, and compassionate.

Planets, luminaries, and the major arcana

Whereas the zodiac signs describe your dominant personality traits, planets and luminaries describe how a specific part of your personality may act. For example, Mercury suggests how you communicate, while Mars suggests how quickly you move through life.

In the following planet descriptions, I explain which part of your personality each planet or luminary defines. As you read through this list, check out the tarot cards that match the planets and luminaries!

Sun

Card: The Sun

The sun defines how you shine — your particular temperament and natural abilities, as well as your heart's desires and what your soul wants to cultivate. The sun defines the traits that help you develop a conscious connection with your higher soul, spirit, Self through life in the physical world (your life purpose).

Moon

Card: The High Priestess

The moon defines the unconscious side of your personality: your instincts, habits, and intuitions, as well as memories from this life and (perhaps) other lifetimes.

Mercury

Card: The Magician

Mercury defines your intellectual faculties: how you think, express yourself, adapt, communicate your ideas, and learn.

Venus

Card: The Empress

Venus defines your emotional disposition and sensitivities: what you feel passionate about; how you express your feelings; what you imagine is desirable, harmonious, comfortable, beautiful, and attractive; and how you attract others and maintain relationships.

The Moon and the moon

The most confusing thing about the links between the tarot, the zodiac signs, the planets, and luminaries is that the moon is associated with The High Priestess card, while The Moon card is associated with the sign of Pisces. Here are a few hints to help keep these straight: 1) The high priestess rests her foot on a crescent moon. 2) The priestess is also crowned by a full moon and waxing and waning moons. 3) Pisces is the last sign of the 12 signs of the zodiac, and The Moon card is just about at the end of the major arcana (as card number 18) — no other astrological signs follow it in the major arcana.

Mars

Card: The Tower

Mars defines your sense of initiative and how you go after what you want: how you take physical action and move through life, whether slowly, quickly, or spontaneously.

Jupiter

Card: Wheel of Fortune

Jupiter defines how willing you are to gather experience and expand your horizons, as well as what opportunities and gifts you receive from others and the world at large. It defines your personal philosophy of life and how you learn your life lessons.

Saturn

Card: The World

Saturn defines how you conserve your energies and how you impose and deal with limitations, rules, and regulations. It defines your sense of responsibility, your greatest ambitions, and how you persevere, structure your life, and discipline yourself.

Uranus

Card: The Fool

Uranus defines how you receive insight from your higher soul, spirit, Self — your ingenuity, originality, inventiveness, and sense of intuition. It defines what inspires you and how you free yourself from what's obsolete.

Neptune

Card: The Hanged Man

Neptune defines your mystical and psychic tendencies and supersensitivity: how you lose yourself to find your Self. It defines what you're willing to make sacrifices for — what awakens your sympathies and compassion — as well as your ability to rise above your feelings and do what's in the best interest of yourself or another.

Pluto

Card: Judgement

When all else fails, Pluto defines what transforms you — how you regenerate and renew yourself or, like the phoenix, rise from the ashes. It defines what you feel compelled to do, what part you play in "the group" (family, cultural group or race, society, and humanity) and how you contribute to that group.

Wheeling through the Zodiac and the Tarot's Number Cards

Each of the number cards in the tarot's minor arcana corresponds with one-third of the time period covered by a sign of the zodiac. When I first learned this, I realized that I could cast astrological charts in new ways — through the tarot!

Because this book isn't a text on astrology, I don't explain how an astrological chart is set up. I also only briefly explain *houses* (the places where the planets "live" in your astrological chart) in Chapter 13. If you want to find out more about astrology, Rae Orion's *Astrology For Dummies* (Hungry Minds, Inc.) can fill you in.

Dividing the zodiac pie

The minor arcana number cards are linked with the signs of the zodiac, as follows:

✔ Like any circle, the circle of the zodiac contains 360 degrees. Imagine the circle of the zodiac as a pie.

✔ The circle is divided into 12 parts: one for each of the 12 signs (and houses) of the zodiac. Each of the 12 parts contains 30 degrees. (30 degrees multiplied by 12 signs = 360 degrees, or a whole circle.) Imagine the pie divided into 12 slices.

✔ Each zodiac sign's 30 degrees is broken into 3 parts, with each part containing 10 degrees. Imagine that instead of 12 guests, 36 show up for pie. You now have to cut each of the 12 slices into 3 servings — less calories for everyone!

✔ Each ten degrees (or thin sliver of pie) is represented by one number card of the minor arcana. Whew! Round and round we go, and where we stop you'll soon know.

Finding your number card

Following is an easy way of finding the number card that corresponds with your own, or anyone's, birthday! For fun, I've included the names of some well-known people whose birthdays fall in each period. The numbers at the beginning of each listing refer to the first, second, and third ten-degree period in each zodiac sign. I've provided a brief explanation of the concepts or characteristics associated with each ten-degree period.

Aries

1. March 21–30: **Two of Wands** (Mariah Carey)

   You tend to be spirited, energetic, pioneering, and assertive.

2. March 31–April 9: **Three of Wands** (Daniel Ellsberg)

   You tend to be vital, self-centered, spontaneous, and idealistic.

3. April 10–April 19: **Four of Wands** (Herbie Hancock)

   You tend to be confident, ambitious, enthusiastic, and generous.

Taurus

1. April 20–30: **Five of Pentacles** (Carmen Electra)

   You tend to be affectionate, feeling, artistic, charming, and sensual.

2. May 1–May 10: **Six of Pentacles** (Tommy Roe)

   You tend to be practical, purposeful, thoughtful, and conserving.

3. May 11–May 21: **Seven of Pentacles** (Lorraine Hansberry)

   You tend to be persevering, obedient, prudent, and dutiful.

Gemini

1. May 22–May 31: **Eight of Swords** (Henry Kissinger)

   You tend to be curious, articulate, and display intellectual versatility and agility.

2. June 1–June 10: **Nine of Swords** (Sonia Braga)

   You tend to be flirtatious, clever, refined, and inclined to think dualistically.

3. June 11–June 21: **Ten of Swords** (Wallis Simpson)

   You tend to be clearheaded, convincing, smart, and a good problem solver.

Cancer

1. June 22–July 1: **Two of Cups** (King Henry VIII)

   You tend to be moody, receptive, nurturing, and imitative.

2. July 2–July 12: **Three of Cups** (Giorgio Armani)

   You tend to be imaginative, intense, sensitive, and protective.

3. July 13–July 22: **Four of Cups** (Anthony Edwards)

   You tend to be generous, intuitive, sympathetic, and ritualistic.

Leo

1. July 23–August 1: **Five of Wands** (Haile Selassie)

   You tend to be dignified, sincere, outgoing, and loyal.

2. August 2–August 12: **Six of Wands** (Billy Bob Thornton)

   You tend to be generous, understanding, dramatic, and looking for recognition.

3. August 13–August 22: **Seven of Wands** (Henri Cartier-Bresson)

   You tend to be fearless, outspoken, excitable, and tireless.

Virgo

1. August 23–September 2: **Eight of Pentacles** (Branford Marsalis)

   You tend to be discerning, thoughtful, attentive, and knowledgeable.

2. September 3–September 13: **Nine of Pentacles** (Jane Curtin)

   You to tend to be industrious, a worrier, prudent, and calculating.

3. September 14–September 22: **Ten of Pentacles** (Don Felder)

   You tend to be serviceable, opinionated, romantic, social, and critical.

Libra

1. September 23–October 2: **Two of Swords** (Phil Rizzuto)

   You tend to be pleasing, cultured, romantic, and a lover of beauty.

2. October 3–October 13: **Three of Swords** (John Lennon)

   You tend to be diplomatic, reliable, disciplined, and committed.

3. October 14–October 23: **Four of Swords** (Eleanor Roosevelt)

   You tend to be fair-minded, uncertain, analytical, and logical.

Scorpio

1. October 24–November 2: **Five of Cups** (Pablo Picasso)

   You tend to be passionate, transformative, intense, forceful, and energetic.

2. November 3–November 12: **Six of Cups** (Calista Flockhart)

   You tend to be resourceful, magnetic, expansive, and willful.

3. November 13–November 22: **Seven of Cups** (Björk)

   You tend to be intuitive, reactive, cool, intense, and manipulative.

Sagittarius

1. November 23–December 2: **Eight of Wands** (Shirley Chisholm)

   You tend to be honest, optimistic, philosophical, and generous.

2. December 3–December 11: **Nine of Wands** (Moby Grape)

   You tend to be adventurous, independent, aspiring, and passionate.

3. December12–December 21: **Ten of Wands** (Cicely Tyson)

   You tend to be free-spirited, good-humored, a lover of experience, and broad-minded.

Capricorn

1. December 22–December 31: **Two of Pentacles** (Andre Kostelanetz)

   You tend to be ambitious, capable, cautious, and diplomatic.

2. January 1–January 10: **Three of Pentacles** (Grandmaster Flash)

   You tend to be conservative, sensual, cool, and controlling.

3. January 11–January 19: **Four of Pentacles** (Martin Luther King, Jr.)

   You tend to be systematic, focused, conventional, and rigid.

Aquarius

1. January 20–January 29: **Five of Swords** (Olga Markova)

   You tend to be inventive, unique, nonconformist, and individualistic.

2. January 30–February 8: **Six of Swords** (Joey Bishop)

   You tend to be inspirational, inflexible, humane, and social.

3. February 9–February 18: **Seven of Swords** (Laura Dern)

   You tend to be friendly, rebellious, companionable, and dispassionate.

Pisces

1. February l9–February 28/29: **Eight of Cups** (Sidney Poitier)

   You tend to be mystical, compassionate, self-destructive, and generous.

2. March 1–March 10: **Nine of Cups** (Carol Bayer Sager)

   You tend to be sacrificing, sentimental, impressionable, and sensitive.

3. March 11–March 20: **Ten of Cups** (Amber Jayanti)

   You tend to be emotional, restless, intuitive, reclusive, confident, ambitious, enthusiastic, and loyal.

Matching the Court Cards to the Zodiac

This section may seem a little more complicated at first, but stick with me — it's worth the effort!

Reslicing the zodiac pie

In the earlier section, "Dividing the zodiac pie," I explain that each number card in the minor arcana corresponds with a ten-degree slice of the zodiac circle. Each of the court cards in the minor arcana corresponds to more than one ten-degree slice. In most cases, a court card corresponds to three ten-degree slices, but not the same three that constitute a single zodiac sign.

Therefore, each court card corresponds to more than one zodiac sign. In most cases, one of the card's ten-degree slices connects with one sign, and its other two slices connect with a second sign. For example, The Queen of Wands represents the three ten-degree slices that run from July 13 to August 12, which means that card is associated with *both* Cancer and Leo.

The page cards are unusual. Rather than correspond to three ten-degree slices of the zodiac pie, the page cards span an entire season (spring, summer, fall, or winter).

When a court card comes up in a tarot spread, I consider the first of the signs it spans as the wisdom and understanding you bring from the past, and the second sign as the qualities you are presently developing. (With the page cards, which span three signs, the third sign can signify the traits you may develop in the future.)

For example, say The Knight of Pentacles appears in your tarot spread. The first part of the The Knight of Pentacles is in the sign of Leo, so it can be interpreted as your having already developed Leo's generosity and outspokenness. The second part of The Knight of Pentacles is in the sign of Virgo, suggesting that you are now developing Virgo's discernment and industriousness.

Finding your court card

In this section, I list the signs of the zodiac and the three ten-degree slices of time associated with each of them. I indicate in bold the court card that corresponds with each slice, and in parentheses, I remind you of the number card that connects with that slice. For a reminder of the key concepts associated with each ten-degree slice of the zodiac, see the earlier section, "Finding your number card."

After the zodiac signs, I list the four seasons and the page cards associated with each sign. Because each page card covers so much of the zodiac cycle, I provide characteristics and concepts associated with these cards.

As you read this section, you may want to take a look at the number card that corresponds with each court card.

Aries

1. March 21–March 30: **King of Wands** (Two of Wands)
2. March 31–April 9: **King of Wands** (Three of Wands)
3. April 10–April 19: **Queen of Pentacles** (Four of Wands)

Taurus

1. April 20–April 30: **Queen of Pentacles** (Five of Pentacles)
2. May 1–May 10: **Queen of Pentacles** (Six of Pentacles)
3. May 11–May 21: **Knight of Swords** (Seven of Pentacles)

Gemini

1. May 22–May 31: **Knight of Swords** (Eight of Swords)
2. June 1–June 10: **Knight of Swords** (Nine of Swords)
3. June 11–June 21: **King of Cups** (Ten of Swords)

Cancer

1. June 22–July 1: **King of Cups** (Two of Cups)

2. July 2–July 12: **King of Cups** (Three of Cups)

3. July 13–July 22: **Queen of Wands** (Four of Cups)

Leo

1. July 23–August 1: **Queen of Wands** (Five of Wands)

2. August 2–August 12: **Queen of Wands** (Six of Wands)

3. August 13–August 22: **Knight of Pentacles** (Seven of Wands)

Virgo

1. August 23–September 2: **Knight of Pentacles** (Eight of Pentacles)

2. September 3–September 13: **Knight of Pentacles** (Nine of Pentacles)

3. September 14–September 22: **King of Swords** (Ten of Pentacles)

Libra

1. September 23–October 2: **King of Swords** (Two of Swords)

2. October 3–October 13: **King of Swords** (Three of Swords)

3. October 14–October 23: **Queen of Cups** (Four of Swords)

Scorpio

1. October 24–November 2: **Queen of Cups** (Five of Cups)

2. November 3–November 12: **Queen of Cups** (Six of Cups)

3. November 13–November 22: **Knight of Wands** (Seven of Cups)

Sagittarius

1. November 23–December 2: **Knight of Wands** (Eight of Wands)

2. December 3–December 11: **Knight of Wands** (Nine of Wands)

3. December 12–December 21: **King of Pentacles** (Ten of Wands)

Capricorn

1. December 22–December 31: **King of Pentacles** (Two of Pentacles)

2. January 1–January 10: **King of Pentacles** (Three of Pentacles)

3. January 11–January 19: **Queen of Swords** (Four of Pentacles)

Aquarius

1. January 20–January 29: **Queen of Swords** (Five of Swords)

2. January 30–February 8: **Queen of Swords** (Six of Swords)

3. February 9–February 18: **Knight of Cups** (Seven of Swords)

Pisces

1. February 19–February 28/29: **Knight of Cups** (Eight of Cups)

2. March 1–March 10: **Knight of Cups** (Nine of Cups)

3. March 11–March 20: **King of Wands** (Ten of Cups)

Spring

March 21–June 11: **Page of Wands** (Ace of Wands)

You are energetic, individualistic, bossy, reliable, goal-oriented, creative, stubborn, self-indulgent, persuasive, changeable, and superficial. You love what's new, and you anger easily.

Summer

June 23–September 22: **Page of Cups** (Ace of Cups)

You are sensitive, moody, tenacious, likable, fun loving, generous, creative, vulnerable, warm, self-critical, competent, and health conscious. You need emotional security.

Fall

September 23–December 22: **Page of Swords** (Ace of Swords)

You are easygoing, social, likable, easily upset, powerful, melodramatic, penetrating, secretive, restless, independent, and direct. You love art and music, and you are interested in religion, spirituality, and philosophy.

Winter

December 23–March 20: **Page of Pentacles** (Ace of Pentacles)

You are competitive, ambitious, disciplined, careful, principled, open-minded, inventive, cool, imaginative, sympathetic, receptive, self-sacrificing, psychic, intuitive, indecisive, and a dreamer.

Running the Numbers

The tarot is the study of symbolism, and numerology is a symbolic system. Like the tarot, numerology is a form of shorthand. Numerology is shorthand for the secret meanings of numbers and their influence on human life.

The tarot offers a unique way of interpreting the meaning of numerals. If you've looked through Chapter 10, you're already familiar with the power of numbers.

Numbering the major arcana

In this section, I provide a list of numerological correspondences to the major arcana tarot cards. I offer brief comments suggesting how the numbers and cards work together.

Keep in mind that you can approach double digits in a couple of ways. You can get the meaning of a double-digit number, say 10, by *combining* the meanings of the two single numbers. For the number 10, The Magician (1) is combined with The Fool (0).

If you're feeling more adventurous, you can also add the two numbers together for more insight. For example: 12, the Hanged Man, is comprised of The Magician (1) and The High Priestess (2) cards. Adding 1 and 2, you get The Empress card (3).

Table 16-1 lists each major arcana card and its numerological correspondence. As you become familiar with the major arcana, perhaps you'll find ways to add to this list.

The Fool card can be numbered as either 0 or 22, because it is considered both the beginning and end of the major arcana (see Chapter 10).

Table 16-1	Numerology and the Major Arcana	
Number	*Card*	*Correspondence*
0	The Fool	Unlimited potential. The number 0 has no beginning or end. The Fool depicts your infinite and eternal nature — your soul.
1	The Magician	Individuality. The number looks like the letter I. The Magician illustrates your particular personality or ego, what Qabalists call self-conscious awareness.
2	The High Priestess	Duplication. Reflection. The High Priestess depicts your subconscious mind. Your subconscious reflects what you pay attention to.
3	The Empress	Creation. Creative imagination. The blending of 1 and 2 gives birth to a new entity. The Empress illustrates your creative imagination, which synthesizes ideas and makes patterns for things to come.

Number	Card	Correspondence
4	The Emperor	Stability. Order. Organization. Reasoning. The emperor protects the world that the empress creates. The word *emperor* means "he who sets in order."
5	The Hierophant	Mediation. Truth. The fifth element, ether, or spirit. The Hierophant shows the Wise One who lives in your heart — your intuition, inner teacher, or conscience.
6	The Lovers	Equilibrium. Reciprocation. The unity of all life. The Lovers suggests how your understanding of differences leads to your understanding of sameness. All differences eventually come together in oneness.
7	The Chariot	Victory. Initiation. Accomplishment. The Chariot illustrates that victory is present within your every defeat. It also depicts that your spiritual growth and development are always right on schedule.
8	Strength	Interconnection. Strength suggests the courage it takes to embrace and accept all aspects of yourself, as these are really the one Self.
9	Hermit	Completion. The Hermit depicts you realizing that you need help and seeking it out — whether it's the tarot cards, the Bible, an astrological reading, or time with a wise friend. Realizing that you need help is a wonderful accomplishment that leads to self-completion.
10	Wheel of Fortune	The Magician (1) plus The Fool (0). The Wheel of Fortune shows that life's changes and cycles aim at aligning your personality with your higher soul, spirit, Self. Also, 1 + 0 gives you 1, The Magician.
11	Justice	The Magician (1) and The Magician (1). Justice illustrates the wisdom of your personality acting in alignment with the one universal will. Also, 1 + 1 gives you 2, The High Priestess.

(continued)

Table 16-1 *(continued)*

Number	Card	Correspondence
12	The Hanged Man	The Magician (1) and The High Priestess (2). The Hanged Man depicts how expansions in your consciousness bring your subconscious patterns to conscious awareness. Also, 1 + 2 gives you 3, The Empress. When your consciousness is raised, new ways of viewing the world are born.
13	Death	The Magician (1) and The Empress (3). Death shows how, as your personal consciousness grows, your mind opens to imagining more realistic ideas about death — and life. Also, 1 + 3 gives you 4, The Emperor.
14	Temperance	The Magician (1) and The Emperor (4). Temperance depicts how your willingness to see things from different angles results in purification and spiritual growth. Also, 1 + 4 gives you 5, The Hierophant.
15	The Devil	The Magician (1) and The Hierophant (5). The Devil illustrates how, when you're willing to free yourself from erroneous and limited mental constructs, you tune into what's real. Also, 1 + 5 gives you 6, The Lovers.
16	The Tower	The Magician (1) and The Lovers (6). The Tower suggests what happens when you insist on hanging onto positions or points of view because you *must* be right. Also, 1 + 6 gives you 7, The Chariot.
17	The Star	The Magician (1) and The Chariot (7). The Star illustrates you recognizing a power that's greater than your personal self and then surrendering to living by it. Also, 1 + 7 gives you 8, Strength.
18	The Moon	The Magician (1) and Strength (8). The Moon shows what happens when you're willing to accept your life path completely. Also, 1 + 8 gives you 9, The Hermit.

Number	Card	Correspondence
19	The Sun	The Magician (1) and The Hermit (9). The Sun depicts what occurs when you focus on and absorb the hermit's light — you become that light. Also, 1 + 9 gives you 10, the Wheel of Fortune, *and* 1 + 0 gives you 1, The Magician. Magic does happen!
20	Judgement	The High Priestess (2) and The Fool (0). Judgement depicts what transpires when you're automatically attuned to your higher soul, spirit, Self. Also, 2 + 0 gives you 2, The High Priestess.
21	The World	The High Priestess (2) and The Magician (1). The World shows the result of the evolution of your consciousness — your subconscious and conscious minds unite. Also, 2 + 1 gives you 3, The Empress.

Adding up the minor arcana and court cards

The correspondences between numbers and the major arcana can be applied to the number or *pip* cards of the minor arcana as well. For example, if you pull The Two of Wands, refer to Number 2 in the preceding table.

The court cards can be numbered as follows:

> pages = 11
>
> knights = 12
>
> queens = 13
>
> kings = 14

As an alternative to the reference numbers of these court cards, you can flip back to the chart in Chapter 10 where each court card is numbered from 1 through 16. Experiment with using these numbers for the court cards.

Chapter 17

Connecting the Tarot to Alchemy and Your Life Journey

· ·

In This Chapter

▶ Understanding the science and philosophy of alchemy
▶ Transforming through the tarot
▶ Connecting the major arcana to your soul's development

· ·

*A*lchemy is both a science and a philosophy. The science of alchemy was an early form of chemistry, whose goal was to transform base metals into gold.

This chapter focuses on the philosophy of alchemy, not the science. As a philosophy, alchemy is the magical power of transforming one thing into another, such as transforming the ordinary you into the enlightened you.

Because both the science and philosophy of alchemy are aimed at accomplishing transformation, the word *alchemy* has come to be used generally to indicate transformation. Spiritual transformation is a natural consequence of working with such tools as the tarot.

In this chapter, I explain the intimate connection between the tarot and alchemy, and I show you the 12 tarot cards that correspond to the 12 alchemical processes. (These same 12 cards also represent the 12 signs of the zodiac.)

The tarot's major arcana cards can be linked with the four stages of life: childhood, adolescence, adulthood, and elderhood or sagehood. Obviously, moving through the stages of life involves transformation, and in this chapter, I explain how you can use the major arcana to view your own spiritual development.

The Elements of Alchemy

As a synonym for the developmental process of changing the ordinary human being into the extraordinary human being, alchemy is aligned with your *psycho-spiritual* (psychological and spiritual) development.

Alchemy is your evolution

- ✔ from *unconsciousness* (behaving without conscious awareness, or being asleep with your eyes wide open)
- ✔ to *consciousness* (behaving with conscious awareness)
- ✔ to *superconsciousness* or *enlightenment* (behaving with complete spiritual understanding at all times).

The goal of the philosophy of alchemy is the "sacred marriage" of the positive and negative or the male and female aspects of yourself (your polarities). The union of these polarities creates a whole or enlightened being.

The Refiner's Fire

The science of alchemy is likened with *tempering*, strengthening and adding flexibility to a metal by purifying the *dross* (impurities) formed on its surface by alternative heating and cooling.

The philosophy of alchemy encourages subjecting the surface of your being — your personality — to the *refiner's fire*, or life's tests and trials. The goal is to purge the dross (your impurities or perfect imperfections) from your personality. (I say "perfect imperfections" because the personality, with all its flaws, is the perfect vehicle through which you divest yourself of misperceptions and evolve to higher consciousness.) Eventually, the alchemical process strips away everything, leaving only the gold of your true Self.

The science of alchemy actually has another goal — to find a universal remedy for all human ills, a sort of elixir of youth. The science and philosophy of alchemy actually merge around this goal. *Enlightened awareness*, behaving with complete spiritual understanding at all times, is the universal remedy for all disease. Although it's called by different names, every belief system has enlightenment as its goal.

Breaking Down and Building Up

Both the science and philosophy of alchemy involve 12 processes, which I explain in this section. The 12 processes are each linked with a card from the tarot's major arcana. Each of the 12 cards are also coupled with an astrological sign and its element — fire, water, air, and earth. As you read the descriptions of these processes, notice how alchemy's cycles of breaking down and building up purge the dross of personal misconceptions: the impure or immature ways that people think and behave.

Quantum physicists say that when you and I experience different emotions, we change at both the atomic and subatomic levels. Keep this in mind as you read the following descriptions.

1. **Calcination:** Calcination is the heating of a substance to a very high temperature. Psycho-spiritually, it can be likened to you getting fired up about something. When this happens, ideas emerge from your subconscious for examination. Calcination is the mental intensity that melts you down and purifies you. Purging your personality of erroneous thinking can be likened to burning off toxins during a fever — it leaves your body cleaner and clearer. Card: **The Emperor.** Astrological sign: Aries. Element: Fire.

2. **Congelation:** Congelation coagulates or solidifies a substance. After calcination melts your personality down, congelation builds it up again! Psycho-spiritually, congelation reshapes your personality — but like gelatin, you become more flexible, which means that you are more receptive to inspiration. Card: **The Hierophant.** Astrological sign: Taurus. Element: Earth.

3. **Fixation:** In chemistry, a fixer stabilizes a substance. When your attention is fixed, it is focused and stable. Psychologically speaking, fixation is the process of forming an attachment to another person or thing. Psycho-spiritually, fixation merges you and what you are fixated upon, resulting in a type of union or oneness. When differences between people disappear, conflicts disappear, and the true or divine nature of a situation, yourself, or another becomes apparent. Card: **The Lovers.** Astrological sign: Gemini. Element: Air.

4. **Separation:** A substance is isolated or separated when it is removed from a mixture. Psycho-spiritually, separation means isolating yourself. Jungian psychologists speak of the need for individuation. At a certain stage of your development, you separate yourself from others so you may rejoin them (or society) as a more complete individual. Doing this enables you to get acquainted with yourself — with your personality

strengths and weaknesses and with your life purpose in contrast to that of others. Separation also offers you a sense of your *Self,* the spirit behind your personality. Card: **The Chariot.** Astrological sign: Cancer. Element: Water.

5. **Digestion:** Digestion subjects a substance to heat, moisture, or chemical agents. When you digest something, it becomes part of you. After you derive your life purpose from separation, you start to digest it. Psycho-spiritually, digestion breaks down your personality — keeping what you need and eliminating the rest. Remember, you can only digest so much at a time: patience and self-acceptance are key. Card: **Strength.** Astrological sign: Leo. Element: Fire.

6. **Distillation:** Distillation vaporizes a liquid substance by heating it. Vapor is the condensation resulting from distillation. This is the process used in making spirits or alcoholic drinks. Psycho-spiritually, distillation draws out your true essence — it releases your soul from its limited identification with your physical body and personality. Distillation helps you view your Self and life more objectively. Card: **The Hermit.** Astrological sign: Virgo. Element: Earth.

7. **Sublimation:** Sublimation converts the vapor that emerges from the distillery, making it a more refined substance than when it entered. The term *sublimation* comes from the word *sublime,* and it means to raise, refine, and purify. Psycho-spiritually, you base more and more of your thoughts, words, and actions on universal and natural laws and principles, and by doing so, you become more and more spiritually refined. Card: **Justice.** Astrological sign: Libra. Element: Air.

8. **Putrefaction:** Putrefaction, the partial decomposition of a substance by microorganisms, produces a stinking mess. Fruit ripens and drops and then dies and putrefies. Yet, from the putrefied fruit comes the seed for a new fruit tree. Psycho-spiritually, purification signifies how certain aspects of your personality start to die off. When you find yourself feeling "rotten," part of you is rotting away so a new you can be born. Card: **Death.** Astrological sign: Scorpio. Element: Water.

9. **Incineration:** Incineration burns away part of a substance — its waste — leaving only the stable essence. Psycho-spiritually, this stable essence is the truth that one Self is behind *every* aspect of your life. In the process of incineration, you experience a trial by fire, which brings to mind the statement, "That which doesn't kill you makes you stronger." Card: **Temperance.** Astrological sign: Sagittarius. Element: Fire.

10. **Fermentation:** Fermentation is the bubbling or exciting of a solution, allowing the escape of indigestible substances. When you eat or drink something that doesn't mix with your chemistry, your body tries to eliminate it by burping or passing gas. Before breaking through to new psycho-spiritual levels of awareness, your mind throws off what's poisoning you by becoming agitated. Fermentation is also a leavening

process. Adding levity or humor to upsetting circumstances can help you gain a new perspective. Just as being enslaved encourages you to seek freedom, being upset encourages you to stop doing what's upsetting you *and* to stop taking yourself so seriously. Card: **The Devil.** Astrological sign: Capricorn. Element: Earth.

11. **Solution:** Solution reduces solids to their elemental substances. Psycho-spiritually, solution means getting down to the essential or underlying nature of all things. When you realize that everything comes from the one and that the one is in all things, your problem-solving abilities improve. It's wonderful to realize that all problems have solutions! This process makes you solution-oriented rather than problem-oriented. Rising above a problematic situation or personality trait and seeing that all things are really spirits with clothes on can help solve many problems. At this stage in your alchemical transformation, you see how applying cosmic principles to mundane situations results in true and lasting solutions. Card: **The Star.** Astrological sign: Aquarius. Element: Air.

12. **Multiplication:** Multiplication increases the quantity of a substance. As one flame can kindle others, multiplication can spread or propagate your solution. Psycho-spiritually, multiplication requires knowing at a cellular or automatic level that you're divine in essence and origin, and it requires behaving divinely — automatically living by spiritual truths, laws, and principles. Doing this, you spread the word to others nonverbally, and others spread it to others, and so on. Card: **The Moon.** Astrological sign: Pisces. Element: Water.

Traveling from Childhood to Old Sage

The Qabalistic mystery school tradition teaches that the major arcana illustrates the alchemy, or magical evolution, of your soul's development. It depicts the stages that anyone on any spiritual or religious path progresses through to higher consciousness and enlightenment.

Many years ago, I read a statement regarding the tarot by the eminent psychologist Carl Jung in his work called *Alchemical Studies*. His work indicates that the tarot illustrates the descent of the soul into the dark abyss, followed by a conscious ascent and reunion with the light. When reading Jung's words, I thought of my Qabalistic mystery school training in which the fool or the soul stepping off the cliff goes from the world of spirit to the physical world. The cards that follow The Fool in the major arcana illustrate the fool's journey, or the education of his/her soul, that brings self-awareness, higher consciousness, and eventually, enlightenment — Jung's conscious reunion with the light. This also fits in with William Blake's idea that when a fool persists in his folly, he become wise.

Although I was never taught how to lay out the major arcana according to the four developmental stages of life — childhood, adolescence, adulthood, and elderhood or sagehood — I suddenly felt compelled to do so. What follows is my interpretation of these stages through the tarot's major arcana. Over the years, numerous tarot authorities have agreed with this conceptualization.

The evolution of consciousness doesn't necessarily correspond with chronological age. You may know a 15-year-old sage or a 45-year-old adolescent. If you view the alchemical developmental process from the "eternal timeframe," where lifetime melts into lifetime to become one life, your development follows the four stages of life.

In the sections that follow, I explain which major arcana cards correspond with the four stages of life. At the beginning of each section, I present a section of a poem written by the late Portia Nelson entitled "Autobiography in Five Short Chapters." The poem summarizes each of the four stages using a simple metaphor.

On being a child

I walk down the street.

There's a deep hole in the sidewalk.

I fall in.

I am lost . . . I am helpless;

it isn't my fault.

It takes forever to find a way out.

Certain major arcana cards correspond with your soul's childhood in the following ways:

- **The Fool:** Your higher soul, spirit, Self decides that it's time to take a body.

- **The Magician:** Welcome to physical reality! You're born with the perfect personality and body to act out your higher soul, spirit, Self's plan.

- **The High Priestess:** You absorb ideas about who you are and your place in life from parents, friends, and the world around you.

- **The Empress:** Believe it or not, you receive the nurturing that's perfect for your soul's development. You're also discovering what you like to eat, hear, smell, see, and touch. (I call these the "perks" of being in a physical body!)

✔ **The Emperor:** Believe it or not, you're shown ways of regulating your behavior that are *perfect* for your soul's development. You're learning to follow, or not follow, the rules of your family, culture, and society.

✔ **The Hierophant:** You discover a little voice inside of you that does its best to guide you through life. You may or may not pay attention to it.

✔ **The Lovers:** When you won't listen or seek guidance, you do whatever you please. (Think about Eve, Adam, and that apple!) You don't know it yet, but there are no mistakes. Just like in the fairy tales, everything does work out in the end.

✔ **The Chariot:** Ready or not, here I come! You go out and flail around in the world. This stage of development can be summed up by my grandmother's sage words over many a bowl of chicken soup: *"Mamala,"* — a Yiddish word for "little mother" — "remember that you live and learn!"

The Chariot card is like a door that opens in two directions: One side exits childhood and the other enters adolescence.

On being an adolescent

I walk down the same street.

There is a deep hole in the sidewalk.

I pretend I don't see it.

I fall in again.

I can't believe I am in the same place;

but it isn't my fault.

It still takes a long time to get out.

Some major arcana cards correspond with your soul's adolescence in the following ways:

✔ **Strength:** Life is sometimes like a lamb and at other times like a lion. You keep meeting your Self on the road of life, but you don't recognize who you are.

✔ **The Hermit:** When you get into enough pain or trouble, you start looking for help.

✔ **Wheel of Fortune:** Help reveals that you're following certain behavior patterns.

✔ **Justice:** Help reveals that your thoughts, words, and behavior patterns influence what happens to you. Although it's often easier said than done, you realize that changing what you think, say, and do may bring you different results!

✔ **The Hanged Man:** Your mind gets blown open! You start seeing through the eyes of your soul. Finding out what's real, your view of life does a complete turnaround. It's not permanent — you keep reverting to your old behaviors — but you now know that there are other ways of being.

✔ **Death:** Your ego dies little by little, allowing for spiritual rebirth.

The Death card is like a door that opens in two directions: One side exits adolescence and the other enters adulthood.

On being an adult

I walk down the same street.

There is a deep hole in the sidewalk.

I see it is there.

I still fall in . . . it's a habit.

My eyes are open.

I know where I am.

It is my fault.

I get out immediately.

Certain major arcana cards correspond with your soul's adulthood in the following ways:

✔ **Temperance:** Zowie! You're adopting the idea that your higher soul, spirit, Self is *always* with you, and everything that happens in your life is soul work!

✔ **The Devil:** You're coming face to face with your perfectly imperfect self: "You mean to say that I'm mean, jealous, angry, spiteful, hateful, manipulative, and . . . human?"

✔ **The Tower:** If you don't pay attention to your issues, they keep knocking you over the head until you do.

✔ **The Star:** But wait, there's hope for you! Face the truth — seek what's *real.* Look for higher guidance, and then base your thoughts, words, and actions on it.

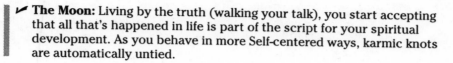

> ✔ **The Moon:** Living by the truth (walking your talk), you start accepting that all that's happened in life is part of the script for your spiritual development. As you behave in more Self-centered ways, karmic knots are automatically untied.

The Moon card is like a door that opens in two directions: One side exits adulthood, while the other enters elderhood or sagehood.

On being an elder or sage

I walk down the same street.

There is a deep hole in the sidewalk.

I walk around it.

Or,

I walk down a different street.

Some major arcana cards correspond with your soul's elderhood or sage-hood in the following ways:

> ✔ **The Sun:** You take your Self wherever you go, and it comes shining through in your thoughts, words, and actions. Those who sense it are drawn to your warm and loving ways.

> ✔ **Judgement:** You are completely aware that divinity lives within you. You look at all life situations from the timeless or eternal point of view. You see what you can and cannot influence. You dedicate your life to relieving human, animal, and environmental suffering. Aware that you're serving as a tool, you're unattached from specific outcomes: All things come in divine time.

> ✔ **The World:** You are fully enlightened and have the option of "going home" — returning to the source or godhead — at will. Your body lives in the physical world, but your thinking, feeling, and doing are completely spiritualized.

Part V
The Part of Tens

The 5th Wave   By Rich Tennant

ALWAYS KEEP YOUR TAROT
DECK IN A SAFE PLACE
AWAY FROM CHILDREN

"What <u>does</u> it mean when Pikachu
appears between two sphinxes?"

In this part . . .

This traditional part of every *For Dummies* book gives you a parting shot at some of the tarot's main principles — with some laughs thrown in. Chapter 18 aims at dispelling some common misconceptions about the tarot in general. In Chapter 19, I introduce you to a de-hexing technique that might work miracles if you pull a card that gives you the creeps.

Chapter 18

Top Ten Tarot Misconceptions

When it came time to write this chapter, I began surveying people who knew little or nothing about the tarot. While I certainly had my own opinions about the top ten tarot misconceptions, I was more interested in finding out what other people thought.

A "tarot misconception" means that someone interprets a tarot concept or card based on incomplete, faulty, or biased information. As you know, misconceptions can be powerful, especially when more people believe them than not. This chapter is devoted to exploring, and hopefully dispelling, the misconceptions associated with the tarot.

The Tarot is a Form of Devil Worship (If 1 Use 1t, 1'll Go to Hell!)

Yes, some people who work with the tarot do worship the devil. And yes, in the hands of someone *intent* upon using it to do harm, the tarot is a devilish tool. But many tarot users are practicing Catholics, Jews, Protestants, Buddhists, Hindus, and Moslem Sufis.

A tool is a tool: A knife can be used for slicing bread or for stabbing someone. The tool itself is not evil; the intention of the person working with the tool determines its use.

If you *believe* that using the tarot will send you to hell, it will. If you *believe* that using the tarot will send you to heaven, it will.

níles

The Tarot is a Religion

Back to the dictionary! If you define religion as the spiritual or emotional attitude of someone who recognizes the existence of a superhuman power or powers, as well as the bond between humanity and divinity, the tarot is a religion. If you define religion as a particular system, the tarot isn't a religion. The tarot is a symbol code that depicts universal and natural laws and principles that are shared by *all* the world's great religio-spiritual traditions.

A paradox: The tarot is *both* a nondenominational and multidenominational system that can enhance and clarify your understanding of whatever religion or spiritual path you follow.

You Must be Psychic to Work with the Tarot

Yes, psychics work with the tarot. But so do hairdressers, secretaries, librarians, painters, rappers, psychologists, engineers, post office employees, teachers, lawyers, and so on. If you can see, and you've got the desire and willingness to see yourself and life in new ways, you can work with the tarot! In truth, everyone has this ability; it's just a question of whether or not you desire to develop it.

You live in a world filled with symbols, from the green light at the intersection to advertisements of the happy family driving a new station wagon. The cards are a symbol system that can assist you in seeing yourself and life situations from new and insightful points of view.

The Purpose of a Tarot Reading is to Find Out About Your Future

The purpose of a tarot reading is to help you see your past and present thoughts, words, and behaviors more objectively. This sort of understanding can make you more aware of the potential results of your present thoughts, words, and behaviors. Remember that what you think, say, and do today helps to create tomorrow.

The Future is Set in Stone

This is one of the aspects of tarot that scares people, and rightly so. It's a misconception to think that no matter what you say or do, the future's set. True, people and events can follow certain patterns, but you do have one of the greatest freedoms possible — freedom of choice. The bottom line is that your present actions help determine future conditions.

Much of what happens in your life depends on how *you* read and respond to the pictures life presents to you.

The tarot spreads that I show you in Chapter 13 denote cards for your "*possible* future" or "future *possibilities.*" Again, what you do today helps make tomorrow!

Dear Tarot Reader, Please Fix Me!

If you want to have someone to blame if your life doesn't work out as promised, this type of tarot is for you. Shirking responsibility for what happens in your life is an act you'll eventually regret. Shame on the tarot reader who says she/he can "fix" your health problems, career, or legal situation by lighting candles or saying prayers. This person is either out to get your money, playing into the fact that you're in a highly suggestible state, or just plain ignorant.

The tarot cards can help you look at your options and offer hope, but you must do the repair work yourself. The tarot aims to create Self-dependent (dependent on your higher soul, spirit, Self) and interdependent (not co-dependent) relationships.

Your Wife's Having an Affair

The tarot cards reflect *you!* If you're thinking that your wife's having an affair, you'd better take a good long look at your reasons for thinking so. Have you been watching too many TV talk shows? Is your self-esteem in the toilet? Is your sex life nonexistent? Could you actually be projecting the affair *you'd* be having if your wife treated you the way you're treating her? *Remember:* The tarot is a mirror that reflects *your* face!

Curses and Love Spells

One of the tarot's main objectives is to *do no harm*. Putting a curse on your enemy actually puts a curse on you. Trying to force someone into a relationship against their will eventually backfires. Watch your motivation. What goes around, comes around!

Reversed Means the Opposite

Thinking that reversed cards mean the exact opposite of what they mean upright is like thinking that people cry only when they're unhappy. If you've ever cried tears of joy, you know that this type of thinking is limited.

For instance, the reversed Strength card in the position of your "past experiences" can indicate weakness, yet it can also show that you've refrained from using physical force. The Five of Pentacles reversed in the position of "future possibilities" can indicate a chance to consciously examine inherited ideas about poverty that you hold in your subconscious. The Four of Wands reversed might not mean disruption but rather the holding of a nontraditional attitude or event.

When interpreting reversals, take the position of a reversed card in a spread, the surrounding cards, and other circumstances or influences into consideration. See Chapter 6 for more information about reversed cards.

My Life's This Way Because . . .

I often hear people say, "I can't have a good love life because my Venus, planet of love, is in such and such sign or house of the zodiac," or, "I have trouble communicating because my Mercury, planet of communication, is in . . ."

You'd be surprised at how many people follow the same route with the tarot. Believing that certain tarot cards are to blame for the state of your life is a huge misconception. ("My day was a mess because I pulled the Judgement card this morning.") If your day was a mess, it's because of how *you* handled what came your way. If you started the day with a seemingly negative card, it was your job to be on the lookout for the chance to be awake and creative.

The tarot aims to assist you in taking responsibility for yourself, not in laying the blame elsewhere.

A Few Extras

Although the following misconceptions didn't fall in the top ten spots, they did call out for consideration.

The tarot is dangerous

Much like the traditional Rorschach inkblots and the imagination-stimulating pictures of the Thematic Apperception Test (TAT) reflect your unconscious mind, so does the tarot. The tarot's archetypes depict every possible state of consciousness and every facet of the human personality. When individuals look at the tarot cards and recognize (unconsciously) an unacceptable facet of their personality, they get frightened. Fear also comes from thinking that the image is predicting dire circumstances.

The tarot images can be upsetting and/or possibly dangerous in the hands of someone who is psychologically unbalanced.

Each tarot card has a specific, predetermined meaning (how boring!)

Although each card reflects some core truths, thinking that each tarot card is *always* read the same way is a misconception and plain old boring. What you see in the card is always a reflection of your physical, mental, emotional, and spiritual state at *that* time. When these states change, your interpretations change with them. Because you are a constantly transforming being, you may read a card one way today and then see the picture quite differently next month or next year. Beware of building inflexible constructs!

A tarot reading a day can keep the doctor away

It's a misconception to think that the tarot can fully diagnose or treat an illness. At best, the cards can point out a weakness, but there's absolutely no replacement for getting the appropriate medical tests and diagnosis.

The tarot does not rule out alternative healing or health care; it supports your making the best decisions about treating a health problem.

Who needs investment counseling?

It's a misconception to think that the tarot cards can show you specifically how and where to invest your own, or another's, money. Because the tarot is about self-empowerment, its imagery is more likely to direct you to a class on financial management, publications on money management, or a professional financial consultant (and not the tarot reader's brother-in-law!).

The tarot supports self-empowerment, which means asking for professional assistance when needed, but doing so only after carefully examining your options.

The tarot has no practical use

The belief that the tarot is "for fortune-telling only" has reinforced the attitude that the tarot has no practical use. Knowledge is useless unless it's applied. The tarot is designed to be lived! Thousands of people have been able to live happier, healthier, and more satisfying lives by living the tarot's principles (or taking the tarot's teachings out of the world of intellectual concepts and into the world of the practical application).

Instead of just thinking about how often The Magician card keeps reminding you of the value of paying attention to what's going on in front of your nose, try to apply what you've learned to something as simple as walking your dog and see how different the experience can be.

Chapter 19

The Ten Cards Most Likely to Cause a Freak-Out

o you have a hex remover? An old friend of mine removes hexes by circling whatever she thinks is hexed with a raw egg. After whispering a few words under her breath (that I never understand), she immediately throws the egg into the garbage and washes her hands. As you start working with the tarot, perhaps you'll think that you need a hex remover, too, because some cards are pretty much guaranteed to make you feel hexed, jinxed, or cursed.

Although some of the tarot images certainly do look grim, your reaction to them has more to do with your perspective and preconceptions about the images than with the images themselves. For example, if you draw The Devil card, your first instinct may be to panic and assume that something or someone evil is going to do you harm. However, I once worked with a second-grade class that made up stories about the devil after looking at the card, and they talked about what a "funny looking animal he is with his wings and claws and tail and horns." The children did not have preconceived ideas about the devil, so the card didn't feel threatening.

As I discuss in Chapter 1, how you respond to a card is related to the archetypes or models held in your subconscious mind and the collective unconscious. Until you replace or transform these concepts, your tendency will be to react to a card in a very specific way. As you become increasingly self-aware, even cards that contain seemingly ominous images can stimulate an entirely different set of ideas.

The more fearful you are of a card, the more likely it is to appear. I can't tell you how many times clients have said, "I'll be fine so long as The Devil, Death, and The Hanged Man don't come up in my cards." And, of course, they do.

Noticing how frequently these "freak-out cards" would appear when a client was fearful, I decided to keep track of how often this actually happened. Over a four-year period, these cards turned up more than 70 percent of the time when a client was fearful.

Remember that the tarot shows *tendencies* based upon your present way of thinking, and those tendencies are *always* subject to change. In this chapter, I demonstrate the potential for this shift by taking you from a freak-out to a review of some of the cards that people fear most. So dust off your hex remover — your own open mind — and take a closer look at some of these persistent bugaboos.

The Tower

Freaking out: My life's falling apart! The bank's foreclosing on my house. My relationship's breaking up. I'm going to get an eviction notice. I'm heading for a nervous breakdown. There's going to be a disaster, tragedy, or catastrophe.

Re-viewing: Take a good look at the card (see Chapter 7). What's wrong with this picture? Of course, the tower's foundation is weak. If you were perched on something as skimpy as the tower's foundation, you'd be coming down too. The appearance of the tower is like the appearance of an unsafe building waiting for a wrecking crew to knock it over. When something's built on a weak foundation, it eventually collapses. Believing that you're better, smarter, richer, or more important than others is setting yourself up for another kind of fall. (We all know the saying "Pride comes before a fall.") Pulling this card gives you the chance to ask yourself stuff like, "What am I thinking or doing that might be putting me at risk for a fall? Would I rather be right than happy? What changes can I make to avoid disaster?"

The tower's bricks are made of clay. Adam, the first human, was made of clay. This symbolizes how your own evolution brings down your used-up ways of thinking and doing. The only constant is change!

I pulled The Tower as my touchstone card (see Chapter 13) on the morning we had a major earthquake in California. As our home was bouncing around on its foundation, glass was shattering, and canned goods were crashing off the shelves, I thought, "Okay, what I didn't secure is falling down." This incident shows that The Tower can indicate acts of God and nature — natural catastrophes. What these situations call for is figuring out how to help yourself and others!

Shake-ups are wake-ups. You're getting a warning. An alarm is sounding. You have a chance to deal with a situation that you've been avoiding. You're getting the opportunity to ward off an impending disaster. The red light's flashing, telling you to stop, look, and listen. There's no denying that you're getting a reality orientation. Might you be more careful about moving so fast? Not only are you missing some important stuff, but you could have an accident. Remember, when you won't make a needed change for yourself, you can count on the universe to step in.

The Nine of Swords

Freaking out: Oh no, more sleepless nights lie ahead! Looks like I'm heading into another deep depression. I'm trapped. Night terrors are coming up. I'm spending my nights worrying about my days. (It's not surprising that some tarot books call this the "nightmare card.")

Re-viewing: Look at the card very closely (see Chapter 8). That's right, hold it out at arm's length, put on your glasses, or take out that magnifying glass. Voilà! The quilt is decorated with cosmic symbols, suggesting that help and protection are with you — *if* you reach for them.

Might the swords be prompting you to turn to a higher source? With a little mental adjustment, the person in the card is in prayer or deep meditation. This card intimates the principle of Ageless Wisdom that says, "Seek what's real."

Chapter 8 explains that the suit of swords is associated with making mental patterns. Difficult as it might be, you may benefit from reformulating a plan or decision. The number nine is linked with mastery. The greatest mastery is Self-mastery.

Death

Freaking out. Who's going to die? Am I going to die? What's dying and when?

Re-viewing: First, keep this in mind: Of course you're going to die, but so am I and *every* living thing on this earth — in it's time! And yes, death can be very sad, because there's an empty space where that person once was. Please, please keep in mind that *the tarot does not predict specific time frames!*

Now, look at the card (see Chapter 7). Is the sun rising or setting? Because it's in the eastern corner of the card, it's rising. When the sun sets in one part of the world, it rises in another. Of course, the Death card can indicate physical death, yet in most instances people are already aware of its proximity. More often than not, the Death card signifies the passing away of some misperception so that a new perception can take form. It's the dying off of an old part of yourself so that something new has room to be born in its place.

Death is transformation from one state into another. Even physicists teach that matter (the physical body) can be destroyed, while energy (the soul) only changes form.

Three of Swords

Freaking out: My heart's broken or is gonna get broken. The pain is overwhelming! My sorrow is endless. I'm being betrayed. I'm never gonna love or be loved again. Waaaaaa . . . poor me!

Re-viewing: Yes, a broken heart is dreadful, but if you look at the card *closely* (see Chapter 8), you see that the cloud has a silver lining. This card is connected with the third sphere of the Qabalistic Tree of Life, Understanding (see Chapter 15). When all else fails, pain and sorrow open you up to understanding yourself, others, and life situations from a more expansive point of view. Again, the suit of swords goes with making plans. It's likely that you made a plan that was out-of-whack with reality, and as always, reality prevails. When this card comes up, so many people say something like, "I was in denial about the depth of my relationship."

The Devil

Freaking out: I'm in hell! I'm gonna go to hell! Life is hell! I'm chained and can't break free. I'm damned. I'm going to have a hell of a time, no matter what happens. The devil's making me do it. Having dark and negative thoughts and feelings makes me an awful person.

Re-viewing: Look at the card (see Chapter 7). The chains around the people's necks are loose, and they can lift them off. Hell is a state of mind. The **Aquarian Deck for the New Age** calls The Devil "The Thinker."

Your mental constructs bind you and free you.

The devil breeds ignorance, narrow-mindedness, inflexibility, and stubbornness. Giving your will over to another person and/or running power trips on others are guaranteed ways of feeling hellish! When your life becomes a living hell, you want to free yourself. Eventually, misery leads to liberation.

Darkness is as much a part of creation as is light. All of us, including you and me, have light and dark or mature and immature personality traits. These are part of the same higher soul, spirit, Self. The devil has the ears of an ass, suggesting that you take a break from denying or punishing and shaming yourself for your dumbass behaviors. Try laughing at your humanness.

Accepting the immature side of your Self is the beginning of wisdom. It's normal to have negative thoughts and feelings. What you *do* about them matters most. Speaking of matter, excessive materialism and greed are other devilish qualities. Now, why do you think devil is the word *lived* spelled backwards?

Five of Pentacles

Freaking out: I'm gonna be out in the street and destitute! I'll never have a place I can call home! Life's tough and getting tougher. My back injury's going to cripple me. Feelings of depression and disenfranchisement are creeping up again. I'm never gonna get a decent job. I have all these things and money, and I still feel down and out.

Re-viewing: Look at the whole picture (see Chapter 8). The people are so engrossed in their "stuff" that they're walking right by an illuminated window! Is turning away from the light (a symbol of some universal truth and your higher soul, spirit, Self) putting you out in the cold? If you're biochemically depressed, more medical assistance is available now than ever before. Might facing some truth about yourself bring you in from the cold?

Are help and refuge available, but not in a form that you recognize or want them to take? Okay, so you won't accept any assistance that has strings attached, but are you sure that there *are* strings instead of just your fear of strings? (How about asking some direct questions?)

Are you proud to the point of being egotistical, possibly making what's difficult even worse? Being receptive and allowing others to assist you is like giving them a gift. Could you be feeling stingy about giving someone this chance? Are you thinking that it's giving that person power over you?

Pentacles deal with physical results and products. Are you reevaluating what makes you feel secure? Some wealthy people are poor in spirit and feel impoverished. Some poor people are rich in spirit and feel wealthy.

The Eight of Swords

Freaking out: I'm trapped! I'm being restrained. I don't have any power. I'm unable to assert myself.

Re-viewing: Look at the card (see Chapter 8). The swords don't actually fence the woman in. What fences you in? If you look at the whole picture, you see that she's come a long way from where she started. The tower is in the background. Is it possible that a long-standing pattern of narrow-mindedness and/or feeling mentally inhibited is being thought of as out of existence? In other words, is your mind opening? You may not be *seeing* the results of this change, but are you thinking and feeling them?

Perhaps your next step is recognizing that freedom is not just a state of physical freedom; it's a state of mind. (One of the freest people I know is living on death row.)

If you keep thinking that you're trapped, you're trapped. If you keep thinking that you're finding a way out of difficulty, you're getting out.

The Ten of Swords

Freaking out: I'm gonna get stabbed in the back! Someone's definitely out to get me. I'm ruined!

Re-viewing: Look, the day is breaking! (See Chapter 8.) Another swords card and another set of ideas. What ideas are breaking through your consciousness? What ideas have been pinning you down? What new ideas are you surrendering to? How might giving up on a lost cause liberate you? What or who do you think might be coming back to "get you"? Would apologizing for some harsh or unconscious words be appropriate? Could surrendering to the truth about yourself or a situation avert what might be coming?

Try looking at it this way: You're receiving a cosmic acupuncture treatment that's relieving trapped energy. Ahhhhh, release! Perhaps you need a good cry?

The number ten symbolizes the beginning of a new cycle. A new day is here; be present! Is there some reason for hanging on to the past? A chance for resolution is here. If you let go of the past, the worst may be over.

The Hanged Man

Freaking out: I'm hung-up, strung-up, and done-up! I can't move!

The Hebrew letter associated with this card is *mem,* meaning water. The card has also been called the "Drowned Phoenician Sailor." This combo suggests someone drowning in their own feelings (all of the "freak-out" reactions).

Re-viewing: Hmmmm, the hanged man actually looks pretty relaxed (see Chapter 7). There's even a halo over his head. What happens if *you* turn upside down? Yes, yes, blood rushes to your head, what's loose falls out of your pockets, *and* everything looks different! The card suggests exactly what you're doing with each of the cards in this chapter: changing your perspective. Children are given timeouts to think about their behavior. When I can give myself a timeout from issues or circumstances that are hanging me up (also known as taking a mental vacation) and do something to center myself, what's unnecessary drops off and I get to the heart of the situation. Doing this, I get a new or renewed view of what's important.

The Hierophant

Freaking out: That's exactly what I hate about religion: someone sitting up there and telling me what I should and shouldn't do! Go bother someone else and leave me alone! Who are *you* to tell *me* what I should do? Stop ordering me around!

In Chapter 6, I mention *blinds:* situations where teachers purposefully mislead, withhold, obscure, or give misinformation. This is done when a teacher wants to entice you into sleuthing out a truth for yourself. Doing this involves you making contact with your inner teacher — a very worthwhile undertaking. The Hierophant represents one of these blinds.

Re-viewing: The word *hierophant* comes from the Greek *hierophantes,* meaning "to reveal, show, or make known" and "one who brings to light." The hierophant's hand signals you to be still and listen to the truth that lies within *you* — not within him/her, but you! (See Chapter 7.) I know, you're used to interpreting such gestures as meaning "quiet down and listen to *me*." Here it means "quiet down and listen to *you!*" (Now this *could* mean listening to another's advice, but it's *your* decision to do so.)

The hierophant is your own higher soul, spirit, Self in pope's clothing. He's your intuition, the inner teacher that lives in your heart. As my yoga teacher consistently told his students, "Honor and worship your Self — God lives within you as you!"

The *phant* in *hierophant* also means "figment." The hierophant is a figment of your imagination; he's whatever you imagine him to be!

The hierophant embodies Willy Shakespeare's wise words, "To thine own self be true."

Appendix

Seeking Additional Resources

So, you're already wanting more tarot? Excellent! There are lots of ways to learn more about this subject: books, tapes, CDs, videos, interactive programs, teachers, workshops — even comic books. In this appendix, I show you how to search out resources that work for you.

Books

Because my tastes may be different from yours, I won't direct you to specific book titles. Instead, I suggest that you visit the tarot sections in several bookstores and peruse the tarot books on the shelf to figure out which books speak to you. Before you buy another book on tarot, ask yourself these questions:

- **Is the book written in language I understand?** Some of the more esoteric books may use different terms than you're used to. Consider whether you're interested in learning this new vocabulary or would prefer a book that you can understand immediately.

- **Does the book use a tarot deck that I'm familiar with?** If the answer is "no," ask yourself whether or not the book depicts a deck you're interested in learning more about.

- **Is the scope of the book narrow or wide?** This means determining whether the information in the book applies only to the deck it depicts, or if it can be applied to other decks.

- **Is the book too radical a departure from the tarot?** Oracular or fortune-telling decks — those that have more or fewer cards than the traditional 78 — are fabulous. However, you may not recognize the cards in the book, and you could get frustrated. But who knows, maybe you'll get turned on to a whole other system!

Comic Books

A couple years ago, one of my students turned me on to a tarot-oriented comic book called "Promethea." In 1999, Alan Moore, J.H. Williams III, and others launched this fascinating series. As in the tarot and all comics, what the words don't tell you, the pictures do. I must admit that I've become like a little kid, in that I pester the comic book store to find out when the new issues will arrive.

Electronic Media

Instructional tapes, CDs, videos, and interactive software programs can be fun and informative. Shop carefully. These tools can be pricey, so get a sample look or listen *before* buying. (If a sneak peek at the product isn't possible, make sure the store offers a money-back guarantee for a certain period of time.) Ask yourself the same types of questions that I have listed for books in the previous section.

Teachers and Schools

If you live in a big city, there's probably a tarot teacher or school somewhere close by. Here are some ideas on how to find one:

- ✔ Call your local spiritual bookstore.
- ✔ Peruse the Yellow Pages under "Tarot" or "Schools."
- ✔ Browse through local entertainment, community, or spiritually oriented newspapers and magazines for ads. Some examples are New York City's *Village Voice,* San Francisco Bay Area's *Common Ground,* and Seattle's *Wisdom of the Ages* and *New Times.*
- ✔ Of course, there's always the Internet. Just type in the keywords *tarot* and *classes* and you're off on an adventure!

Before committing to anything, interview your potential teacher with the following suggestions in mind:

- ✔ It's best to have an idea of what aspect of the tarot you want to learn more about: readings, the major arcana, the minor arcana, the court cards, the Tree of Life, and so on. Ask the teacher if he or she offers what you want.
- ✔ Find out how long the teacher's been teaching and what his or her background is. For example, you may find it easier to learn from a tarot teacher who has a background in comparative religions and tarot rather than in sociology and tarot.
- ✔ Get a reference or two. Of course, teachers will refer you to students who loved their classes, but asking a student *what* they loved about them can prove helpful.

Questions such as these can give you an idea of how someone teaches and whether or not the potential of getting what you're looking for from the class is there. Sometimes just talking with the teacher will give you a sense of whether or not you vibe together.

Find out whether the teacher will permit you to try one class (for a fee, of course) before signing up for a whole series. Doing this can help you get a taste of the teacher's methods and prevent you and the teacher from getting locked into a situation that doesn't work for either of you.

Correspondence Courses

There are some excellent tarot correspondence courses available. Unfortunately, there are also some scam courses available. You can find correspondence courses advertised in the back of spiritually and psychically oriented magazines and newspapers, and on the Internet.

Although I benefited tremendously from doing 13 years of Builders of the Adytum courses, I'm not sure this route is for everyone. Check out correspondence courses much as you would any book, teacher, or teaching tool.

Try to determine what you want from a correspondence course before signing up. Some courses aim at assisting your spiritual development, others are geared toward teaching you how to read the tarot cards, and still others show you how to become a tarot teacher. Some courses offer everything and can provide only some of it, while others are outright scams. Read all guarantees and disclaimers before signing up, and don't be afraid to ask seemingly silly questions.

If a school, organization, or individual promises you tarot mastery in a short amount of time and/or for a large fee, run in the other direction!

Community Programs

More and more community programs, such as the YMCA and YWCA, are offering classes on tarot at low fees. Check out catalogs for continuing education from community colleges and universities, as well as catalogs for community and adult education programs.

Community programs offer great opportunities to meet like-minded people, network, and "interview" teachers without spending a lot of time and money doing so.

Institutes

If you have the time, interest, money, and inspiration for traveling, many places such as Esalen Institute in Big Sur, California; Naropa University in Boulder, Colorado; and the Omega Institute in Rhinebeck, New York offer a variety of short workshops. These are wonderful places for learning, relaxing, and spending time in nature.

Institutes are outgrowths of the human potential movement. They encourage self-awareness and optimum health and foster personal and social transformation. They offer alternative education, and most are not accredited. Institutes offer cutting-edge views of science, the humanities, and religion and spirituality as a means of facilitating personal and planetary healing. In addition to courses on such subjects as massage, yoga, Tai Chi, healthy eating, various forms of meditation, and psychological and spiritual healing, institutes offer you the environment in which to have a mentally, emotionally, and physically regenerating retreat.

I can't guarantee that a particular institute is providing tarot workshops at any given time, but I know that their teaching staffs are usually excellent. If an institute isn't presently giving tarot workshops, you might suggest that they contact a teacher about offering one!

Tarot Organizations

Several tarot associations and societies also offer workshops. Because these organizations tend to be cliquish, "members only," or sponsored by a particular publisher, many excellent teachers are often excluded. For this reason, I suggest that you take an eclectic approach to these groups. Until you know exactly what you want from a tarot class or workshop, I recommend sampling what you think are the best offerings from among the diverse sources, systems, and styles available.

Index